PENGUIN PASSNOTES

Chemistry

Vivien Boorman was educated at Chelsea College, University of London, where she obtained a B.Pharm. (Hons). She then took her Post Graduate Certificate of Education at Bulmershe College. She has since taught in a wide variety of institutions in both secondary and further education. She is an examiner in Chemistry at O-level for a major examining board.

PENGUIN PASSNOTES

Chemistry

VIVIEN BOORMAN

ADVISORY EDITOR: STEPHEN COOTE, M.A., PH.D.

PENGUIN BOOKS

Penguin Books Ltd, Harmondsworth, Middlesex, England
Viking Penguin Inc., 40 West 23rd Street, New York, New York 10010, U.S.A.
Penguin Books Australia Ltd, Ringwood, Victoria, Australia
Penguin Books Canada Limited, 2801 John Street, Markham, Ontario, Canada, L3R 1B4
Penguin Books (N.Z.) Ltd, 182–190 Wairau Road, Auckland 10, New Zealand

First published 1984
Reprinted 1984, 1986

Made and printed in Great Britain by
Richard Clay (The Chaucer Press) Ltd, Bungay, Suffolk
Filmset in Monophoto Times Roman by Northumberland Press Ltd, Gateshead

The publishers are grateful to the following Examination Boards for permission to reproduce questions from examination papers used in individual titles in the Passnotes series:

Associated Examining Board, University of Cambridge Local Examinations Syndicate. Joint Matriculation Board, University of London School Examinations Department, Oxford and Cambridge Schools Examination Board, University of Oxford Delegacy of Local Examinations.

Contents

Introduction

This book is written to help you understand your chemistry course so that you can learn it. It is impossible to learn and remember something you do not understand. Chemistry is not always easy to grasp: to begin with you are talking about atoms and molecules that are so small that you can never see them; you just have to imagine them.

At the end of each chapter there are examination questions from different boards, followed by model answers. Unless stated to the contrary these questions are taken from the long answer questions, which are usually part of the second paper issued by each examining board. In order to make the questions relevant to the chapter, only those which refer to the preceding topics have been used. However, many examination questions will link together ideas, which you may have learnt separately. For example, questions on the reactivity of elements may be related to their atomic structure. Alternatively a question on electrolysis may involve problems on redox reactions.

This means that you must familiarize yourself with your particular syllabus and also with past papers from your examining board. Different examining boards ask questions in different ways and use different phrases. The main topics, which are common to most syllabuses, have been covered, but you must *check* what other topics are in your course. For example, knowledge of transition elements and the variation of the solubility of a salt with temperature may be included.

Revision

No one can tell you how to revise; you must work out a system that is effective for you. Nevertheless the following points should be considered.

1. Plan a timetable of revision, so that you spend enough time on each of your subjects, otherwise you might end up in a panic.

2. Remember that you cannot concentrate and learn effectively by

working *all* day. Plan breaks and relax by doing something completely different.

3. You will never learn work by just reading it through. You must make yourself recite it, or write it out, with your textbook closed. It is a good idea to summarize facts and then check these summaries.

4. Learn all the definitions thoroughly. There is no excuse for not gaining full marks in an examination question for these facts. Moreover some questions depend on your knowing a definition before you can answer them. Take this book with you on any journey; anyone could test your knowledge of the definitions found in the glossary.

5. It is unnecessary to memorize all the experimental details of many of the experiments you have carried out during your course. You should learn what these experiments demonstrate. Check over past papers and you will soon realize that there are only a few experiments which you would be asked to describe in detail: for example, the preparation of ethanol and experiments to demonstrate rates of reactions seem popular.

6. Look at past examination papers, write outline answers to questions and then check these with your textbook or with a teacher, if available.

The Examination Paper

Most examining boards require you to answer two question papers. Paper 1 is usually a multiple choice paper, where you must answer all the questions. Paper 2 is divided into two sections:

structured questions, which are all compulsory; and
longer questions, where you have a choice.

Oxford Examining Board has a different arrangement. Paper 1 resembles the Paper 2 of most boards. Paper 2 is either a practical paper or another theory paper, which concentrates on examining the practical work you have covered in your course. Your school decides which paper you take.

Most examining boards do not set a practical paper. However, this does *not* mean that questions about this work will be omitted. Therefore you should memorize the glossary which contains tests for identifying substances.

Multiple Choice Paper

1. Although every question in a multiple choice paper carries the same number of marks, some are more difficult than others. Work steadily through the paper and initially leave out any questions which you find difficult.

2. Keep an eye on the time. You should be half way through the paper by half time.

3. When you have finished your first attempt, return to the difficult questions. Read every answer and try eliminating one or two of them. The difficulty often lies in deciding which of two answers is correct. If in doubt, then make a sensible guess. You will get no marks if you leave a question unanswered, whereas your sensible guess may be correct and gain you a mark.

4. Finally, if you have any time left, check through your answers.

Structured Questions

Structured questions are compulsory and one question consists of several short sections which require concise answers.

1. The number of marks allocated to each question is usually indicated; the higher this number of marks the more detail you must include. If in doubt, you will not be penalized for writing too much, but marks will be lost if you do not write enough.

2. Remember that however much you know about one topic you must have answered all the questions in the time indicated. So divide your time equally provided that all the questions carry equal marks. If they are not all equally important then work steadily through the paper.

3. If you find one question looks difficult, then leave it until the end and return to it, but you *must* attempt it since the first few marks of these questions are usually easy to obtain, whereas the last few marks are difficult.

4. If you are short of time, or space, then answer a question in note form. For example, if you have to describe the preparation of ethene, you might want to say: Some ethanol is placed in a flask, fitted with a thistle funnel full of concentrated sulphuric acid. This acid is added dropwise to the ethanol and the flask is shaken and cooled. The flask is then heated on a sand bath. The gas evolved is passed through sodium hydroxide solution to remove any impurities, before it is collected by displacement of water.

This could be written in note form as: Ethanol and concentrated sulphuric acid are heated together and the gas produced is passed through sodium hydroxide solution to remove impurities and collected by displacement of water.

5. Make sure you answer the question the examiner asks rather than the one you *think* he asks! For example:

Question: Give the formula of one basic oxide; one amphoteric oxide; one acidic oxide. (3)

This is a quick answer, you merely have to write the formula of three correct examples. You are *not* asked for any definitions *or* names of compounds.

Question: Name two essential substances which together are necessary to cause iron to rust.

This requires two names, *not* formulae.

Question: (a) Give the names of two gases which are formed when hot air is passed through hot coke. (b) Write an equation to illustrate the formation of one of them.

(a) Requires just two names, not formulae.

(b) Requires a balanced equation for *one* of them.

6. If you have to carry out any calculations then you *must* show your essential workings. The more marks that are allocated to a calculation the more necessary it is to show all your workings.

Long Questions

In this section you have a choice of questions, but each one must be answered in 15 to 30 minutes, depending on the examining board.

1. Read through each question and decide which ones you will answer. It is easier to answer a question if it is broken up into sections for you. The marks are then allocated to each section and you do not have to decide on your own subdivisions.

2. If a question looks suitable, except for one small section, then it is often worth answering it. You will gain high marks on most of your answer and possibly several marks for your attempt at the small section.

3. Questions involving calculations are easy to obtain high marks on if you are good at mathematics; disastrous if not. You know your own capabilities.

4. It is usually sensible to attempt the questions you are confident about first and then finally attempt your last choice. You may disagree about this, but it is upsetting to start off answering a question which you find difficult, and this may affect the quality of your other answers.

5. Attempt the correct number of questions, even if you feel one of your answers will be weak. Otherwise you will lose all those valuable extra marks that you will gain even from a weak answer.

6. It is very important to answer the questions accurately. Plan out a long answer before you start writing; it is always worthwhile to organize your thoughts.

If you are describing an experiment, draw a diagram even if you are not asked to do so. Conversely if the question says, 'describe, with the aid of a diagram ...' then you *must* draw this diagram.

7. Always write an equation for any reaction you describe, even if you are not asked to do so. If the question states 'write an equation for the reaction' then you *must* do so.

In conclusion, remember – an examiner *wants* you to pass, but he cannot award you marks if you do not attempt a question or do not write down your thoughts.

1. *Particles and the Movement of Particles*

Particles

Particles are the 'building blocks' from which all substances are made, they may be atoms, molecules or ions (for definitions see Glossary 3) so the word particle is a general word covering atoms, molecules or ions.

An atom is the smallest particle into which an element can be divided without losing the properties of an element (page 24).

A molecule is a group of atoms which are bonded together and which can exist as a separate unit.

The atoms in a molecule may be of the same kind or of several different kinds.

States of Matter

Chemicals can exist in three different states, forms or phases: a solid, liquid or gas. They can be converted from one state to another by the following changes:

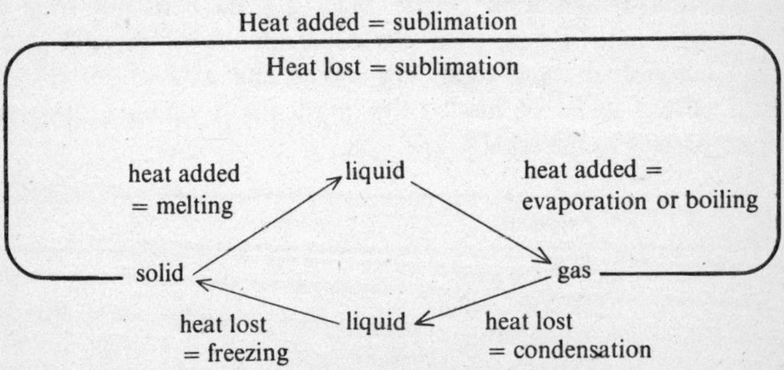

These types of change are called physical changes.

A physical change is a reversible reaction where no new substance is formed but the chemical merely changes its state.

Melting point. This is the temperature at which a solid turns to a liquid.

Pure samples of the same solid will melt at the same temperature, while different solids have different melting points.

Boiling point. This is the temperature at which a liquid turns to a vapour at normal atmospheric pressure.

Pure samples of the same liquid will boil at the same temperature, but if the atmospheric pressure is decreased this will decrease the boiling point. Different liquids have different boiling points.

Notes:

1. On boiling, molecules of a liquid turn to vapour molecules throughout the whole volume of the liquid (compare with evaporation as defined below).
2. A volatile liquid is one which turns to a vapour at a low temperature, e.g. ether.
3. The word 'vapour' is often used instead of the word 'gas'. A vapour is a gas, which can be compressed into liquid without cooling it, e.g. steam, but not chlorine gas, which is naturally a gas at room temperature.

Evaporation. Evaporation occurs when the *surface* molecules of a liquid change to vapour molecules below the boiling point of the liquid. As the temperature of the liquid increases so will the rate of evaporation, until finally the boiling point is reached.

Condensation. Condensation occurs when a vapour cools down and becomes a liquid.

Sublimation. Sublimation occurs when a solid does not melt but turns directly into a gas, or a gas cools and turns directly into a solid. Examples of these solids are iodine and ammonium chloride.

Each of the states of matter has particular properties and these are summarized in the table below.

State	*Properties*
Solid	Definite mass Definite volume A fixed shape
Liquid	Definite mass Definite volume which takes up the shape of its container
Gas	Definite mass Changing volume which increases to occupy a given space

The previous table can be understood by looking at the structure of the three states of matter. All three states of matter are made up of particles, but the arrangement of these particles and the energy they possess are different.

Kinetic Theory

Kinetic Theory and the States of Matter

The kinetic theory discusses the motion of particles. In a solid the particles are held together in a definite fixed pattern because there are strong forces of attraction between them. This ordered arrangement of particles is called a lattice (see page 50). When energy (heat) is supplied to these particles they will break into clusters so that they can move over each other. Now there are gaps between the groups of particles and the forces between them are weaker. This is the liquid state where the particles have more energy. Finally, when more energy is supplied to these clusters of particles they separate and move around rapidly. This is the gaseous state, which has no structure.

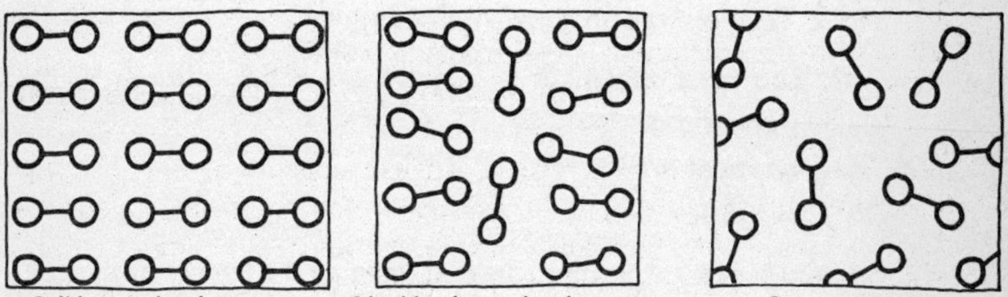

Solid: an ordered structure — Liquid: a less ordered structure — Gas: no structure

A diagram of the states of matter

Kinetic Theory and the Gas Laws

The kinetic theory can be used to explain the Gas Laws, which show the relationship between the temperature, pressure and volume of a gas.

The pressure caused by a gas can be explained by the kinetic theory. The gas molecules, which are in constant motion, bombard (hit with a force) the walls of their container and this causes the pressure of this gas.

Boyle's Law

The volume of a fixed mass of gas is inversely proportional to the pressure, if the temperature remains constant; that is

$$\text{Pressure} \propto \frac{1}{\text{volume}}$$

or $P_1V_1 = P_2V_2$

P_1 = initial pressure of the gas
V_1 = initial volume of the gas
P_2 = final pressure of the gas
V_2 = final volume of the gas

If the temperature of a gas is kept constant, then the molecules would not gain any more energy of movement (kinetic energy). If the volume of this gas was decreased these molecules would be more likely to bombard one of the container walls and so the pressure would increase. If the volume was halved the pressure would be doubled.

Charles' Law

The volume of a fixed mass of gas is directly proportional to its temperature, on the Kelvin scale, if the pressure remains constant; that is

Volume $\propto$ Temperature (in Kelvin *not* °C).

Note: You must remember to convert any temperature in °C to Kelvin (symbol K).

0 °C = 273 K
100 °C = 373 K

If the pressure of a gas is kept constant, then as the temperature rises the volume will increase to prevent the molecules, which have gained kinetic energy, bombarding the walls of the container more rapidly, so increasing the pressure.

Third Gas Law

If the temperature of a certain volume of gas is increased, then the molecules will gain kinetic energy and so move more rapidly and bombard the walls of the container more frequently and more vigorously, so increasing the pressure.

Pressure $\propto$ Temperature (in Kelvin)

Note: There is no named law for this relationship. These laws are combined in the general gas equation.

General Gas Equation

$$\frac{P_1V_1}{T_1} = \frac{P_2V_2}{T_2}$$

$P_1V_1T_1$ = initial pressure, volume and temperature

$P_2V_2T_2$ = final pressure, volume and temperature

Note: A gas at standard temperature and pressure (s.t.p.) refers to a temperature of 273 K and 760 mm (76 cm) mercury pressure.

Evidence for the Movement of Particles

Brownian Motion

Brownian motion or movement is the random movement of minute pieces of solid caused by their irregular bombardment from the surrounding invisible gas or liquid molecules.

Experiment to Demonstrate Brownian Motion

When a smoke cell (small pieces of carbon suspended in air) is looked at through a microscope you can see bright pinpricks of light moving jerkily against a black background. These pinpricks of light are the illuminated pieces of carbon. They are moving because they are being bombarded by the *invisible* gas molecules, which are in constant motion. This movement would be impossible to see without a microscope and is important evidence for the movement of particles.

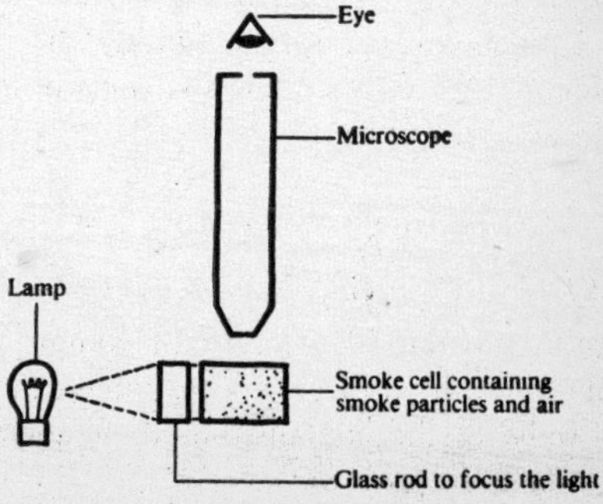

A diagram of the smoke cell

Diffusion

Diffusion is the spreading of one sort of particle through another. Particles move from a region of high concentration to a region of low concentration.

Experiments to Demonstrate Diffusion

If a small drop of liquid bromine is placed in a sealed gas jar after a few minutes the jar will be filled with a brown vapour. Bromine is a volatile liquid so it vaporizes and then the vapour spreads, mixing with the air particles.

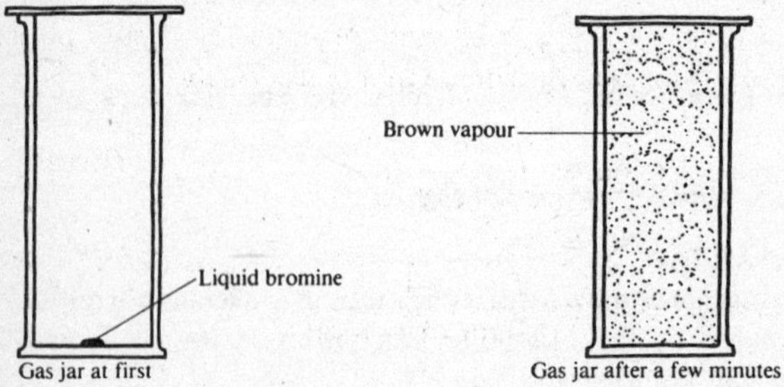

If a small crystal of potassium permanganate is placed at the bottom of a beaker of water, the colour will start to move very slowly through the liquid until eventually the whole liquid is pink. This diffusion of a solid through a liquid is slower than the diffusion of a gas through a gas.

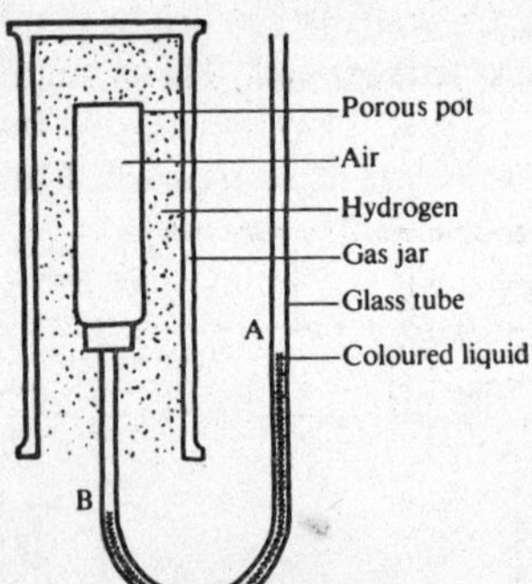

When the apparatus is set up, the hydrogen and air start to diffuse in and out of the porous pot respectively. The pressure in the pot is seen to increase since the level of the coloured liquid at A rises while the level at B decreases. This is because the hydrogen particles are diffusing into the porous pot faster than the air particles are diffusing out.

When this experiment is repeated, using carbon dioxide instead of hydrogen, the liquid at B rises while the level at A decreases, showing that carbon dioxide particles diffuse more slowly than air particles as they are denser (heavier) than air.

This is expressed by the following law.

Graham's Law of Diffusion

The rate of diffusion of a gas at constant temperature and pressure is inversely proportional to the square root of its density.

$$\text{Rate of diffusion} \propto \sqrt{\frac{1}{\text{density}}}$$

or

$$\text{Rate of diffusion} \propto \sqrt{\frac{1}{\text{molecular mass}}}$$

or

$$\frac{\text{rate of diffusion of A}}{\text{rate of diffusion of B}} = \sqrt{\frac{\text{density of B}}{\text{density of A}}}$$

Experiment to Compare the Rate of Movement of Gas Particles

A long glass tube, sealed at both ends, is set up as shown in the diagram below:

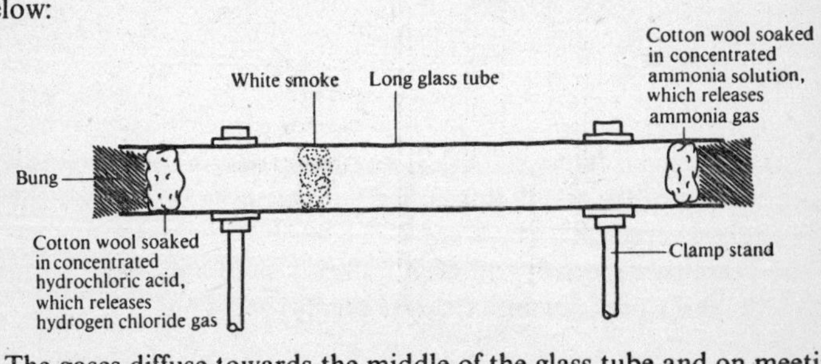

The gases diffuse towards the middle of the glass tube and on meeting form a white smoke of ammonium chloride

$$NH_3(g) + HCl(g) \rightarrow NH_4Cl(s)$$

This is found to occur, not in the middle of the glass tube, but nearer to the cotton wool soaked in acid. This is because the lighter ammonia molecules (mass 17) have diffused further than the heavier hydrogen chloride molecules (mass 36.5).

Examination Questions

Examining boards do not compose many complete structured and essay questions on these topics. However, they feature in parts of questions and in multiple choice papers.

1. Part of a question (*Oxford, Autumn 1977*).

A drop of bromine is placed at the bottom of a tall cylindrical vessel, a lid fitted to prevent disturbance by air currents and the vessel allowed to stand. What would you see after a while? What explanation can you give?

Answer

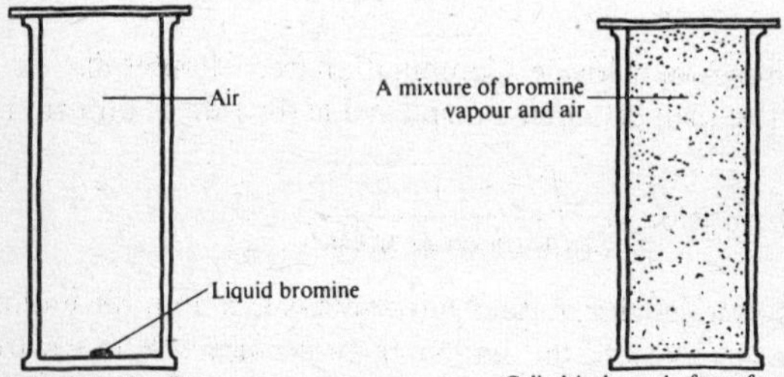

Cylindrical vessel at first   Cylindrical vessel after a few minutes

At first the vessel is full of colourless air, then a brown coloration is seen at the bottom of the vessel; this gradually rises until finally the vessel is full of brown vapour.

The bromine vaporizes and then diffusion occurs as these particles mix with the air particles until they are evenly spread out.

2. Part of a question (*Oxford, Autumn 1977*).

This figure represents the apparatus used in a laboratory experiment.

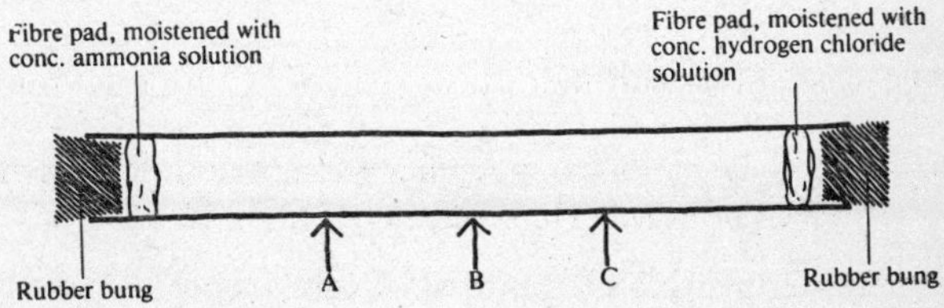

Some minutes after the suitably moistened fibre pads have been simultaneously placed in the tube a white disc of smoke appears:

(i) *What is the 'disc' and by what chemical reaction is it formed?*

(ii) *At which of the points A, B or C in the tube would you expect the disc to form? Give an explanation and state what property of matter is being displayed.*

Answer

(i) Ammonium chloride. Combination (see Chapter 8).

(ii) C. The property being displayed is the rate of diffusion.

$$\text{Rate of diffusion} \propto \sqrt{\frac{1}{\text{molecular mass}}}$$

Since the molecular mass of ammonia is less than the molecular mass of hydrogen chloride, the ammonia molecules will move towards the middle of the tube faster and so meet the other particles at C.

2. Elements, Compounds and Mixtures, Purification

Elements, Metals and Non-Metals

An element. An element is a substance which cannot be split up chemically into anything simpler. It is made up of atoms, which all have the same atomic number (page 35).

Just over one hundred elements have been discovered and they are the 'building blocks' of all substances. Elements may be solids, liquids or gases and can be divided further into metals, non-metals and substances in between the two. The important differences between metals and non-metals are listed below. Most metals will possess most of the properties listed, but there are sometimes exceptions and no single property alone should be used to decide whether a substance is a metal or non-metal.

A table of the differences between metals and non-metals

Metals	*Non-metals*
Usually have 1–3 electrons in their outer shell	Usually have 4–8 electrons in their outer shell
Physical properties	
1. Good conductors of heat and electricity	Poor conductors of heat and electricity (except carbon in graphite form which is a good conductor of electricity)
2. When freshly cut, they are shiny	Dull, even when freshly cut
3. Ductile (can be drawn out into a wire)	Usually brittle (they shatter and break)
4. Malleable (can be beaten into shape)	

	Chemical properties
1. Form positive ions (see Chapter 3)	Do not form positive ions except for hydrogen
2. Form basic oxides and form alkalis if soluble in water (see Chapter 7)	Form acidic or neutral oxides
3. Replace the hydrogen in acids forming salts (and hydrogen) (see Chapter 7)	Do not liberate hydrogen from acids
4. Their chlorides are ionic compounds and therefore electrolytes (see Chapter 6)	Their chlorides are covalent compounds and therefore non-electrolytes (see Chapter 6)

Compounds. A compound is a substance made up of two or more elements which are joined together and so cannot be separated by a physical process.

A chemical change. A chemical change occurs when two substances join together to form a new substance.

A table to summarize the differences between chemical and physical changes

Physical changes	*Chemical changes*
1. No new substance is formed; there is merely a change in state	A new, often very different, substance is formed
2. Easily reversible	Not easily reversible
3. No great energy changes occur	Large energy changes occur
4. No change in mass occurs	A change of mass often occurs

Naming Compounds

1. Compounds ending in -ide consist of two elements; the ending of the non-metal is changed to -ide:

e.g. sodium chloride contains the elements sodium and chlorine; iron sulphide contains the elements iron and sulphur.

2. Compounds ending in -ate usually consist of three elements; the ending means that one of those elements is oxygen. The ending of the non-metal is changed to -ate:

e.g. copper(II) sulphate contains the elements copper, sulphur and oxygen; sodium nitrate contains the elements sodium, nitrogen and oxygen; magnesium carbonate (note carbonate not carbate) contains the elements magnesium, carbon and oxygen.

3. The exception to No. 2 above occurs when metals combine with the hydroxide group (this group contains the elements hydrogen and oxygen) but the compounds are called metal hydroxides:

e.g. sodium hydroxide contains the elements sodium, hydrogen and oxygen.

Potassium hydroxide contains the elements potassium, hydrogen and oxygen.

4. Sometimes further information is given in a name:

(a) carbon *di*oxide means that not only does this compound contain carbon and oxygen but that every atom of carbon is joined to two atoms of oxygen.

(b) aluminium *tri*iodide (or aluminium iodide) means that every atom of aluminium is joined to three atoms of iodine.

(c) carbon *tetra*chloride means that every atom of carbon is joined to four atoms of chlorine.

Mixtures

A mixture consists of two or more different substances which are not chemically combined, so they can be separated by physical processes, e.g. a mixture of sand and salt. Solutions and suspensions are special examples of mixtures.

A solution is formed when a solid, liquid or gas is mixed with a liquid to give a clear solution.

The substance which is being dissolved is called the *solute*, while the substance which does the dissolving is called the *solvent*.

Example:

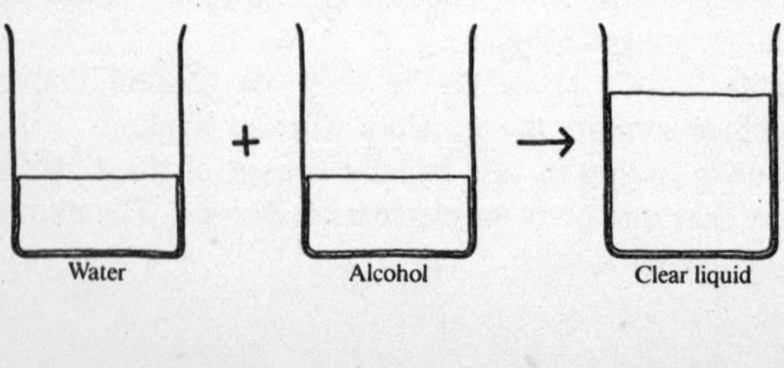

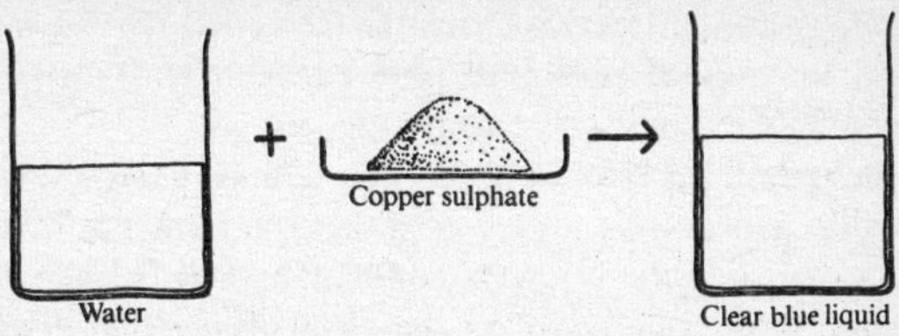

A suspension is formed if two substances are mixed and the resulting mixture is not clear; that is, the substances are present in different states.

For example:

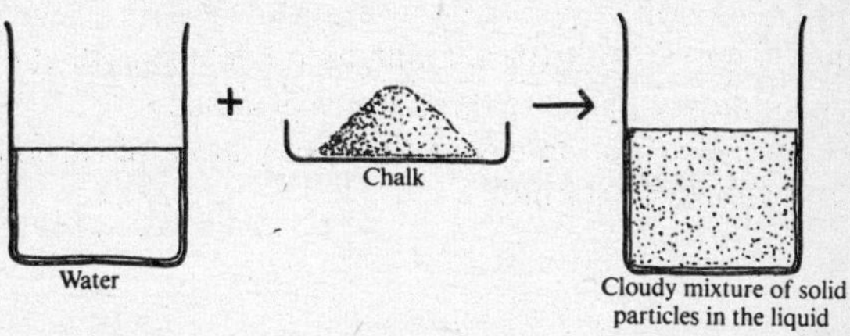

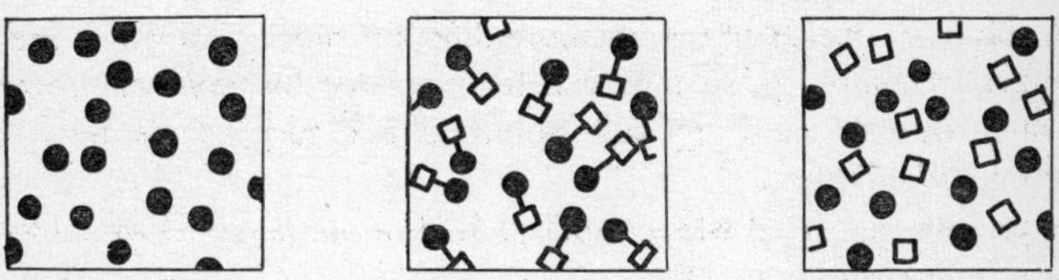

An element: all atoms are the same kind

A compound: two (or more) elements are joined together

A mixture: two (or more) elements mix but are not joined

A diagram to represent the differences between elements, compounds and mixtures

A table to summarize the differences between compounds and mixtures

	Compounds	Mixtures
1.	Always the same composition throughout	May or may not be the same composition throughout, e.g. water and ethanol (same composition); iron and sulphur (not necessarily the same composition if the elements are unevenly distributed)
2.	The elements are present in fixed and definite amounts	Can have any amounts of the substances present
3.	A fixed melting point and boiling point	The melting point and boiling point will vary, depending on the composition of the mixture
4.	Cannot be split up by physical processes	Can be split up by physical processes
5.	The properties of the compound are different from the properties of the elements which it contains	The properties of the mixture are related to the substances present

Purification Techniques

Chemicals made in the laboratory usually contain impurities; that is they are mixtures of substances which can be separated by one of the following physical processes.

Solution, Filtration and Crystallization

A mixture of two solids can be separated by dissolving them in a solvent that will only dissolve one of the compounds; this solvent may be hot. This solution is then filtered so that the insoluble substance is left behind on the filter paper (the residue). The clear solution (the filtrate) is heated slowly on a water bath, so that some of the solvent evaporates. The concentrated solution that is left is cooled and allowed to crystallize so that pure crystals are formed. If the residue is required it is washed with distilled water before it is dried.

Note: This method is only suitable when one substance does not dissolve in the solvent used.

e.g. (i) a mixture of sand and salt can be separated using water which dissolves the salt only;

(ii) a mixture of sugar and salt can be separated using alcohol which dissolves the sugar only.

Heating Two Substances

This is of very limited use as it can only be used to separate a mixture if one of the substances will sublime. For example, if a mixture of sodium chloride and ammonium chloride is heated in a test tube, the ammonium chloride will vaporize and can be seen as a white powder at the top of the test tube, while the sodium chloride is left unchanged at the bottom of the test tube.

Mixtures containing iodine as one of the substances can also be separated by this method, as it sublimes.

Distillation

(a) Simple distillation.

This is the separation of two liquids that mix together to give a clear solution (miscible liquids). The mixture is heated and, because the liquids have different boiling points, the one with the lowest boiling point will vaporize first. This vapour (known as the distillate) is condensed and collected in a different container.

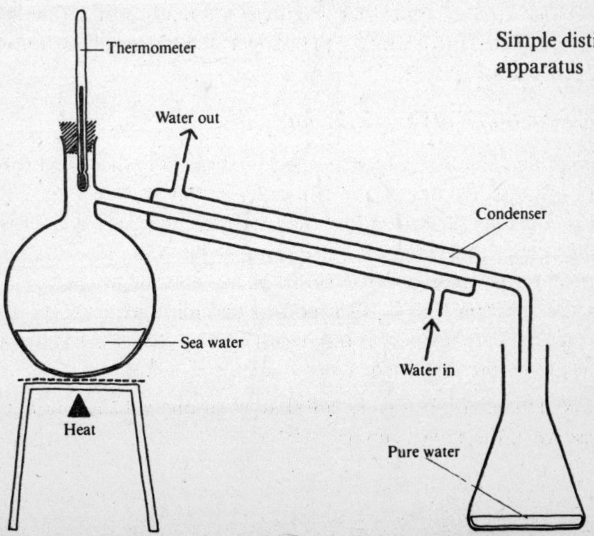

Simple distillation apparatus

This process can be used to separate alcohol and water or produce pure water from sea water.

(b) Fractional distillation.

Simple distillation is not always very efficient. When the boiling points of the substances in the mixture are similar then some of the molecules of the liquid with the higher boiling point tend to vaporize as well, so they contaminate the distillate. When this occurs, as it does with a water–ethanol mixture, then fractional distillation is used instead; this is just repeated distillation. A fractionating column is used, packed with glass beads to provide a large surface area. As the mixture vaporizes it rises up this column, but the higher it rises the cooler the column is so

Fractional distillation apparatus

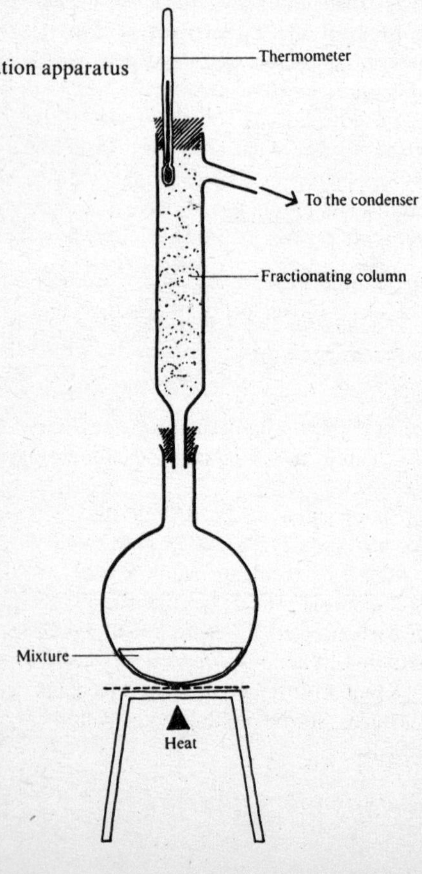

eventually it condenses and trickles back into the flask. During the experiment the column warms up, so the most volatile substance in the mixture (the one with the lowest boiling point) will eventually remain as a vapour and enter the condenser. Molecules of the less volatile substance will never receive enough heat energy so that they remain as a liquid in the fractionating column.

Distillation is also used to separate oxygen and nitrogen from liquid air (see page 168) and in the oil industry to separate oil into its different fractions.

Chromatography

This is the separation of a mixture by taking advantage of the different rates of movement of its substances, which are in the same solvent, over an absorbing material.

For example, a mixture of inks can be separated by placing a spot of the mixture at the bottom edge of a piece of chromatography (filter) paper, which is then placed in a small amount of solvent at the bottom of a closed container. As the solvent rises the ink separates into different colours.

> *Note:* You should be able to describe experiments to separate a mixture of inks or green leaf or grass pigments.

Purity

When a substance is pure it contains only one type of substance. Pure substances have definite melting points and boiling points (at normal atmospheric pressure).

For example, pure water melts at 0 °C and boils at 100 °C. Pure sodium chloride melts at 801 °C and boils at 1465 °C. If impurities are present in the substance then the melting point will decrease and the boiling point will increase. This is because pure substances contain only certain types of particles packed together in a regular way, so the energy required to break up this solid is always the same. When a different type of particle is present a different amount of energy will be needed to break up the particles, so the melting point will alter.

Examination Questions

There are not many complete questions on these topics; they feature in part questions and in multiple choice papers.

Part of a question (*London, January* 1982).

Pure water can be obtained from sea water by using the apparatus shown below.

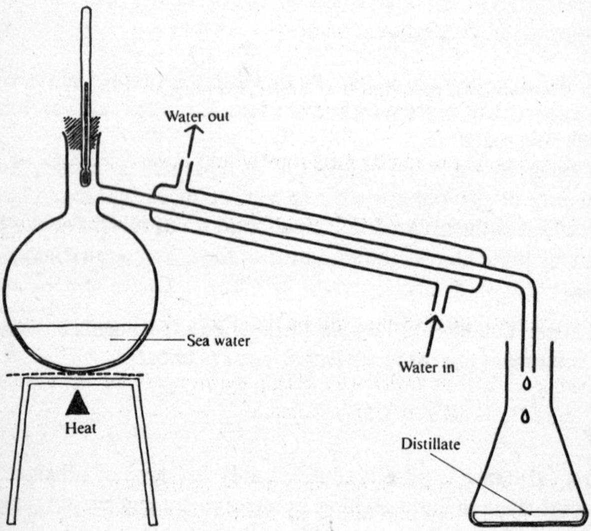

(a) *It is advisable to place a few pieces of broken porcelain in the flask containing the sea water. What purpose does the porcelain serve?* (1)

Answer
To give even boiling throughout the liquid.

(b) *Why is the thermometer placed in the position shown in the diagram?*(1)

Answer
To measure the temperature of the vapour, not the liquid.

(c) *Why would it be unsatisfactory to reverse the water connections to the condenser?*

Answer
The cooling would be less efficient, and the condenser may not fill completely with water.

(d) *The distillate is usually distilled water.*
(i) *Give the names of TWO gaseous impurities that it might contain.*

Answer
1. Oxygen. 2. Carbon dioxide.

(ii) *Why would it be unlikely to contain any dissolved salts?* (3)

Answer
They would be left in the flask as they would never vaporize.

(e) *Suggest ONE reason for collecting the distillate in a conical flask rather than a beaker* (2)

Answer
Evaporation of the distillate will be reduced.

(f) *Suggest TWO reasons why this apparatus would be unsuitable for separating crude oil into its constituents.* (2)

Answer
1. Crude oil is inflammable so could not be heated using a bunsen burner.
2. A fractionating column has to be used to separate crude oil efficiently.

3. *The Structure of the Atom and Bonding*

The Structure of the Atom

The solar system is made up of the sun in the centre with the planets circling around it; most of this system is empty space. Chemists believe that the structure of the atom is rather like this. At the centre of the atom is the nucleus, which has a large mass. Orbiting round this are much lighter particles called electrons.

Protons, Electrons and Neutrons

The nucleus of an atom contains positively charged particles called protons and uncharged particles called neutrons. The mass of these particles is *very* small, so chemists say that a proton and a neutron each have a mass of 1 unit. Protons have a positive charge of one, but neutrons have no charge (are neutral).

The electrons are found in definite orbits or shells around the nucleus; these orbits have different energy levels. Electrons have a mass of 1/1840 (so are much lighter than the other two particles) and a negative charge of one.

The mass of the atom is concentrated in the nucleus.

Particle	*Charge*	*Mass*
Proton	+1	1
Neutron	0	1
Electron	−1	1/1840

For Ordinary level you concentrate on the structure of the first twenty elements in the Periodic Table. Because of this you can assume that:

The innermost shell or orbit labelled 1 or K contains a maximum of 2 electrons.

The next shell or orbit labelled 2 or L contains a maximum of 8 electrons.

The next shell or orbit labelled 3 or M contains a maximum of 8 electrons.

When drawing an atom you need to know the following:

The mass number of an atom is the sum of the number of protons and the number of neutrons in the nucleus of that atom.

The atomic number of an atom is the number of protons in the nucleus of that atom.

Note: Remember that in a neutral (uncharged) atom:

1. Number of protons = number of electrons.
2. Mass number – atomic number = number of neutrons.
3. The numbers of protons and neutrons are not always equal.

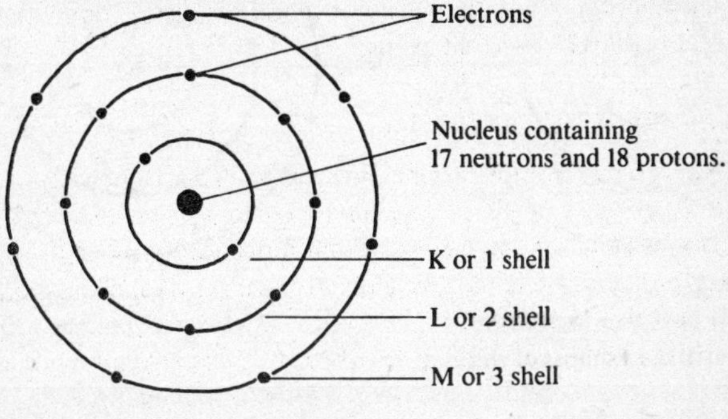

Diagram of an atom (in this case chlorine)

Note: Always label your diagrams, putting in as much information as possible. It is, however, unnecessary to label the shells.

The Periodic Table arranges atoms in order of their increasing atomic number, that is:

Hydrogen has an atomic number of 1 and a mass number of 1, so it contains 1 proton (and so 1 electron) and no neutrons.

Helium has an atomic number of 2 and a mass number of 4, so it contains 2 protons (and 2 electrons) and 2 neutrons.

This information can be written as: ${}^{1}_{1}H$ and ${}^{4}_{2}He$.

Sometimes only mass numbers are needed. These may be written as:

$A_r(H) = 1$ $A_r(He) = 4$ A_r = relative atomic mass (see page 36).

Isotopes

The atom of any element is recognized because it has a certain number of protons. However, some elements have forms with the same number of protons but the number of neutrons varies; these forms are called isotopes. For example, chlorine always contains 17 protons (and 17 electrons) but may contain 18 or 20 neutrons.

Isotopes are atoms of the same element, which contain different numbers of neutrons; that is, they have the same atomic numbers but different mass numbers.

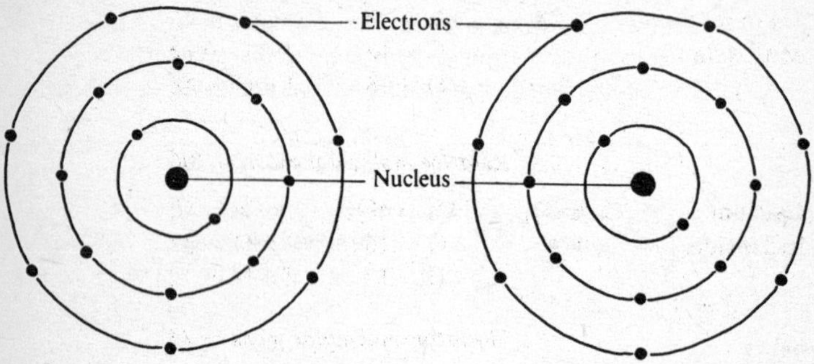

$^{35}_{17}Cl$ Mass number = 17 protons + 18 neutrons

$^{37}_{17}Cl$ Mass number = 17 protons + 20 neutrons

A diagram of the isotopes of chlorine

Relative Atomic Mass

Chlorine gas is a mixture of the above isotopes in the ratio of 3 parts of $^{35}_{17}Cl$: 1 part $^{37}_{17}Cl$. So the 'average' atom of chlorine has a mass number of $\frac{(3 \times 35) + 37}{4} = 35.5$. So 35.5 is the relative atomic mass (R.A.M.) of chlorine *not* its mass number.

The relative atomic mass of an element is the 'average' mass of an atom of the element compared with that of an atom of $^{12}_{6}C$, the mass of which is taken as 12 units.

This can be written as e.g. $A_r(Cl) = 35$. The mass number of an element only refers to a particular isotope or type of atom and is always a whole number. It is also compared to the mass of an atom of $^{12}_{6}C$. Thus the chlorine isotope $^{35}_{17}Cl$ is nearly three times as heavy as an atom of carbon.

Relative Molecular Mass

The relative molecular mass of a molecule is the 'average' mass of a molecule of an element or compound compared with that of the mass of $^{12}_{6}C$. This can be written as $M_r(CO_2) = 44$.

The relative molecular mass (R.M.M.) can be calculated from the formula of the compound provided you know the relative atomic mass of each atom in that compound.

Compound	Formula	Relative atomic mass	
Sodium carbonate	Na_2CO_3	Na = 23	2 × Na = 46
		C = 12	1 × C = 12
		O = 16	3 × O = 48
		Relative molecular mass	*= 106*
Calcium hydroxide	$Ca(OH)_2$	Ca = 40	1 × Ca = 40
		O = 16	2 × O = 32
		H = 1	2 × H = 2
		Relative molecular mass	*= 74*

The Bonding of Atoms

Atoms of the inert (noble) gases have the maximum number of electrons in their outer shell so are very unreactive under normal conditions.

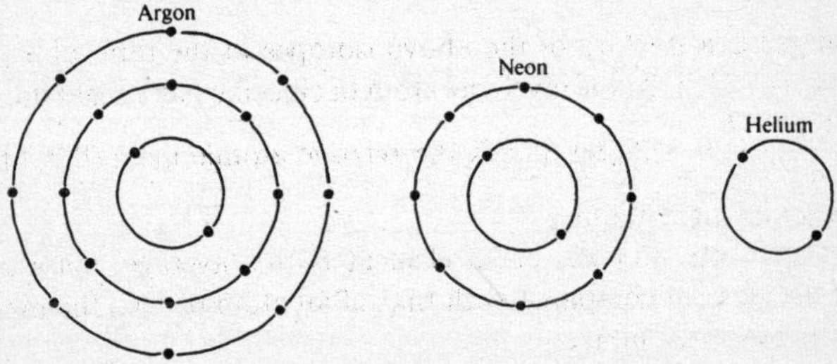

A diagram of the electronic structure of three inert gases

Chemists realized that when atoms join together to form compounds, they join in such a way that the atoms concerned end up with 8 electrons in their outer shell. This may be achieved in two different ways:

1. *Ionic Bonding*

Metals usually have 1, 2 or 3 electrons in their outer shell, e.g. sodium, magnesium and aluminium, so it is easier for them to lose these electrons and end up with the structure of an inert gas.

Non-metals usually have 5, 6 or 7 electrons in their outer shell and so find it easier to gain electrons in order to attain an inert gas structure, e.g. nitrogen, oxygen and chlorine.

Thus if a metal atom and a non-metal atom join, the metal atom will lose electron(s) and the non-metal atom will gain electron(s).

Definitions

An ion is a charged atom or molecule. It does not contain an equal number of protons and electrons.

A cation is a positively charged ion (it has more protons than electrons).

An anion is a negatively charged ion (it has more electrons than protons).

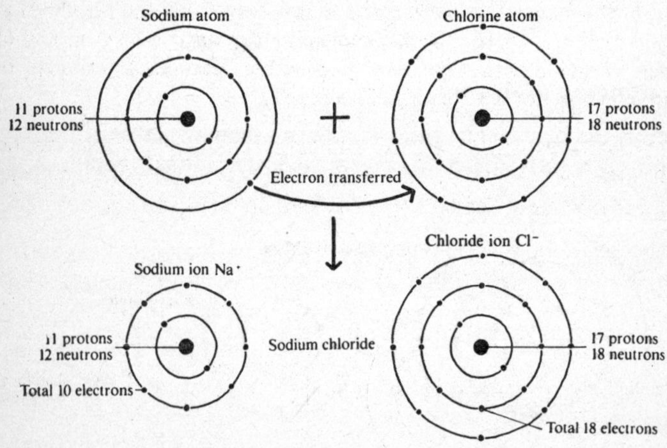

A diagram of the formation of sodium chloride

Note: The formula is NaCl as 1 atom of sodium reacts with 1 atom of chlorine, giving a sodium ion (cation) and a chlorine ion (anion).

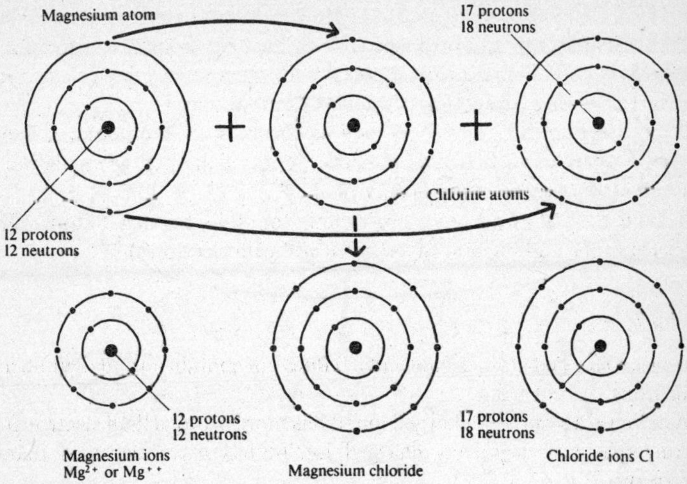

A diagram of the formation of magnesium chloride

This time the magnesium atom needs to lose 2 electrons, but the chlorine atom needs only 1 electron to complete its outer shell. Two atoms of chlorine combine with 1 atom of magnesium, forming 1 molecule of magnesium chloride; so the formula is $MgCl_2$.

> *Note:* When an ion has more than one charge the charge can be written as M^{2+}, M^{++}, X^{2-}, or $X^{=}$. M^{2+} is preferable as it is quicker and the reader does not have to count up the charges.

A diagram of the formation of magnesium oxide

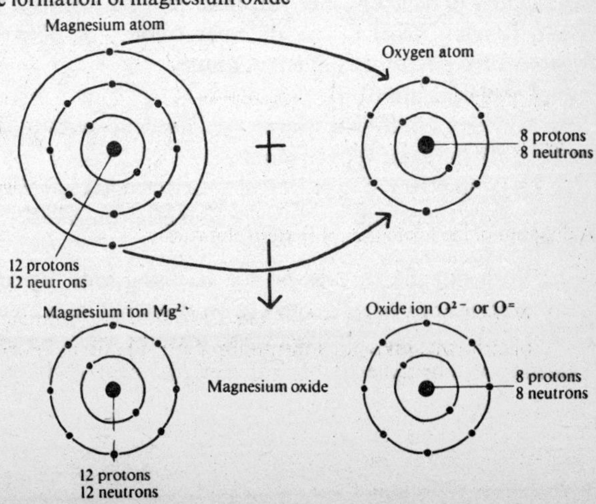

This time the oxygen atom needs to gain 2 electrons to complete its outer shell while the magnesium atom provides these 2 electrons. So the formula is MgO.

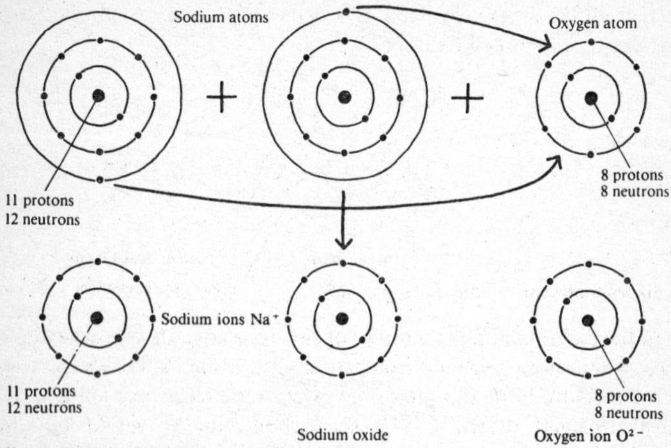

A diagram of the formation of sodium oxide

The formula is Na_2O.

To draw out this type of bonding, you should follow this procedure:

1. Work out the formula of the compound from the atomic number, which is usually given (number of electrons = number of protons in a neutral atom).
2. Draw the electronic structure of the atoms. You need not include the number of neutrons, but you must put the electrons in their correct shells. It often helps to use different colours or different symbols to represent the electrons of different atoms.
3. Label each atom.
4. Add any additional atoms you need by putting them beside or underneath the same type of atoms.
5. Draw in arrow(s) to represent the electron(s) transferred.
6. Redraw the 'atoms' as they are after electron-transfer, labelling them clearly.
7. Work out the charges on the resulting ions. Remember that the number of protons is unchanged, so an atom that loses 1 electron becomes an ion with a single positive charge (cation), while an atom that gains 1 electron will become an ion with a single negative charge (anion).

2. *Covalent Bonding*

This type of bonding occurs when 2 atoms (often non-metals) both need to gain electrons. Electrons are not lost or gained by any atoms but shared, so that all the atoms involved have a complete outer shell of electrons. For example carbon dioxide (CO_2).

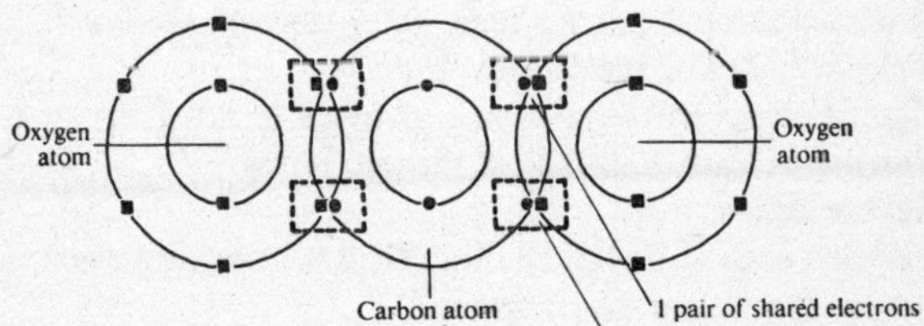

A diagram of a carbon dioxide molecule

In the diagram above each pair of electrons consists of 1 electron from the carbon atom and one from an oxygen atom. These electron pairs are shared by both the atoms involved. One electron pair is a single covalent bond drawn C—O; so carbon dioxide would be drawn O═C═O.

> *Note:* No electrons are gained or lost so *no* ions are produced, the product is uncharged, but all atoms have 8 electrons in their outer shell.

The formula is NH_3.

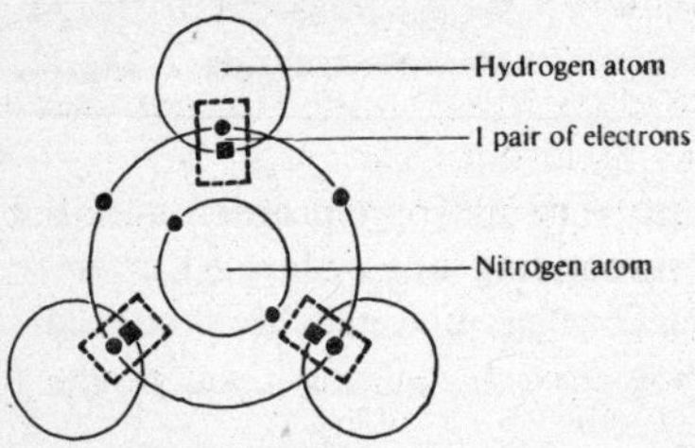

A diagram of an ammonia molecule

The formula is CH_4.

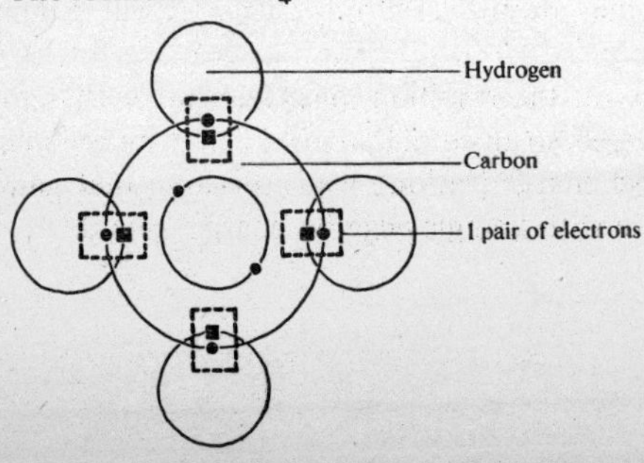

A diagram of a methane molecule

When drawing covalent compounds you should follow this procedure:

1. Work out the formula of the compound.
2. Draw the outer shell of each atom involved. If 3 or more atoms are present in a molecule, the one which is present in the smallest number should be placed in the centre of the diagram. The other atoms should be evenly placed around it, with their outer electron shells overlapping the outer electron shell of the central atom.
3. Draw the electrons of the atoms involved, making sure you show the electron pairs clearly and enclose them in boxes.
4. Label the atoms.
5. Check that each atom has an outer shell containing 8 electrons.
6. Write the formula of the compound.

You should be able to draw the following covalent compounds: oxygen (O_2), nitrogen (N_2), hydrogen chloride (HCl) and water (H_2O).

Note: Some non-metals can form ionic or covalent bonding, depending on the other atoms involved.

	Examples			
Element	*Covalent bonding*		*Ionic bonding*	
Chlorine	Hydrogen chloride	HCl	Magnesium chloride	$MgCl_2$
	Carbon tetrachloride	CCl_4	Sodium chloride	NaCl
Oxygen	Carbon dioxide	CO_2	Magnesium oxide	MgO
			Sodium oxide	Na_2O
Nitrogen	Nitrogen	N_2	Magnesium nitride	Mg_3N_2

These two types of bonding cause very different properties of the compounds formed. In the case of ionic bonding ions are formed, whereas no charged particles are formed when covalent molecules are produced.

Properties of ionic and covalent compounds

Ionic compounds	*Covalent compounds*
1. Usually crystalline solids (as oppositely charged ions attract each other and form a regular lattice structure)	Usually gases or liquids

2. Conduct electricity when molten or in solution (as charged ions carry this electricity)	Do not conduct electricity (no ions present to carry the electricity)
3. High melting and boiling points (as difficult to overcome the attraction between the ions in the lattice)	Low melting and boiling points (only have to overcome the forces between the molecules, which are weak)
4. Usually soluble in water but not in organic solvents	Usually insoluble in water but soluble in organic solvents

Valency

This is the combining power of an element. By learning these values in the following table, you can write the formula of any compound. Most compounds consist of a metallic and non-metallic part; the non-metallic part may be an element or group (radical). For example, sodium has a valency of +1, whereas chlorine has a valency of −1 (the valency of an element is usually the number of electrons that it must lose or gain so that it reaches a stable atomic structure).

Valency table

Name	*Symbol*	*Ion*
Elements and groups with a combining power of +1		
Ammonium	NH_4	NH_4^+
Copper(I)	Cu	Cu^+
Hydrogen	H	H^+
Potassium	K	K^+
Silver	Ag	Ag^+
Sodium	Na	Na^+
Elements and groups with a combining power of −1		
Bromine (bromide)	Br	Br^-
Chlorine (chloride)	Cl	Cl^-
Hydrogen	H	H^-
Hydrogencarbonate	HCO_3	HCO_3^-
Hydrogensulphate	HSO_4	HSO_4^-
Hydroxide	OH	OH^-
Iodine (iodide)	I	I^-
Manganate(VII) (permanganate)	MnO_4	MnO_4^-
Nitrate	NO_3	NO_3^-

Name	*Symbol*	*Ion*
Elements and radicals with a combining power of +2		
Calcium	Ca	Ca^{2+}
Copper(II)	Cu	Cu^{2+}
Iron(II)	Fe	Fe^{2+}
Lead(II)	Pb	Pb^{2+}
Magnesium	Mg	Mg^{2+}
Tin(II)	Sn	Sn^{2+}
Zinc	Zn	Zn^{2+}
Elements with a combining power of +3		
Aluminium	Al	Al^{3+}
Iron(III)	Fe	Fe^{3+}
Radical with a combining power of −3		
Phosphate	PO_4	PO_4^{3-}
Elements with a combining power of +4		
Lead(IV)	Pb	Pb^{4+}
Tin(IV)	Sn	Sn^{4+}
Elements with a combining power of 4		
Carbon	C	no ion
Silicon	Si	no ion

You can pretend that a valency of +1 or −1 is one 'hook' protruding from an atom, which must join with another atom. When atoms join, all the 'hooks' which are protruding must be used up before the formula is written. For example:

1. Write the formula of calcium hydroxide.

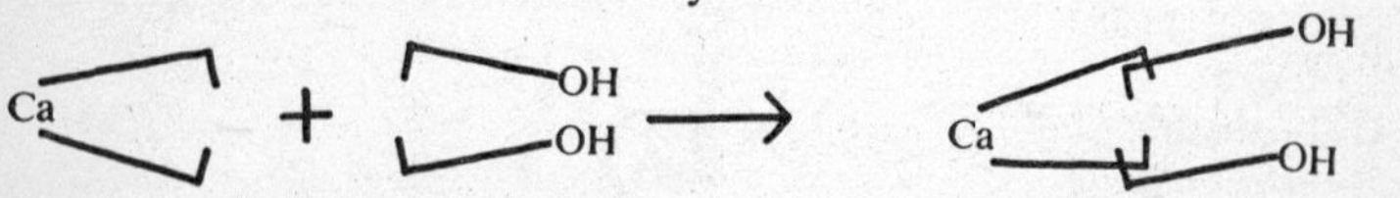

Calcium +2   hydroxide groups 2 × −1

So formula is $Ca(OH)_2$.

2. Write the formula of aluminium oxide.

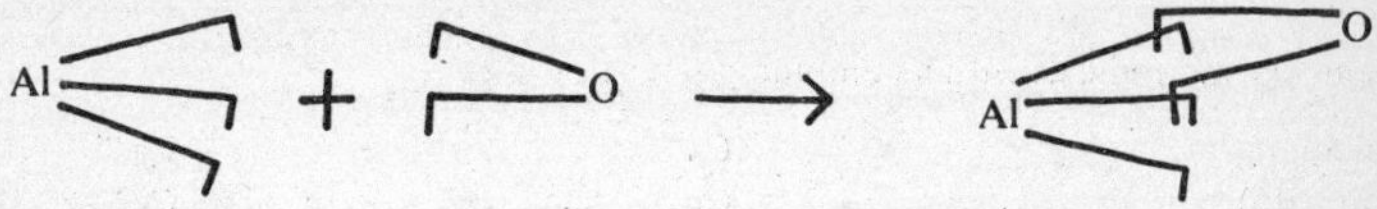

aluminium valency +3 | oxygen valency −2 | one hook from the aluminium is free, so another oxygen is added

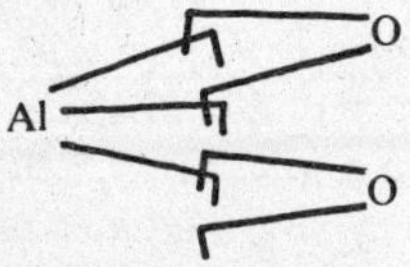

now there are too many oxygen hooks, so add one more oxygen and aluminium

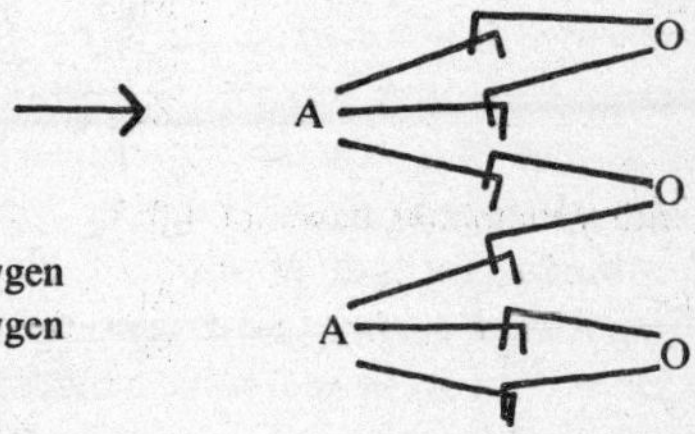

So formula is Al_2O_3.

Note: When elements have a variable valency, this has to be specified when writing down its compounds. For example, copper has a valency of +1 or +2. The formulae CuO and Cu_2O make it obvious that in CuO, copper is present as Cu^{2+} and in Cu_2O, copper is present as Cu^+. Writing down the name copper oxide does not show this, so the names copper(II) oxide and copper(I) oxide respectively are used.

Examination Questions

This is an important topic as it is popular with examiners. You must be able to draw out the two types of bonding.

1. This is a straightforward question from the structured part of a London paper (*June 1982*). **The answers are underlined.**

(a) *Complete the table below.*

	Element X	*Element Y*	*Element Z*
Atomic	11	6	16
Number of protons	11	6	16
Number of neutrons	12	6	16
Mass number (relative mass of atom)	23	12	32
Electronic configuration	2.8.1	2.4	2.8.6

(6)

(b) *Which of the above elements X, Y and Z is a metal?* X (1)

(c) *Element X combines with element Z to form a compound.*

(i) *Write down the most likely formula of this compound using the symbols X and Z* X_2Z

(ii) *What type of bonding exists between the two elements X and Z?* Ionic bonding (2)

(d) *The relative atomic mass of element Z is accurately quoted as 32.1. Suggest why it is not a whole number.* Isotopes of Z must exist which have different mass numbers, so the average mass of Z = 32.1. (1)

2. This is part of a structured question from a specimen A.E.B. paper (*June 1982*). Nitrogen (atomic number 7) and hydrogen (atomic number 1) can combine to form an ammonia molecule.

(a) *Using a small square (□) to represent an electron of a nitrogen atom and a large dot (●) to represent an electron of a hydrogen atom, draw a diagram to show how the outer shell electrons are arranged in an*
(2) *ammonia molecule* (3)

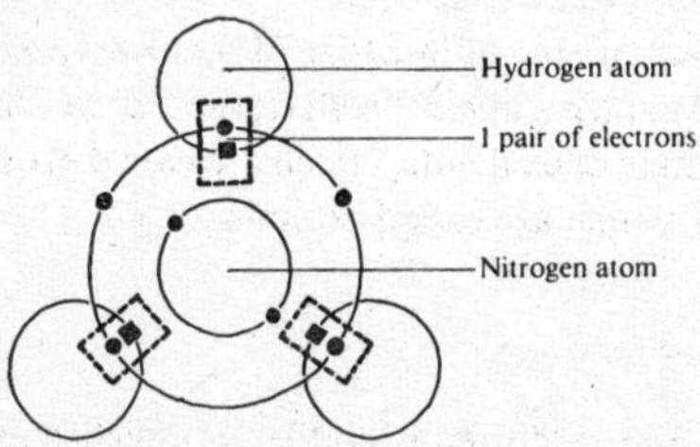

(b) *What type of bonding is present in this molecule?* Covalent. (1)

4 The Periodic Table and Structure

There are over a hundred elements known to man. From the nineteenth century onwards many chemists have tried to divide these elements into groups of similar substances. Mendeleef, who formulated the Periodic Table, even left gaps for elements which he predicted would later be discovered but perhaps not during his lifetime. He was proved correct.

The Periodic Table

The table overleaf shows the electronic structure of the first twenty elements of the Periodic Table.

The elements are arranged in order of their increasing atomic number and this arrangement is called the Periodic Table. This table is divided into vertical columns of elements, which are called groups, and horizontal rows of elements, which are called periods.

Groups

The elements in any group have similar properties as they all have the same number of electrons in their outer shell. Groups 1, 2 and 3 are metals, so they have 1, 2 or 3 electrons respectively in their outer shell. They need to lose 1, 2 or 3 electron(s) to form a stable structure.
Group 1 contains elements called the alkali metals.
Group 2 contains elements called the alkaline earth metals.
Group 4 elements are non-metals and metals, but they all have 4 electrons in their outer shell, so they need to form stable compounds by sharing electrons.
Groups 5, 6 and 7 are non-metals and they need to gain 3, 2 or 1 electron(s) respectively to form stable structures.
Group 7 contains elements called the halogens.
Group 8 or 0 contains the inert (or noble) gases, and they each contain 8 electrons in their outer shell.

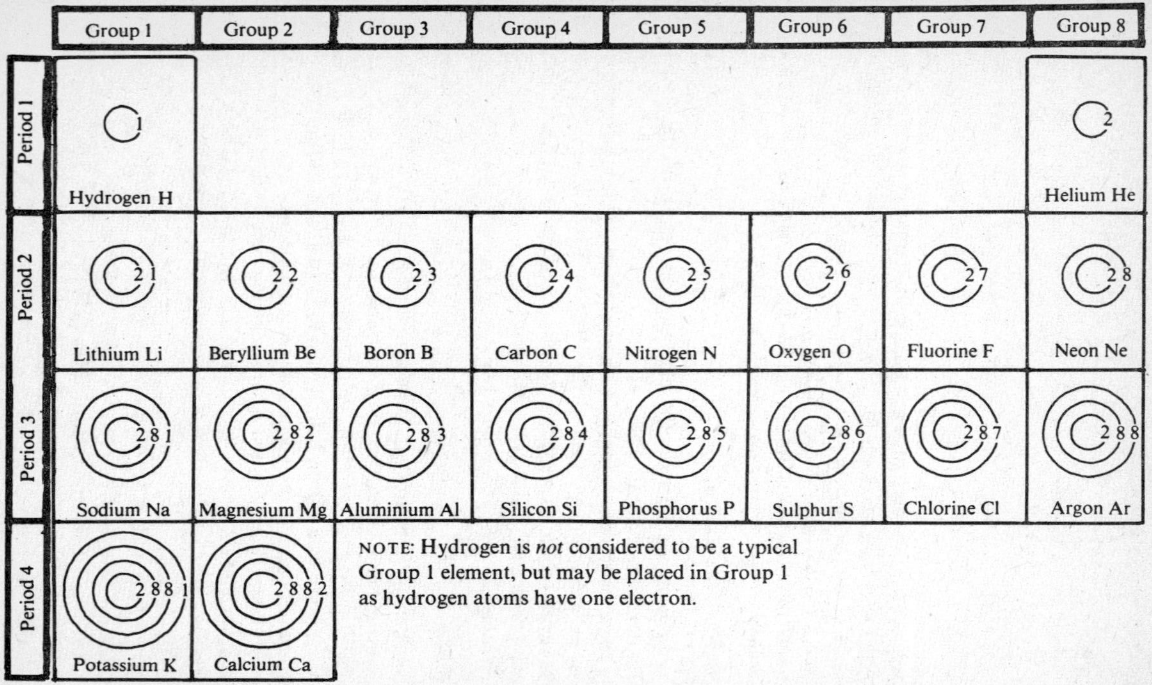

NOTE: Hydrogen is *not* considered to be a typical Group 1 element, but may be placed in Group 1 as hydrogen atoms have one electron.

Hydrogen is often excluded from group 1. It has 1 electron in its outer shell but because of its small size, its properties are not similar to those of group 1 metals.

Periods

As you go across a period, from group 1 to group 7, you are adding electrons to the same outer shell. In group 1 the elements are metals, the following elements become less metallic and finally non-metallic as you move across a period.

Changes across a Period

When you take one period of the Periodic Table and move from group 1 to group 2, the metal in group 1 is chemically more reactive than the metal in group 2, as it is easier for an atom to lose 1 electron (and so form a stable structure) than it is for an atom to lose 2 electrons. Using the same reasoning the group 3 metal would be less reactive than the group 2 metal, while in group 4 chemical activity is at its lowest. Group 5 atoms need to gain 3 electrons in order to reach a stable structure, while groups 6 and 7 need to gain 2 and 1 electron(s) respectively. These elements are becoming progressively more reactive, as it is easier to gain 1 electron (and so form a stable structure) than it is to gain 2 electrons.

These facts are summarized in the following graph:

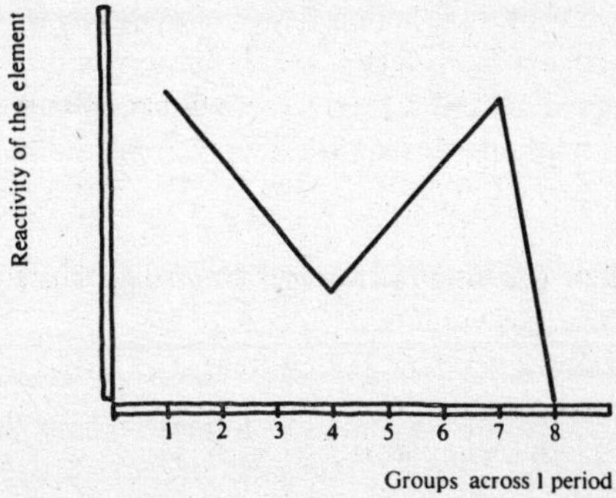

A graph to show the reactivity of elements across one period

Changes down one Group of the Periodic Table

The atomic number of the elements increases down a group, so although each atom has the same number of electrons in its outer shell, the number of complete electron shells will increase. Therefore the atomic radius of each atom will increase.

The larger the radius of a metallic atom, the further away the outermost electron(s) are from the attractive power of the nucleus, and the easier it is for that atom to lose electrons; so chemical reactivity increases down a group.

The opposite situation occurs in groups 5, 6 and 7. As these atoms become larger the positive nucleus will have more difficulty in attracting the necessary electron(s) to attain a stable structure, so their reactivity will decrease as the atomic number increases.

All these facts can be summarized as follows:

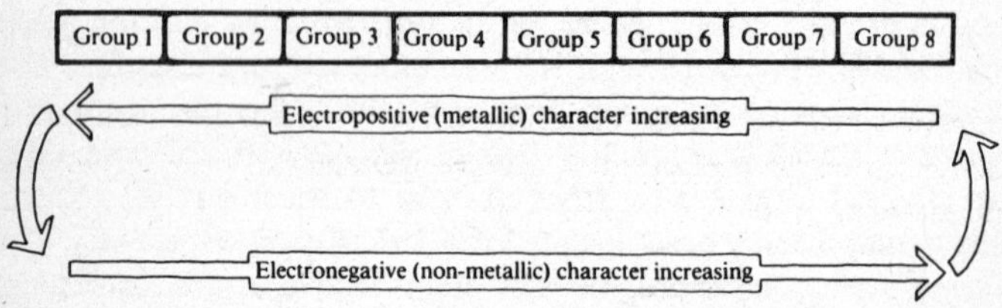

Transition Elements

Some syllabuses ask for a basic knowledge of these elements – so check.

Transition elements are metals which have variable valencies, for example Fe^{2+} and Fe^{3+}, and they usually form coloured compounds. The elements are hard and dense with high melting and boiling points.

The Structure of Elements related to their Properties

1. *Metallic Lattices*

The atoms in a sample of a metal are thought to have lost their outer shell electron(s) so that they become positive ions. These positive ions repel each other (like charges attract) but they are held together by the 'sea' of free electrons. These electrons can move anywhere in the lattice: they are called delocalized electrons.

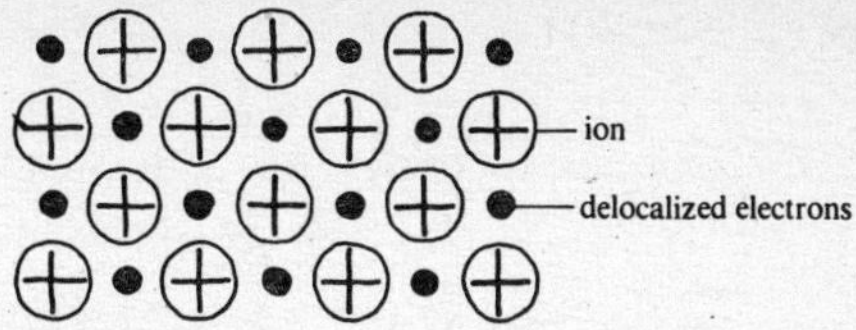

A diagram of a metallic lattice

In this metallic lattice structure, the layers can slide over each other. So metals are malleable and ductile.

Since there are freely moving electrons present in a metallic lattice, these electrons can pass on electrical and heat energy: so metals are good conductors of heat and electricity.

The melting and boiling points of metals are high as, for these processes to occur, the strong bonds in the metallic lattice must be broken.

2. *Giant Atomic Lattices* (*Macromolecules*)

Elements which have this sort of structure are covalently bonded. The example, which is important, is carbon. Carbon can exist in two forms – diamond or graphite.

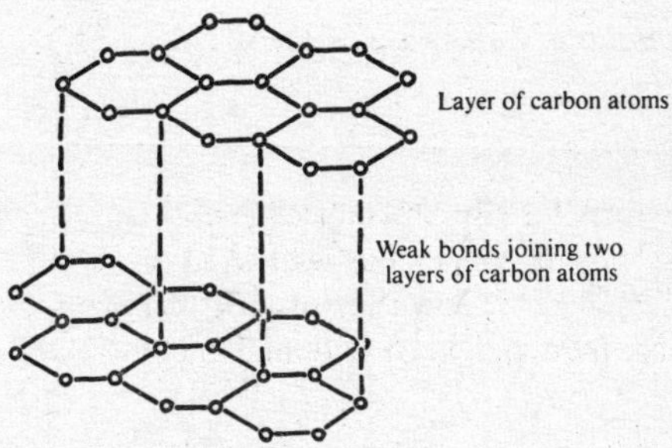

A diagram of the structure of graphite

Graphite has layers of carbon atoms arranged in regular hexagonal patterns; these layers have very strong bonds. However, the bonds *between* the layers are weak, so graphite is soft as these layers can slide over each other (it is used as a lubricant).

Graphite can conduct electricity, as not all the electrons are involved in the bonding, so they are free to convey electricity. It has high melting and boiling points as a lot of energy is needed to break up the structure.

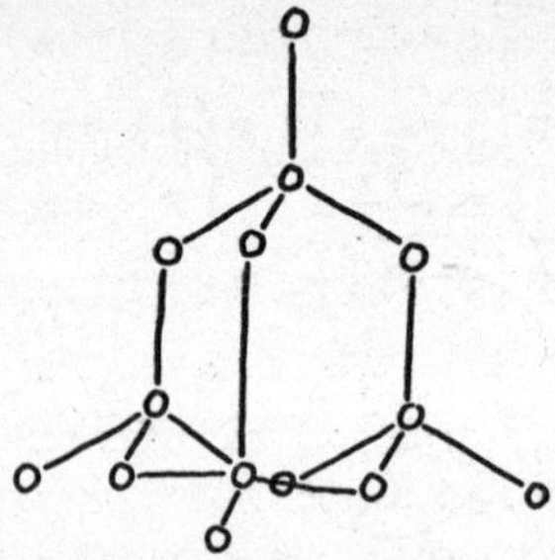

A diagram of the structure of diamond

In this form of carbon all the atoms are bonded by four covalent bonds. This results in a very rigid structure, so diamond is very hard. It has very high melting and boiling points as it is extremely difficult to break these strong bonds.

Allotropy

When an element can exist in more than one form, in the same state, it is said to show allotropy.

3. *Simple Molecular Lattices*

Most of the non-metals have these kinds of structure, e.g. iodine (I_2), sulphur (S_8).

A diagram of the structure of an iodine molecule

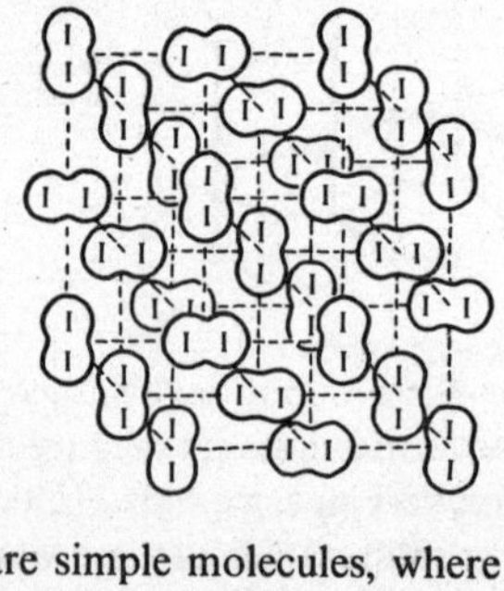

Molecules of iodine are simple molecules, where 2 atoms of iodine are joined together by covalent bonding, so the intramolecular bond (bond within the molecule) is strong. Clusters of these molecules then arrange themselves in a regular order, so the intermolecular bonds (bonds between molecules) are weak. Iodine is easily vaporized, which means that these intermolecular bonds are easily broken giving iodine gas. Iodine is a solid with low melting and boiling points.

A sulphur molecule contains 8 atoms of sulphur joined together.

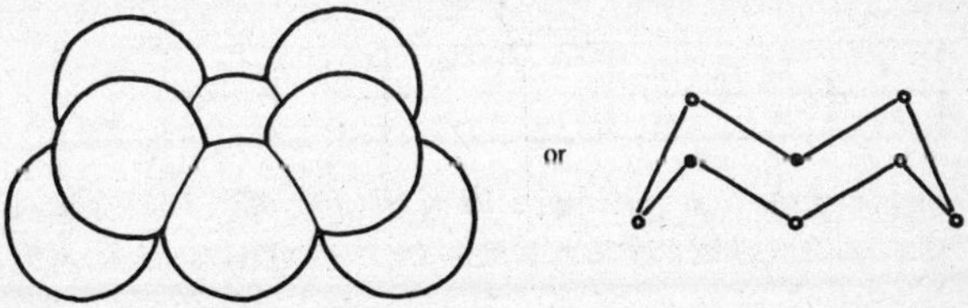

A diagram of the structure of a sulphur molecule

These molecules can be packed together in two different ways, so that there are two allotropes of sulphur. As in iodine, there are weak intermolecular forces and these are easily broken by heating, so sulphur has low melting and boiling points. (Allotropes of sulphur, page 153).

The Structure of Ionic Compounds

When ionic compounds are formed the ions involved arrange themselves into an ionic lattice, with ions held together by their opposite charges.

A diagram of the structure of sodium chloride

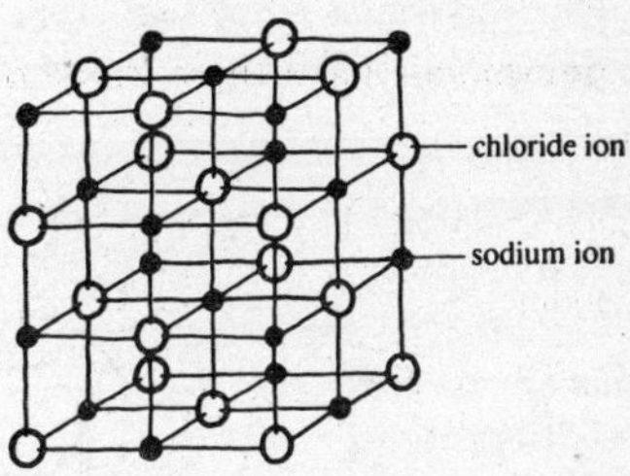

The attraction between these oppositely charged ions is very strong, so these substances will have very high melting points. As all the electrons are involved in the attraction between the ions, these substances will not conduct electricity in the solid state. However, when molten, or dissolved in water, the lattice breaks up, so the ions are free to carry current and so conduct electricity.

Examination Questions

1. (*June* 1978) *Associated Examining Board*

		H	He				
1	Be	B	2	N	O	3	Ne
Na	4	Al	Si	P	5	Cl	6

In this diagram of the first three periods of the Periodic Table the symbols for six of the elements have been replaced by the numerals, 1, 2, 3, 4, 5 and 6.

(a) *Which numeral is occupying the place of* (i) *a halogen,* (ii) *an inert gas,* (iii) *a non-metal with a high melting point,* (iv) *a solid which at room temperature is composed of simple molecules?* (4)

(b) *For the elements represented by 2, 3, 4 and 5, state the number of protons in each nucleus and show diagrammatically the arrangement of electrons around each nucleus.* (4)

(c) *Elements 2 and 3 form a stable compound and so do elements 3 and 4. Show the arrangement of the outer shell of electrons of each element in each of the* two *compounds formed and deduce two properties for each compound.* (11)

(d) *Elements 2 and 5 exhibit allotropy. State clearly the meaning of this term. Suggest how you would prove that two allotropes of an element are chemically the same.* (5)

Answer

(a) (i) 3; (ii) 6; (iii) 2; (iv) 5.

(b) 2 contains 6 protons;
3 contains 9 protons;
4 contains 12 protons;
5 contains 16 protons.

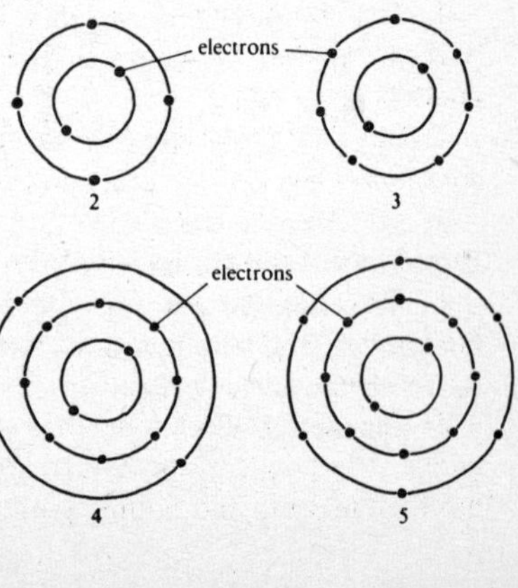

(c)

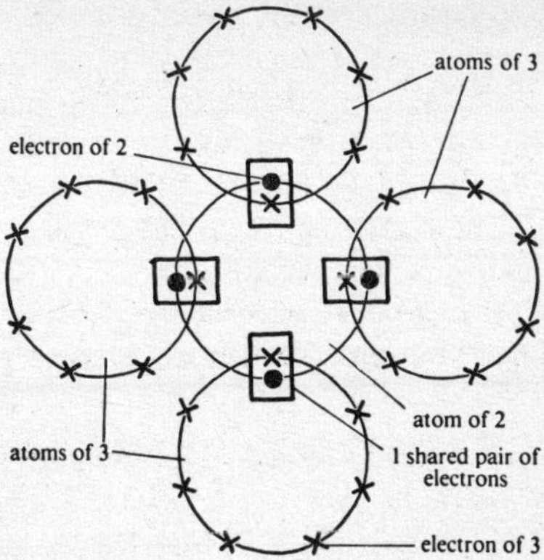

Compound formed from 2 and 3

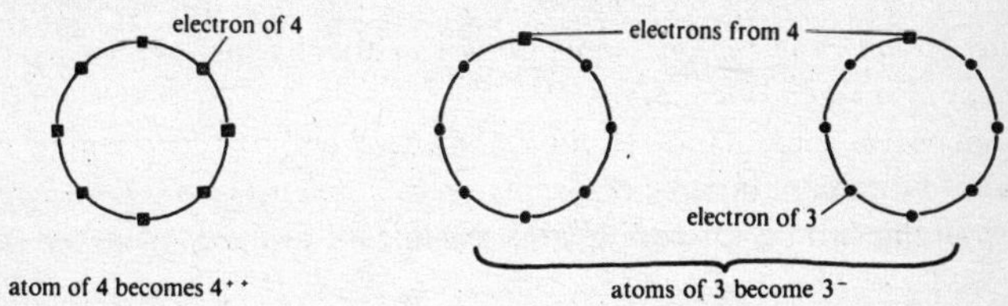

Compound formed from 3 and 4

Note: This is asking you for properties of covalent and ionic compounds, but the question says 'deduce two properties', rather than 'state two properties', so you must explain why these properties apply.

Properties of the compound from 2 and 3

1. This compound has covalent bonding between its atoms, so electron pairs are shared. No charged particles are formed, therefore it does not conduct electricity.

2. Covalent molecules have weak bonds between the molecules, so the compound has low melting and boiling points.

Properties of the compound from 3 and 4

1. This compound has ionic bonding, so charged particles called ions are formed. In the molten state, these particles are free to move, therefore it conducts electricity.

2. The oppositely charged ions attract each other and so form a crystal lattice. The bonds in this lattice are difficult to break, so the compound has high melting and boiling points.

(d) Allotropy. When an element can exist in more than one form, when it is in the same state, then it is said to show allotropy. For example, carbon, which is a solid, can exist as the solid diamond or the solid graphite. These two allotropes have different structures.

To prove that two allotropes are chemically the same, the same mass of each could be burnt in excess oxygen. The product and mass obtained from both allotropes should be the same.

2. This is a difficult question from London (*June 1981*). It is difficult because you must decide what to include in your answer.

State FOUR general types of structure taken up by solid elements and compounds. Give TWO examples of each. Use the examples you have been given to discuss the important physical properties possessed by substances with each of these structures. Draw a diagram to show how the particles are arranged in each of the four structures.

Answer

The four types of structure are:

1. Metallic lattice, e.g. sodium; magnesium.

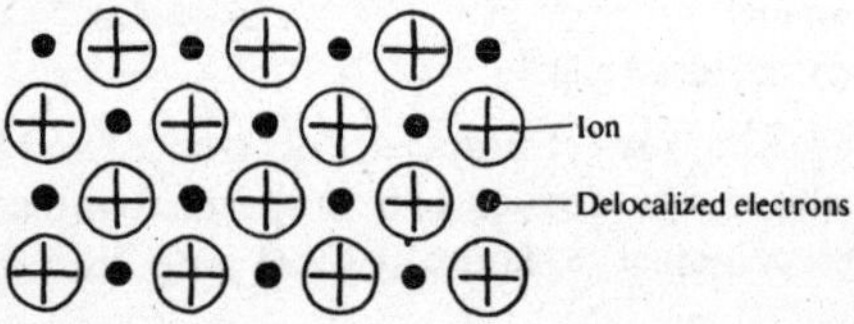

Diagram of metallic structure

2. Ionic lattice, e.g. magnesium chloride; sodium chloride.

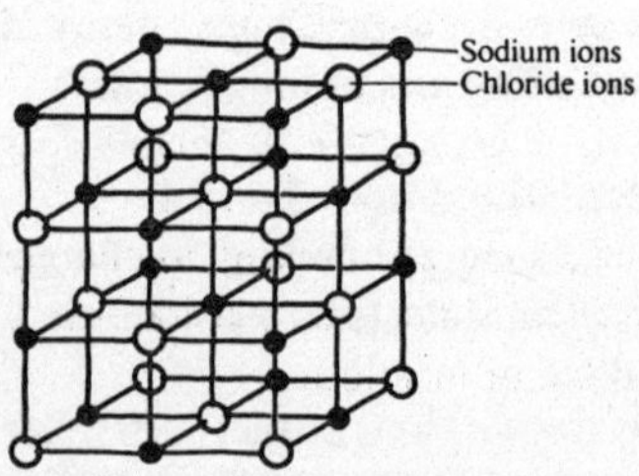

Diagram of
sodium chloride lattice

3. Giant atomic lattices, e.g. carbon; silicon.

Diagram of diamond

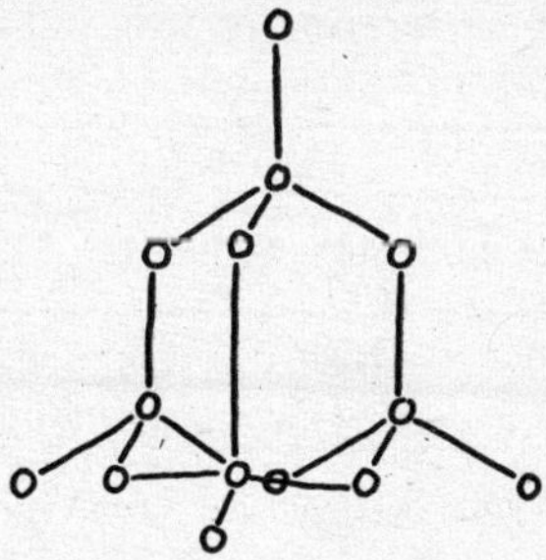

4. Simple molecular lattices, e.g. iodine; sulphur.

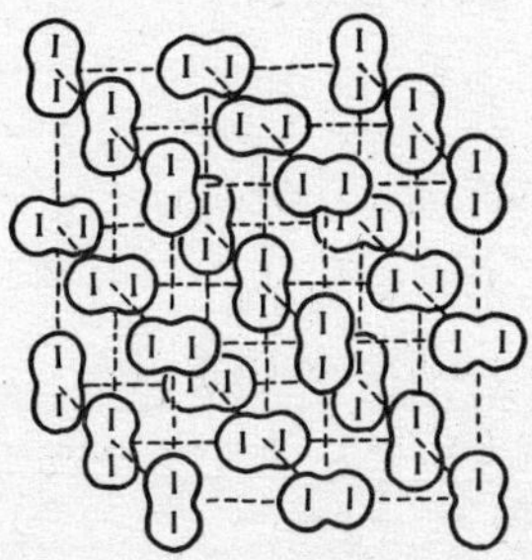

Diagram of iodine

The strength of the bonds in these structures gives rise to different physical properties. If the bonds are hard to break between the atoms, or molecules, and within the molecules, then high melting and boiling points occur.

If the structure is rigid with strong bonds between the atoms or molecules, then the resulting substance is hard, e.g. sodium chloride; whereas in metals the layers of atoms can slide over each other so they are malleable and ductile.

If free electrons or ions are present in the structure then they will conduct electricity. In ionic lattices these ions are only free to move when the substance is molten or in solution.

Note: A table would then summarize these properties in a clear way.

Type of structure	*Bonding*	*Melting point/ boiling point*	*Description*	*Conduction of electricity*
Metallic lattice	Strong	Usually both high	Solid, ductile and malleable	Yes
Ionic lattice	Strong	High	Hard, brittle	Only when molten
Atomic lattice	Strong	High	Very hard solid	No; exception graphite
Molecular lattice	Weak	Both low	Soft solid	No

5. *The Mole, Formulae and Equations*

The Mole

A bag containing 100 dead rats which has a mass of 15 kg

A bag containing 100 marbles which has a mass of 2.5 kg

Since there are *the same number of articles* in each bag, you can compare the ratio of the masses of rats and marbles.

Ratio of mass   rats : marbles
                15 : 2.5

But ratios are expressed with the smallest value as 1. So dividing each number by 2.5:

Ratio of mass   rats : marbles

$$\frac{15}{2.5} : \frac{2.5}{2.5}$$

$$= 6 : 1$$

This idea of ratio can be applied to atoms (which have a very small mass). Chemists take 6.02×10^{23} atoms or 602000000000000000000000 atoms and determine their mass. When this number of carbon atoms are taken, they have a mass of exactly 12 g. When 6.02×10^{23} atoms of magnesium are taken, they have a mass of 24 g.

But carbon has a relative atomic mass of 12 and magnesium has a relative atomic mass of 24, so in order to find the mass of 1 mole of an element you find the relative atomic mass and express it in grams.

Avogadro's Constant (Avogadro's Number)

There are 6.02×10^{23} atoms of carbon in 12 g of carbon (atomic number 12). This number is known as Avogadro's Constant.

The Mole

The mole is the amount of any substance that contains 6.02×10^{23} particles of that substance.

Note: 1 mole of oxygen could mean 1 mole of oxygen molecules (O_2 so mass 32 g) or 1 mole of oxygen ions (O^{2-} mass 16 g); so the type of particle being considered must be specified. If the type of particle is not clear from a question, then you should assume the substance concerned is in the form you would normally find it.

If you want to calculate the mole of a compound, then you must find the relative molecular mass (R.M.M. or M_r) first. For example, for water R.M.M.

	R.A.M.
2 × hydrogen	2
1 × oxygen	16
	18

So 1 mole of water molecules will have a mass of 18 g.

Note: The R.A.M. or R.M.M. of any substance in grams contains 6.02×10^{23} particles of that substance.

Calculations involving the Mole

1.

Substance	*R.M.M. or R.A.M.*		*Mass of* 1 *mole*
Silver	108		108 g
Sodium hydroxide	23 + 16 + 1	6.02×10^{23} molecules → weigh	40 g
Oxygen (O_2)	16 + 16		32 g
Chlorine (Cl_2)	35.5 + 35.5		71 g

2. Calculate the mass of (a) 10 moles of water; (b) 0.5 mole of iodine (I_2); (c) 2 moles of calcium hydroxide ($Ca(OH)_2$).

(a) Water has an R.M.M. of $2 \times H = 2$

$1 \times O = 16$

18

1 mole of water has a mass of 18 g.

So 10 moles of water has a mass of 180 g.

(b) Iodine has an R.M.M. of $2 \times I = 2 \times 127 = 254$

1 mole of iodine has a mass of 254 g.

So 0.5 mole of iodine has a mass of $\frac{254}{2} = 127$ g.

(c) Calcium hydroxide has an R.M.M. of $1 \times Ca = 40$

$2 \times O = 32$

$2 \times H = 2$

74

1 mole of calcium hydroxide has a mass of 74 g.

So 2 moles of calcium hydroxide has a mass of $74 \times 2 = 148$ g.

Laws of Chemical Combination

The Law of Conservation of Mass

Matter is neither created nor destroyed in a chemical reaction.

This is an important law because it states that when atoms react they rearrange themselves, but nevertheless the initial mass of all the reactants equals the final mass of all the products.

Sometimes there appears to be a decrease in the final mass if a gas is produced and this gas escapes. However, if the mass of this gas is determined, then this law will be obeyed. If this law did not exist then balanced chemical equations could not be written.

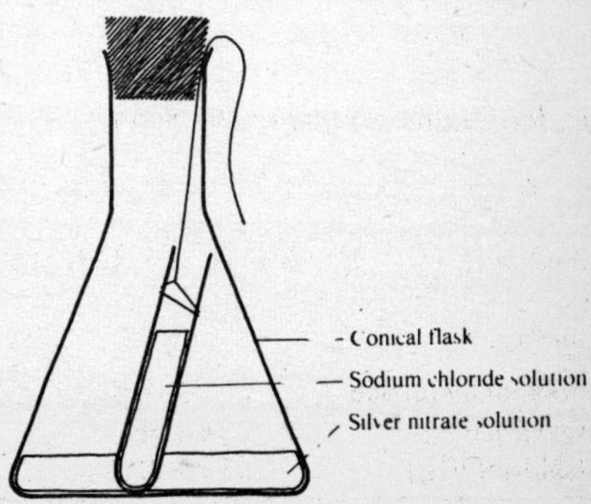

The conical flask is set up as shown in the diagram and placed on a balance to determine its mass. The flask is then tilted so that the two liquids mix. The mass is then redetermined and found to be unaltered, although from the equation it can be seen that different substances are present.

$$AgNO_3(aq) + NaCl(aq) \rightarrow NaNO_3(aq) + AgCl(s)$$

The Law of Constant Composition (or definite proportions)

All pure samples of the same chemical compound contain the same elements combined together in the same proportions by mass.

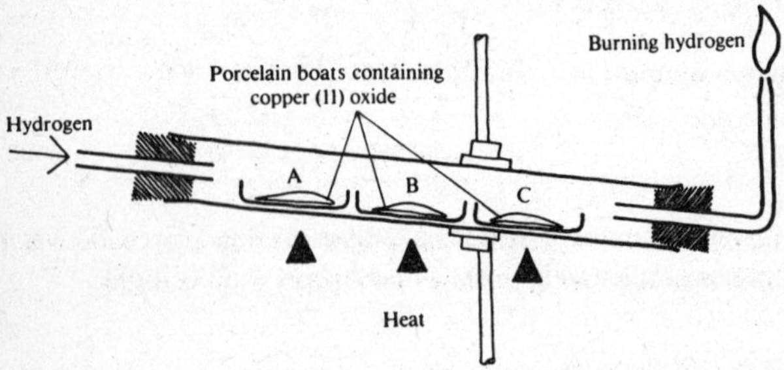

Experiment to prove the Law of Constant Composition by the reduction (removal of oxygen) from copper(II) oxide

Three dry porcelain boats are weighed, filled with copper(II) oxide and then reweighed. They are then put in a sloping combustion tube as shown in the diagram above. (The tube slopes so that the water formed collects in the cooler part of the tube and does not run back into the hotter section, perhaps breaking the tube). These boats are heated while a supply of hydrogen is passed over them. They are then cooled (with the stream of hydrogen still passing over them) and then reweighed.

$$CuO(s) + H_2(g) \rightarrow Cu(s) + H_2O(l)$$

The following is an example of the results obtained with the required calculation:

	Sample A	*Sample B*	*Sample C*
Mass of porcelain boat + copper(II) oxide	4.14 g	4.26 g	3.65 g
Mass of porcelain boat + copper	3.85 g	4.02 g	3.42 g
Mass of porcelain boat alone	2.70 g	3.01 g	2.50 g
Mass of copper(II) oxide	4.14–2.70 g = 1.44 g	4.26–3.01 g = 1.25 g	3.65–2.50 g = 1.15 g
Mass of copper	4.14–3.85 g = 1.15 g	4.26–3.01 g = 1.01 g	3.42–2.50 g = 0.92 g
Percentage copper in copper(II) oxide	$\frac{1.15 \times 100}{1.44}$ = 79.8%	$\frac{1.01 \times 100}{1.25}$ = 80.8%	$\frac{0.92 \times 100}{1.15}$ = 80.0%

In all samples the percentage of copper in copper(II) oxide was found to be the same, so proving the law of constant composition.

The Law of Multiple Proportions

When two elements A and B combine together to form more than one compound, the different masses of A, which combine with a fixed mass of B, are in a simple ratio.

Experiment to Prove the Law of Multiple Proportions

This experiment is similar to the previous one. This time copper(II) oxide and copper(I) oxide are placed in separate porcelain boats and reduced with hydrogen. The masses are determined before and after the experiment.

$$CuO(s) + H_2(g) \rightarrow Cu(s) + H_2O(l)$$
$$Cu_2O(s) + H_2(g) \rightarrow 2Cu(s) + H_2O(l)$$

The following is an example of the results obtained with the required calculation:

	Copper(I) oxide	*Copper(II) oxide*
Mass of boat + oxide	9.80 g	9.40 g
Mass of boat + copper	9.48 g	9.00 g
Mass of boat	7.40 g	7.38 g
Mass of copper	9.80–7.40 g = 2.08 g	9.00–7.38 g = 1.62 g
Mass of oxygen	9.80–9.48 g = 0.32 g	9.40–9.00 g = 0.40 g
	0.32 g of oxygen combines with 2.08 g of copper ∴ 100 g oxygen combines with $\frac{2.08}{0.32} \times 100$ = 650 g copper	0.40 g of oxygen combines with 1.62 g of copper ∴ 100 g oxygen combines with $\frac{1.62}{0.40} \times 100$ = 405 g copper

This ratio is approximately 2:1. So the fixed mass of oxygen (100 g) has combined with copper in the two separate compounds in the ratio of 2:1.

Percentage Composition of Compounds

The following example shows you how to calculate the percentage composition by mass of a compound.

Example: Calculate the percentage by mass of each element in calcium sulphate.

1. Start by calculating the R.M.M. of the compound from the formula $CaSO_4$.

1 × Ca	40
1 × S	32
4 × O	64
	136

2. Express the mass of each element present as a percentage of the total mass.

$$\text{Percentage of calcium} = \frac{40}{136} \times 100 = 29.4\%$$

$$\text{Percentage of sulphur} = \frac{32}{136} \times 100 = 23.5\%$$

$$\text{Percentage of oxygen} = \frac{64}{136} \times 100 = 47.1\%$$

Note: When you have calculated two values, the third could be found by subtracting the two answers from 100%, i.e. percentage of oxygen = 100 – (29.4 + 23.5) = 47.1%. However, if you have made an error in the first two calculations this will give the wrong answer. It is preferable to calculate *all* the percentages and then check they add up to 100%.

Calculation of the Empirical (simplest) Formula of a Compound

Example: Calculate the empirical formula of a compound which has the following percentage composition: sulphur 40.5%, oxygen 30.4% and sodium 29.1%.

First of all you need to find the number of moles of each element present. This procedure should be followed whether you are given the percentage of each element or the mass of each element.

$$\text{The number of moles present} = \frac{\text{mass or percentage of the substance}}{\text{R.A.M. or R.M.M.}}$$

Note: This calculation should be set out as follows. Too many pupils do not show their workings and so lose marks.

	Sodium	*Sulphur*	*Oxygen*
Percentage (or mass in g)	29.1	40.5	30.4
R.A.M.	23	32	16
Number of moles present	$\frac{29.1}{23}$ = 1.26	$\frac{40.5}{32}$ = 1.26	$\frac{30.4}{16}$ = 1.9
Ratio of moles present (divide each value by the smallest number)	$\frac{1.26}{1.26}$ = 1	$\frac{1.26}{1.26}$ = 1	$\frac{1.9}{1.26}$ = 1.5

Note: Since you cannot have 1.5 molecules of oxygen each number must be multiplied by 2. So the empirical formula = $Na_2S_2O_3$.

Water of Crystallization

(For definition see page 173)

Experiment to Determine the Water of Crystallization in a Substance

A hydrated compound is placed in a crucible of known mass. The mass of this crucible and compound is determined before and after heating. The crucible and compound are reheated, then reweighed, until a constant mass is obtained. This means that *all* the water of crystallization has been driven off.

In an experiment to determine the formula of hydrated sodium sulphate, i.e. $Na_2SO_4 \cdot xH_2O$ the following results were obtained:

Mass of crucible + hydrated salt	18.56 g
Mass of crucible + salt after heating to constant mass	16.76 g
Mass of crucible	15.34 g
Mass of salt after heating	16.76–15.34 g = 1.42 g
Mass of water lost	18.56–16.76 g = 1.80 g

	Water	*Sodium sulphate*
Mass in g	1.80 g	1.42 g
R.M.M.	1.8	$(23 \times 2) + 32 + (16 \times 4) = 142$
Number of moles present	$\frac{1.8}{18}$ = 0.1	$\frac{1.42}{142}$ = 0.01
Ratio of moles present (divide each value by the smallest number)	$\frac{0.1}{0.01}$ = 10	$\frac{0.01}{0.01}$ = 1

So the formula of hydrated sodium sulphate = $Na_2SO_4 \cdot 10H_2O$.

Equations

Equations are used by chemists to represent chemical changes in shorthand. They do not always state the conditions of a reaction and they may or may not specify the state of the element or compound; they do not state whether heat is required or whether the substances are concentrated, or how fast a reaction proceeds.

The formulae of compounds have been established from many experiments, where the masses of reacting substances have been determined before and after a reaction.

Balancing Equations

Examples

1. For the reaction between burning magnesium ribbon and oxygen, which forms a white ash of magnesium oxide:

(a) Write down the formulae of the reacting substance(s) and product(s)

$$Mg + O_2 \rightarrow MgO$$

left-hand side of the equation	right-hand side of the equation

These formulae are fixed from the valencies of the elements.

Note: Elements, which are gases (exception inert gases) join together to form molecules and therefore oxygen is written as O_2 *not* O.

(b) According to the above equation 1 atom (or 1 mole) of magnesium reacts with 1 molecule (or 1 mole) of oxygen to give 1 molecule (or 1 mole) of magnesium oxide. But the Law of Conservation of Mass says that matter is neither created nor destroyed in a chemical reaction. So the equation in (a) is an 'unbalanced equation' as 1 molecule of oxygen contains 2 atoms of oxygen on the left-hand side of the equation; while on the right-hand side of the equation 1 molecule of magnesium oxide contains only 1 atom of oxygen.

(c) In order to balance this equation you can alter the number of molecules (or moles) reacting with each other, but *you must not alter the formulae*; so first increase the number of oxygen atoms on the right-hand side of the equation:

$$Mg + O_2 \rightarrow 2MgO$$

But this is still 'unbalanced' as there are now two molecules of magnesium oxide on the right-hand side containing 2 atoms of magnesium.

Try again – by doubling the number of moles of magnesium!

$$2Mg + O_2 \rightarrow 2MgO$$

This is now 'balanced' as there are the same number of magnesium and oxygen atoms on both sides of the equation.

2. Ammonia is formed bv heating nitrogen and hydrogen together:
(a) Write down the formulae of the reacting substance(s) and product(s)

$N_2 + H_2 \rightarrow NH_3$

This is an 'unbalanced equation' as 1 molecule of nitrogen (containing 2 atoms of nitrogen) reacts with 1 molecule of hydrogen (containing 2 atoms of hydrogen) to give 1 molecule of ammonia (containing 1 atom of hydrogen and 3 atoms of nitrogen). So there are more atoms of hydrogen on the right-hand side of the equation.
(b) Balance the number of hydrogen atoms on both sides:

$$N_2 + 3H_2 \rightarrow 2NH_3$$

number nitrogen atoms = 2	number nitrogen atoms = 2
number hydrogen atoms = 6	number hydrogen atoms = 6

So this equation is now 'balanced'.

Note: Other elements which exist as molecules are chlorine (Cl_2) and fluorine (F_2). Two other elements are bromine liquid, which is written as Br_2, while iodine solid is written as I_2.

Further information can be added to equations by the following symbols, which are placed after a formula

(g) = gas
(l) = liquid
(s) = solid
(aq) = a substance which is dissolved in water.

So Examples 1 and 2 can be written:

$2Mg(s) + O_2(g) \rightarrow 2MgO(s)$
$N_2(g) + 3H_2(g) \rightarrow 2NH_3(g)$

Ionic Equations

As the heading suggests, these are equations showing the ions involved in a reaction; they are shorter than full equations and are popular with examiners, although they often cause students trouble.

1. The test for the presence of a chloride ion involves the addition of silver nitrate solution to a solution of the suspected chloride. The full equation would be written as:

$$AgNO_3(aq) + NaCl(aq) \rightarrow AgCl(s) + NaNO_3(aq)$$

This suggests that solid silver chloride and a solution of sodium nitrate have been formed. In fact the sodium and nitrate ions are present as separate ions. This equation is written with ions:

$$Ag^+(aq) + NO_3^-(aq) + Na^+(aq) + Cl^-(aq) \rightarrow$$
$$AgCl(s) + Na^+(aq) + Cl\ \ (aq)$$

The sodium and nitrate ions have not changed during the reaction, so they are called 'spectator' ions. It is unnecessary to include them in an ionic equation, so this is rewritten:

$$Ag^+(aq) + Cl^-(aq) \rightarrow AgCl(s)$$

This is 'balanced' as there is one positive ion and one negative ion on the left-hand side of the equation, which 'balance' each other.

2. When sodium hydroxide solution is added to a solution of iron(III) chloride a reddish-brown precipitate of iron(III) hydroxide is formed. The ionic equation is written:

$$Fe^{3+}(aq) + OH^-(aq) \rightarrow Fe(OH)_3(s)$$

This equation is not 'balanced' as the iron ion has three positive charges, while the hydroxide ion has only one negative charge. Since these charges must balance, three hydroxide ions are needed:

$$Fe^{3+}(aq) + 3OH^-(aq) \rightarrow Fe(OH)_3(s)$$

3. When chlorine gas is bubbled through potassium bromide solution an orange-brown colour appears as the bromine is displaced (page 162). This reaction can be written ionically:

$$Cl_2(g) + Br^-(aq) \rightarrow Cl^-(aq) + Br_2(aq)$$

This is not 'balanced' as there are not the same number of chlorine and bromine atoms and ions on both sides of the equation.

$$Cl_2(aq) + 2Br^-(aq) \rightarrow 2Cl^-(aq) + Br_2(aq)$$

This is now 'balanced', since there are the same number of particles on each side of the equation.

Calculations using Equations

Calculation of Reacting Masses

Once an equation is balanced it can be used to calculate the mass of the reactant(s) (the substance(s) that will react together) and the product(s) (the substance(s) which are produced).

1. Examine the equation:

$$2Mg(s) + O_2(g) \rightarrow 2MgO(s)$$

2 moles of magnesium ribbon will react with 1 mole of oxygen to produce 2 moles of magnesium oxide.

(a) First, convert these numbers of moles to masses:

1 mole of magnesium has a mass of	24 g
So 2 moles of magnesium has a mass of	48 g
1 mole of oxygen (O_2) has a mass of	32 g
1 mole of magnesium oxide has a mass of (24 + 16) =	40 g
2 moles of magnesium oxide has a mass of	80 g

So 48 g of magnesium will react with 32 g of oxygen to produce 80 g of magnesium oxide.

2. You might need to determine how many grams of a product would be present after a reaction. For example, what mass of ammonia is evolved (given off) when 2 g of ammonium sulphate is boiled with excess sodium hydroxide solution?

(a) Write down the balanced equation, if it is not given in the question.

$$(NH_4)_2SO_4(aq) + 2NaOH(aq) \rightarrow Na_2SO_4(aq) + 2NH_3(g) + 2H_2O(l)$$

This question is only concerned with the masses of ammonium sulphate and ammonia so it is *unnecessary* to work out any other masses.

(b) From the equation 1 mole of ammonium sulphate reacts and produces 2 moles of ammonia. Converting these moles into masses:

1 mole of ammonium sulphate has a mass of	132 g
calculated as 2 × N	28
8 × H	8
1 × S	32
4 × O	64
	132
1 mole of ammonia has a mass of (14 + 3)	17 g
2 moles of ammonia has a mass of	34 g

So 132 g of ammonium sulphate will react and produce 34 g of ammonia

So 1 g of ammonium sulphate will produce $\frac{34}{132}$ g ammonia

So 2 g of ammonium sulphate will produce $\frac{34 \times 2}{132}$ g ammonia = 0.5 g

> *Note:* Problems of this type are very similar. You may have to calculate the mass of any product or reactant but usually you do not have to work out *all* the masses.

Calculations of Strength of Solutions

A standard solution is a solution of known concentration.
A molar solution (M) of a compound is one which contains 1 mole of the compound in 1 cubic decimetre (dm^3) of the solution.

Example: Calculate the volume of hydrochloric acid 1 M, which would be required to dissolve 2 g of magnesium ribbon.
(a) Write down the balanced equation

$$Mg(s) + 2HCl(aq) \rightarrow MgCl_2(aq) + H_2(g)$$

(b) From the equation 1 mole of magnesium reacts with 2 moles of hydrochloric acid.
(c) Convert the number of moles to a mass for magnesium only to find the fraction of 1 mole of magnesium, which is used.
1 mole of magnesium has a mass of 24 g, so rewriting the above sentence:

24 g of magnesium provides 1 mole of magnesium
1 g of magnesium provides $\frac{1}{24}$ mole of magnesium
2 g of magnesium provides $\frac{1}{24} \times 2$ mole of magnesium
$= \frac{1}{12}$ mole of magnesium

(d) From the equation, $\frac{1}{12}$ mole of magnesium is used; therefore $2 \times \frac{1}{12}$ $= \frac{1}{6}$ mole of hydrochloric acid is required. But 1 mole of hydrochloric acid is contained in 1 dm^3(1000 cm^3) 1 M HCl
so $\frac{1}{6}$ mole of hydrochloric acid is contained in $1000 \times \frac{1}{6}$ 1 M HCl
= 166.3 cm^3 1M HCl

Calculations of Volumes of Gases

It is more usual to determine the volume of a reacting gas rather than its mass.

Avogadro's Law

Equal volumes of all gases, under the same conditions of temperature and pressure, contain the same number of molecules. From this we can define:

The Molar Volume of a Gas

1 mole of any gas occupies a volume of 22.4 dm^3 (22400 cm^3) at s.t.p. s.t.p. is an abbreviation for standard temperature and pressure which are specified as 0 °C and 76 cm of mercury.

Thus 1 mole of ammonia gas (mass 17 g) or 1 mole of oxygen gas (mass 32 g) will occupy a volume of 22400 cm^3 at s.t.p.

Examples

1. What volume of carbon dioxide would be produced if 10 g of calcium carbonate reacts with excess hydrochloric acid at s.t.p.?

(a) Write the balanced equation

$CaCO_3(s) + 2HCl(aq) \rightarrow CaCl_2(aq) + H_2O(l) + CO_2(g)$

So 1 mole of calcium carbonate will react with hydrochloric acid to produce 1 mole of carbon dioxide.

(b) Converting moles of calcium carbonate to a fraction of a mole.

		R.A.M
1 mole of calcium carbonate has a mass of	1 × Ca	40
	1 × C	12
	3 × O	48
		100 g

So 10 g of calcium carbonate is $\frac{10}{100} = \frac{1}{10}$ mole.

(c) If only $\frac{1}{10}$ mole of calcium carbonate reacts with hydrochloric acid then only $\frac{1}{10}$ mole of carbon dioxide will be produced.

1 mole of carbon dioxide occupies a volume of 22400 cm^3

$\frac{1}{10}$ mole of carbon dioxide occupies a volume of $\frac{22400}{10} = \underline{2240\ cm^3}$

2. When carbon dioxide is passed over heated carbon, carbon monoxide is produced according to the equation $CO_2(g) + C(s) \rightarrow 2CO(g)$. What volume of carbon monoxide can be produced from 3 g of carbon?

(a) From the equation 1 mole of carbon will react to produce 2 moles of carbon monoxide.
(b) 1 mole of carbon has a mass of 12 g
or 12 g of carbon is 1 mole of carbon.
So 3 g of carbon is $\frac{1}{12} \times 3$ moles of carbon = 0.25 mole of carbon.
(c) 1 mole of carbon monoxide will occupy a volume of 22.4 dm^3.
So 2 × 0.25 mole of carbon monoxide will occupy a volume of

$$22.4 \times 2 \times 0.25$$
$$= \underline{11.2\ dm^3}$$

Gay-Lussac's Law

When gases react together they do so in volumes which are related to each other simply, and to the product if gaseous. All the measurements are made at the same temperature and pressure.

This means that if 100 cm^3 of gas A react with 200 cm^3 of gas B then the ratio of their reacting volumes would be 1:2. That is, the ratio is a simple one rather than a complicated one like $1:1\frac{2}{3}$.

Calculations based on this law are popular.

Examples

1. What volume of oxygen would be required to burn 0.5 mole methane completely? What volume of carbon dioxide would be formed?
(a) Write the balanced equation

$$CH_4(g) + 2O_2(g) \rightarrow CO_2(g) + 2H_2O(l)$$

1 mole of methane would need to burn in 2 moles of oxygen and produce 1 mole of carbon dioxide. If only 0.5 mole methane was used then 1 mole of oxygen and 0.5 mole carbon dioxide would be involved.
(b) Converting moles to volumes
1 mole of oxygen occupies a volume of 22.4 dm^3
1 mole of carbon dioxide occupies a volume of 22.4 dm^3
0.5 mole of carbon dioxide occupies a volume of $\underline{11.2\ dm^3}$

Note: The volume of water produced occupies a negligible volume as it will condense from steam to water.

2. 60 cm^3 oxygen was added to 24 cm^3 of carbon monoxide and the mixture ignited. The product occupied 72 cm^3. Show that this calculation illustrates Gay-Lussac's Law.

(a) $2CO(g) + O_2(g) \rightarrow 2CO_2(g)$

2 moles 1 mole 2 moles

Since only 24 cm^3 of carbon monoxide is present only 12 cm^3 of oxygen will be used up, so the oxygen is present in excess. Excess oxygen = initial volume − volume used up.

$60\ cm^3 - 12\ cm^3 = 48\ cm^3$

(b) The amount of carbon dioxide can be calculated in two ways

(i) Amount of gaseous product − excess oxygen = amount of carbon dioxide

$72\ cm^3 - 48\ cm^3 = 24\ cm^3$

(ii) Since 24 cm^3 of carbon dioxide reacted with the oxygen, from the equation 24 cm^3 of carbon monoxide will be produced. The reacting volumes of the gases are:

	oxygen	carbon monoxide	carbon dioxide
Reacting volumes	12 cm^3	24 cm^3	24 cm^3
Ratio reacting volumes	1	2	2

These reacting volumes are in a simple ratio and so illustrate Gay-Lussac's Law.

Examination Questions

Calculations frequently occur in questions and parts of questions. It is easy to obtain full marks on calculations provided that you show *all* your workings.

1. Part of a question (*Associated Examining Board, June 1981*).

An oxide of a metal M $A_r(M) = 118$, was weighed in a porcelain boat and placed in a combustion tube. The oxide was then reduced to the metal by heating it in a stream of hydrogen gas. The boat, with the metal in it, was allowed to cool with the hydrogen still passing over it and it was then reweighed. It was reheated in hydrogen, cooled and weighed once again. The masses obtained were as follows:

mass of boat	*5.20 g*
mass of boat + metal oxide	*8.20 g*
mass of boat + metal (1)	*7.56 g*
mass of boat + metal (2)	*7.56 g*

(i) *Why was hydrogen still passing over the boat while it was cooling?*
(ii) *Why was the boat and metal reheated and reweighed?*
(iii) *What mass of oxygen was originally combined with the metal?*
(iv) *Calculate the empirical formula of the metal oxide (showing clearly how you arrive at your answer), and write an equation for the reaction of the oxide with hydrogen.* (8)

Answer

(i) So that the metal was not oxidized by any oxygen in the air to the oxide.

(ii) So that a constant mass was obtained. This meant that all the oxide had been reduced to the metal.

(iii)	mass of boat + oxide	8.20 g
	mass of boat + metal	– 7.56 g
	mass of oxygen	0.64 g
(iv)	mass of boat + metal	7.56 g
	mass of boat	– 5.20 g
	mass of metal	2.36 g

So 2.36 g of metal has combined with 0.64 g oxygen.

	Oxygen	*Metal*
Mass in g	0.64	2.36
R.A.M.	16	118
Number of moles	$\frac{0.64}{16}$	$\frac{2.36}{118}$
Ratio of moles present	= 0.04	= 0.02
(divide each value by the smallest number)	= 2	= 1

The empirical formula is therefore MO_2.
The equation for the reaction is

$$MO_2 + 2H_2 \rightarrow M + 2H_2O$$

2. (*Oxford, Summer 1978*)

(a) *The reaction between sodium and water is represented by the equation*

$$2Na + 2H_2O \rightarrow 2NaOH + H_2$$

4.60 g of sodium are completely dissolved in water.

Calculate:

(i) *the mass of hydrogen produced*

(ii) *the number of moles of hydrogen produced*

(iii) *the volume of hydrogen at s.t.p. produced*

(iv) *the volume of* 1.00 *M hydrochloric acid needed to neutralize the sodium hydroxide solution produced.*

(b) *Three samples of copper*(II) *oxide prepared by three different methods were found to contain* 20.1% *of oxygen by weight. Name and state the law upheld by these results.*

(c) (i) *Name* three *reducing agents which could be used to reduce copper*(II) *oxide to copper.*

(ii) *Draw a simple diagram of the apparatus you would use to reduce an oxide of copper.*

Answer

(*a*) (i) From the equation 2 moles of sodium react to produce 1 mole of hydrogen (mass 2 g).

A mass of 46 g of sodium will provide 2 moles of sodium, so a mass of 4.6 g of sodium will provide $\frac{2}{10}$ mole of sodium. Therefore $\frac{2}{10}$ mole sodium $\rightarrow \frac{1}{10}$ mole hydrogen = 0.2 g.

(ii) From above, $\frac{1}{10}$ mole or 0.1 mole hydrogen is produced.

(iii) 1 mole of any gas at s.t.p. occupies 22.4 dm^3, so 0.1 mole hydrogen gas at s.t.p. occupies 2.24 dm^3.

(iv) From the equation 0.2 mole of sodium reacts to produce 0.2 mole of sodium hydroxide.

$$NaOH + HCl \rightarrow NaCl + H_2O$$

From this equation 0.2 mole sodium hydroxide will react with 0.2 mole hydrochloric acid.

1 mole of hydrochloric acid is contained in 1 dm^3 of 1 M hydrochloric acid, so 0.2 mole HCl is contained in 1 × 0.2 dm^3 of 1 M hydrochloric acid = 0.2 dm^3.

(b) The Law of Constant Composition. All pure samples of the same chemical compound contain the same elements combined together in the same proportions by mass.

(c) (i) carbon monoxide; hydrogen; methane.

(ii)

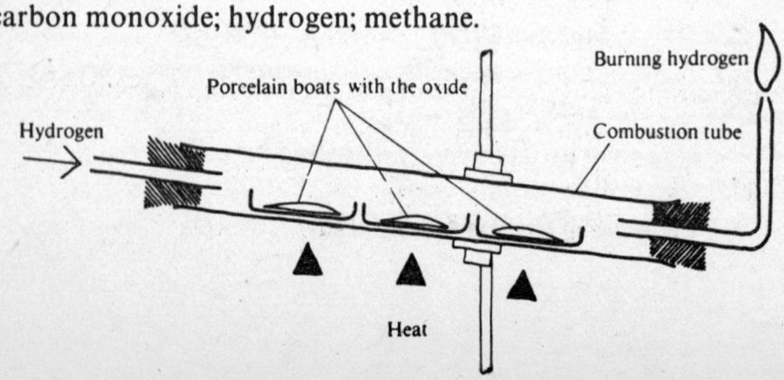

6. *The Reactivity of Metals, Electrolysis and Redox Reactions*

The Reactivity of Metals

The common metals in the Periodic Table can be arranged in an order of chemical reactivity. To do this the reactions of the metals with water, oxygen and acids as well as displacement reactions (page 106) are considered.

> *Note:* These experiments are important; you should know the results and be able to relate them to the reactivity series.

A Summary of the Reactions of Metals with Water

Metal	*Results and equations*
Sodium	Reacts vigorously with cold water; gives hydrogen and an alkaline solution $2Na(s) + 2H_2O(l) \rightarrow 2NaOH(aq) + H_2(g)$
Potassium	Reacts even more vigorously with cold water; burns with a purple flame; gives alkaline solution $2K(s) + 2H_2O(l) \rightarrow 2KOH(aq) + H_2(g)$
Calcium	Reacts quickly with cold water, giving a less soluble hydroxide suspension and hydrogen $Ca(s) + 2H_2O(l) \rightarrow Ca(OH)_2(aq) + H_2(g)$
Magnesium	Only reacts after several days with cold water; reacts rapidly with steam $Mg(s) + H_2O(g) \rightarrow MgO(s) + H_2(g)$
Aluminium	No reaction with water or steam, as the surface is covered with a protective oxide layer
Zinc	Reacts rapidly with steam only $Zn(s) + H_2O(g) \rightarrow ZnO(s) + H_2(g)$

Iron	Reacts reversibly with steam $3Fe(s) + 4H_2O(g) \rightleftharpoons Fe_3O_4(s) + 4H_2(g)$
Lead Copper	No reaction with steam

A Summary of the Reactions of Metals with Acids

Metal	*Results and equations using hydrochloric acid*
Sodium Potassium	Too reactive to risk reacting with acids
Calcium Magnesium	Rapid effervescence (fizzing) with cold acid forming hydrogen $Ca(s) + 2HCl(aq) \rightarrow CaCl_2(aq) + H_2(g)$
Aluminium	Reacts very slowly with cold acid as the oxide layer is present; reacts rapidly when heated with acid $2Al(s) + 6HCl(aq) \rightarrow 2AlCl_3(aq) + 3H_2(g)$
Iron	Reacts slowly with cold acid and faster on heating $Fe(s) + 2HCl(aq) \rightarrow FeCl_2(aq) + H_2(g)$
Lead Copper	No reaction

Note: If an element is above hydrogen in the reactivity series then it will replace the hydrogen in an acid; that is, it will react with the acid.

Displacement Reactions

When a metal is added to a solution of a salt of a different metal, and the metal is more reactive than the metal in solution, it displaces it ('pushes it out' of the compound). For example, when magnesium ribbon is placed in copper(II) sulphate solution the magnesium slowly dissolves so the solution becomes magnesium sulphate (which is colourless), while the copper is seen as a brown precipitate.

$$Mg(s) + CuSO_4(aq) \rightarrow MgSO_4(aq) + Cu(s)$$

A summary of some typical displacement reactions

	Solutions				
Metal	*Magnesium sulphate*	*Zinc sulphate*	*Iron*(II) *sulphate*	*Copper* (II) *sulphate*	*Lead nitrate*
Magnesium		D	D	D	D
Zinc	NR		D	D	D
Iron	NR	NR		D	D
Copper	NR	NR	NR		NR
Lead	NR	NR	NR	D	

NR = no reaction D = displacement

The Reactivity Series

From all the above experiments the reactivity series of metals can be compiled, starting with the most reactive metal:

Potassium
Sodium
Calcium
Magnesium
Aluminium
Zinc
Iron
Tin
Lead
(Hydrogen)
Copper
Mercury*
Silver*
Gold*
Platinum*

Note: An easy sentence to help you remember this series is: *P*oisoned *s*ausages *c*an *m*ake *a* *z*ulu *i*ll; *t*herefore *l*et *h*ighly *c*lever *m*en *s*lay *g*ood *p*igs.

The first letter of every word corresponds to the first letter of the metal. Those metals marked with an asterisk are unnecessary for O-level purposes, but they complete the sentence.

The Electrochemical Series (e.c.s.)

The reactivity series of metals has been decided by investigating the chemical activities of the metals. The electrochemical series (in which the metals are in the same order) has been determined by placing each metal in a solution of a salt of the metal and measuring the voltage of the system when compared with a reference substance.

Electrolysis

Electrolysis occurs when an electric current is passed through a solution, or a molten (melted) substance, and a chemical change takes place. This can be demonstrated by the following apparatus.

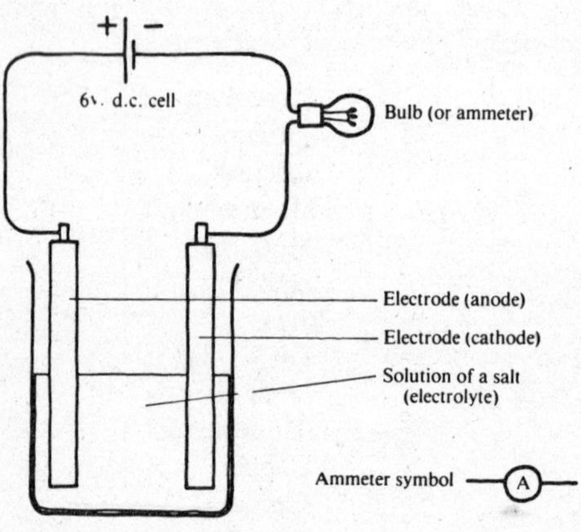

The current passes from the cell through the wire to the anode, then through the solution to the cathode and back to the cell, through the bulb. When the bulb glows this means a current is flowing in the circuit.

You need to know the following definitions:

An electrolyte is a solution, or a molten substance, which conducts an electric current and is decomposed by it.

Electrodes are metal or carbon rods where the current enters or leaves the electrolyte.

The anode is the positive electrode where the electrons leave the electrolyte.

The cathode is the negative electrode where the electrons enter the electrolyte.

A cation is a positively charged ion, which is attracted to the cathode during electrolysis.

An anion is a negatively charged ion, which is attracted to the anode during electrolysis.

An Explanation of Electrolysis

1. *A Solid*

When you try to pass electricity through an ionic solid the bulb in the circuit will not light up, showing that these substances do not conduct electricity. However, when they are heated, the ions, which are present in the solid structure, separate and are free to move towards the electrodes; so electrolysis occurs.

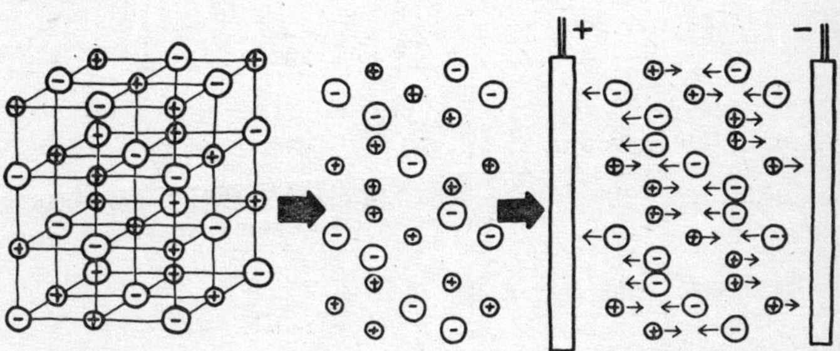

Solid sodium chloride

Molten sodium chloride

Electrolysis of molten sodium chloride. The arrows show the direction of movement of the ions when electrolysis occurs

A diagram representing the electrolysis of sodium chloride

2. *A Solution*

When a solution is electrolysed (undergoes electrolysis) not only are there ions present but also water, which is ionized to a small extent.

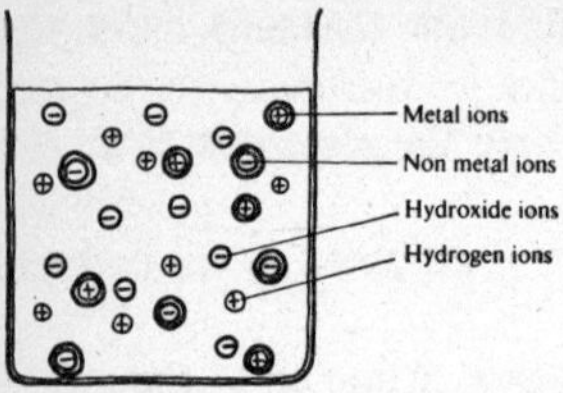

$$H_2O \rightleftharpoons H^+ + OH^-$$

(hydrogen ion) (hydroxide ion)

In a solution all ions are free to move. When electrolysis occurs these ions are attracted towards the electrodes.

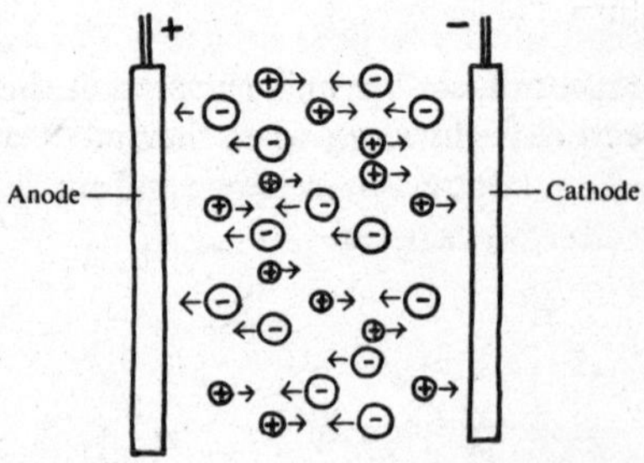

Reactions at the Cathode

When cations reach the cathode, they will gain electron(s) and become neutral atoms.

e.g. $Na^+ + e^- \rightarrow Na$
(electron)

$Ca^{2+} + 2e^- \rightarrow Ca$

When a solution is electrolysed, metal cations and hydrogen ions travel to the cathode. If the metal is above hydrogen in the electrochemical series then hydrogen is produced at the cathode.

$H^+ + e^- \rightarrow H$

then $H + H \rightarrow H_2(g)$

If the metal is below hydrogen in the electrochemical series, then the metal is produced at the cathode.

Since the electrochemical series lists atoms in decreasing order of reactivity, then once the more reactive atoms have formed ions, these ions will be stable and so will not form atoms as readily as the lower metals in the series.

Reactions at the Anode

When anions reach the anode they become neutral by losing electrons.

e.g. $Cl^- \rightarrow Cl + e^-$
then $Cl + Cl \rightarrow Cl_2$
$O^{2-} \rightarrow O + 2e^-$
then $O + O \rightarrow O_2$

If more than one anion is present then the group or anion which is lowest in the list below is discharged (neutralized):

SO_4^{2-}
NO_3^-
Cl^-
Br^-
I^-
OH^-

Sometimes an unexpected cation or anion is discharged from a mixture. This usually happens because this particular ion is present in a high concentration.

Experiments to Demonstrate Electrolysis

You are often asked to describe an electrolysis experiment. You should include the following details:

1. Draw a fully labelled diagram of the apparatus you used. This should include a bulb or ammeter, anode and cathode, an electrolyte and a system to test any gases which are evolved (given off).
2. Write down any changes you would see, i.e. any gases evolved and any change in colour of the electrolyte.
3. Write down the ions present, then write the equations for the reactions at the anode and cathode.

The following table summarizes the experiments, which you need to know:

			Reactions		
Electrolyte	*Electrodes*	*Ions present*	*At the cathode*	*At the anode*	*Changes observed*
Copper(II) sulphate solution	Platinum or Copper	Cu^{2+} SO_4^{2-} H^+ OH^-	$Cu^{2+} + 2e^- \rightarrow Cu(s)$	$OH^- \rightarrow OH + e^-$ $4OH \rightarrow 2H_2O + O_2(g)$	Blue solution slowly becomes colourless
Copper(II) sulphate solution	Copper	Cu^{2+} SO_4^{2-} H^+ OH^-	$Cu^{2+} + 2e^- \rightarrow Cu(s)$	$Cu \rightarrow Cu^{2+} + 2e^-$	Mass of anode decreases Mass of cathode increases
Dilute sulphuric acid	Platinum or Carbon	H^+ SO_4^{2-} H^+ OH^-	$H^+ + e^- \rightarrow H$ $H + H \rightarrow H_2$	$OH^- \rightarrow OH + e^-$ $4OH \rightarrow 2H_2O + O_2(g)$	The acid slowly becomes more concentrated
Sodium hydroxide solution	Platinum or Carbon	Na^+ OH^- H^+ OH^-	$H^+ + e^- \rightarrow H$ $H + H \rightarrow H_2$	$OH^- \rightarrow OH + e^-$ $4OH \rightarrow 2H_2O + O_2(g)$	The solution slowly becomes more concentrated
Sodium chloride solution	Carbon (Platinum anode attacked by chlorine)	Na^+ Cl^- H^+ OH^-	$H^+ + e^- \rightarrow H$ $H + H \rightarrow H_2$	$Cl^- \rightarrow Cl + e^-$ $Cl + Cl \rightarrow Cl_2$ (is present in a far higher concentration than OH^-)	The solution slowly becomes sodium hydroxide solution

Industrial uses of Electrolysis

Reactive metals occur in compounds in the earth's crust. Once they have been extracted from the earth they must be broken up into their elements. This is a very difficult process as the bonding between the elements is very strong and so electrolysis has to be used.

e.g. aluminium is extracted from bauxite (impure Al_2O_3)
sodium is extracted from rock salt (impure NaCl)

The molten ore is electrolysed and the cations travel to the cathode, where they are collected (for details of aluminium, page 125 and sodium, page 124).

The Purification (Refining) of Copper

This process is really a large-scale version of the laboratory electrolysis of copper(II) sulphate solution using copper electrodes. The impure copper is made the anode, while the pure copper is made the cathode. Since only pure copper(II) ions will be attracted to the cathode, the impurities will fall to the bottom of the copper(II) sulphate solution as a sludge.

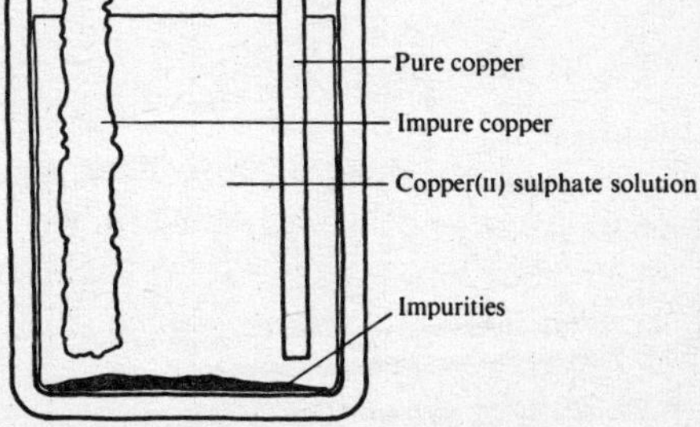

A diagram of the purification of copper

Electroplating

Electroplating is the process whereby an object (usually metallic) is coated with a thin layer of another metal by electrolysis.

This process can be used to silver plate cutlery. The anode is pure silver, the electrolyte is a solution of silver ions, while the article to be plated is the cathode. Nickel and chromium or nickel and copper can be used to electroplate iron in order to prevent corrosion.

Faraday's Laws of Electrolysis

These laws show that the amount of an element deposited during electrolysis depends on:

(i) the amount of current flowing
(ii) the time this current is flowing
(iii) the charge on the ion of the element.

The quantity of electricity flowing is measured in coulombs (C)

$$\text{Number of coulombs used} = \begin{matrix}\text{current} \\ \text{(in amps) (A)}\end{matrix} \times \begin{matrix}\text{time} \\ \text{(in seconds)}\end{matrix}$$

1 Faraday (F) of electricity (or 96 500 C) consists of 1 mole of electrons.

1 Faraday of electricity is needed to discharge (neutralize) 1 mole of monovalent ions (e.g. Na^+) during electrolysis.

2 Faradays (2 × 96 500 C) are needed to discharge 1 mole of divalent ions (e.g. Mg^{2+}) during electrolysis.

3 Faradays are needed to discharge 1 mole of trivalent ions (e.g. Al^{3+}).

Faraday's First Law

The mass of a substance produced in electrolysis is proportional to the quantity of electricity passing through the electrolyte.

For example

Current (in amps)	*Time (in seconds)*	*Mass of copper deposited (in grams)*
0.5	600	0.099
1.0	600	0.198
1.5	600	0.297

Faraday's Second Law

When the same quantity of electricity is passed through solutions of different electrolytes the number of moles of the elements deposited are inversely proportional to the charges on the ions of the elements.

e.g. If a current of 0.45 A is passed for 12.5 minutes through equal volumes of solutions of, first, 0.05 M copper(II) sulphate, and then 0.05 M silver nitrate, the masses deposited will be copper 0.221 g; silver 0.755 g.

$$\text{Number of moles of copper deposited} = \frac{\text{mass}}{\text{R.M.M.}} = \frac{0.221}{63.5}\,\text{g}$$
$$= \underline{0.0035 \text{ mole}}$$

$$\text{Number of moles of silver deposited} = \frac{0.755}{108}\,\text{g}$$
$$= \underline{0.0070 \text{ mole}}$$

Twice as many moles of silver are deposited because the ions present are Ag^{+} and Cu^{2+}.

Calculations

1. How many Faradays are required to produce
(a) 8 g of oxygen (as O_2)?
(b) 54 g of aluminium?
(c) 23 g of sodium?

(a) 2 F will be required to produce 1 mole of oxygen as O = 16 g.
2 F will be required to produce $\frac{1}{2}$ mole of oxygen as O_2 = 16 g.
1 F will be required to produce $\frac{1}{4}$ mole of oxygen as O_2 = 8 g.
(b) 3 F will be required to produce 1 mole of aluminium (Al^{3+}) mass 27 g.
6 F will be required to produce 2 moles of aluminium mass 54 g.
(c) 1 F will be required to produce 1 mole of sodium ions (Na^{+}) mass 23 g.

2. Calcium metal may be obtained by electrolysis of fused calcium chloride. How long, to the nearest minute, would a current of 4 A have to be passed in order to deposit 6 g calcium?

2 F (96 500 C × 2) will be required to produce 1 mole of calcium (40 g).

Rearranging this sentence, 40 g of calcium will be deposited by $96\,500 \times 2$ C

So 6 g of calcium will be deposited by $\dfrac{96\,500}{40} \times 6$ C

$= 14475$ C

But the quantity of electricity = current × time

$$\text{Current} = 4 \text{ A}$$

$$\text{Therefore} \quad 14475 \text{ C} = 4 \text{ A} \times \text{time}$$

$$\begin{aligned}\text{time} &= \frac{14475}{4}\\ &= 3618.75 \text{ secs}\\ &= \frac{3618.75}{60} \text{ minutes}\\ &= \underline{60 \text{ minutes}} \text{ (to the nearest minute)}\end{aligned}$$

Note: Examining boards vary in what they require you to know about Faraday's laws – so check your syllabus.

Oxidation and Reduction (Redox Reactions)

There are three different ways of defining oxidation and reduction.

Oxidation occurs during

1. The addition of oxygen to an element or compound.
2. The loss of hydrogen from a compound.
3. The loss of electron(s) from an atom or ion.

Reduction occurs during

1. The loss of oxygen from a compound.
2. The gain of hydrogen by an element or compound.
3. The gain of electron(s) by an atom or ion.

Note: A word to help you memorize the definition involving electron transfer.

O Oxidation
I is
L loss (of electron(s))
R Reduction
I is
G gain (of electrons)

Examples of Redox Reactions

The processes of oxidation and reduction always take place simultaneously.

1. e.g. when calcium is heated in oxygen, calcium oxide is formed

$$2Ca(s) + O_2(g) \rightarrow 2CaO(s)$$

The calcium atom loses two electrons and is therefore oxidized to calcium ions, while the oxygen molecule gains electrons and is therefore reduced to the oxide anion. Alternatively calcium atoms gain oxygen and become oxidized.

2. When hydrogen gas is passed over copper(II) oxide copper and water are produced.

$$CuO(s) + H_2(g) \rightarrow Cu(s) + H_2O(l)$$

The copper(II) oxide loses oxygen, so it is reduced to copper, while the hydrogen gains oxygen and so is oxidized to water. Alternatively the copper ions in copper(II) oxide gain electrons to become copper, so they are reduced, while the hydrogen molecules lose electrons, so they are oxidized.

3. The process of electrolysis is a redox reaction. Consider the reaction at the cathode when a solution of copper(II) sulphate is electrolysed using platinum electrodes

$$Cu^{2+} + 2e^- \rightarrow Cu$$

This is reduction as the copper ions gain electrons and form copper. At the anode

$$OH^- \rightarrow OH + e^-$$
$$4OH \rightarrow 2H_2O + O_2$$

This is oxidation as the hydroxide ions lose electrons and form water and oxygen.

Thus redox reactions occur at the electrodes during electrolysis, while the electrons move through the electrical circuit.

Oxidation Numbers

Many reactions in chemistry are redox reactions, but this may not always be obvious. The idea of oxidation numbers (ON) can be used to identify the elements that are oxidized and reduced.

Each element is given an oxidation number according to the following rules:

1. All elements which are uncombined with any other element have an oxidation number of 0.

2. A simple ion has an oxidation number which is the same size and sign as the charge on the ion.

e.g.

Ion	oxidation number
Na^+	$+1$
O^{2-}	-2

3. Hydrogen has an oxidation number of $+1$ in covalent compounds.
4. Oxygen has an oxidation number of -1 in peroxides.
5. The sum of all the oxidation numbers of the elements in a compound is zero.

e.g. copper(II) sulphate

$$\overset{+2}{Cu}\,\overset{+6}{S}\,\overset{-2}{O_4} \qquad \text{oxidation number values}$$

oxidation numbers total $(+2)+(+6)+(4\times-2)=0$

6. The sum of all the oxidation numbers of the elements in a charged group equals the charge on that group.

e.g. the carbonate ion $\overset{+4}{C}\,\overset{-2}{O_3}{}^{2-}$

$$(+4)+(3\times-2)=-2$$
$$+4-6 \qquad =-2$$

e.g. the sulphate ion $\overset{+6}{S}\,\overset{-2}{O_4}{}^{2-}$

$$(+6)+(4\times-2)=-2$$
$$+6-8\rightarrow=-2$$

Oxidation occurs when the oxidation number of the element increases. Reduction occurs when the oxidation number of the element decreases.

Examples

In the following reactions, what is oxidized and what is reduced?

(a) $$2\overset{+2}{Fe}\overset{-1}{Cl_2} \quad + \overset{0}{Cl_2} \quad 2\overset{+3}{Fe}\overset{-1}{Cl_3}$$

$$(+2)+(2\times-1)=0 \qquad 0 \qquad (+3)+(3\times-1)=0$$

So $\overset{+2}{Fe}\rightarrow\overset{3+}{Fe}$ i.e. an increase in ON. So oxidation has occurred.

$\overset{0}{Cl_2}\rightarrow2\overset{-1}{Cl}$ i.e. a decrease in ON. So reduction has occurred.

(b) $2\overset{+2}{Cu}\overset{-2}{O} + \overset{0}{C} \rightarrow 2\overset{0}{Cu} + \overset{+4}{C}\overset{-2}{O_2}$

So $\overset{+2}{Cu} \rightarrow \overset{0}{Cu}$ i.e. a decrease in ON. So reduction has occurred.

$\overset{0}{C} \rightarrow \overset{+4}{C}$ i.e. an increase in ON. So oxidation has occurred.

$\overset{-2}{O} \rightarrow \overset{-2}{O}$ i.e. no change in ON. So neither oxidation nor reduction has occurred.

(c) $\overset{+4}{Mn}\overset{-2}{O_2} + 4\overset{+1}{H}\overset{-1}{Cl} \rightarrow \overset{+2}{Mn}\overset{-1}{Cl_2} + 2\overset{+1}{H_2}\overset{-2}{O} + \overset{0}{Cl_2}$

Note: If you do not know the oxidation number of an element you can work it out. Since, when this element is present in a compound, the oxidation numbers in that compound must add up to zero or the charge on the ion.

e.g. $Mn\overset{-2}{O_2}$

$(x) + (2 \times -2) = 0$

So $x = +4$

$Mn\overset{-1}{Cl_2}$

$(y) + (2 \times -1) = 0$

$y = +2$

$\overset{+4}{Mn}\overset{-2}{O_2} \rightarrow \overset{+2}{Mn}\overset{-1}{Cl_2}$ The ON of manganese has decreased, so it has been reduced.

The ONs of hydrogen and oxygen are unchanged.

$\overset{+1}{H}\overset{-1}{Cl} \rightarrow \overset{0}{Cl_2}$ The ON of chlorine has increased. So it has been oxidized.

(d) $\overset{+2}{Cu}\overset{-2}{O} + \overset{+1}{H_2}\overset{+6}{S}\overset{-2}{O_4} \rightarrow \overset{+2}{Cu}\overset{+6}{S}\overset{-2}{O_4} + \overset{+1}{H_2}\overset{-2}{O}$

There has been no change in the ON of any of the elements so this is *not* a redox reaction.

Oxidizing and Reducing Agents

In example (c) above the manganese(IV) oxide has been reduced while the hydrochloric acid has been oxidized, so manganese(IV) oxide is said to be acting as an oxidizing agent.

Oxidizing Agents

An oxidizing agent is a substance which causes oxidation of another substance (while it is itself reduced).

Since the manganese(IV) oxide has been reduced by the hydrochloric acid, the hydrochloric acid can be said to be acting as a reducing agent.

Reducing Agents

A reducing agent is a substance which causes reduction of another substance (while it is itself oxidized).

e.g. $\overset{0}{C} + 2\overset{+1}{H_2}\overset{+6}{S}\overset{-2}{O_4} \rightarrow \overset{+4}{C}\overset{-2}{O_2} + 2\overset{+4}{S}\overset{-2}{O_2} + 2\overset{+1}{H_2}\overset{-2}{O}$

$\overset{0}{C} \rightarrow \overset{+4}{C}\overset{-2}{O_2}$ The ON of C has increased. So oxidation has occurred.

$\overset{+1}{H_2}\overset{+6}{S}\overset{-2}{O_4} \rightarrow \overset{+4}{S}\overset{-2}{O_2}$ The ON of S has decreased. So reduction has occurred.

The ONs of oxygen and hydrogen are unaltered. Thus carbon is oxidized to carbon dioxide by sulphuric acid, so sulphuric acid is an oxidizing agent; or sulphuric acid is reduced to sulphur dioxide by carbon, so carbon is a reducing agent.

A table of some oxidizing and reducing compounds

Reducing agents		*Equation*	*Changes observed*
1. Hydrogen sulphide (H_2S)	it is oxidized to sulphur	$\overset{+1}{H_2}\overset{-2}{S} \rightarrow \overset{0}{S}$	Yellow solid formed
2. Aqueous sulphur trioxide (SO_3)	oxidized to sulphate ions	$\overset{+4}{S}\overset{-2}{O_2} \rightarrow \overset{+6}{S}\overset{-2}{O_4}{}^{2-}$	
3. Carbon monoxide (CO)	oxidized to carbon dioxide	$\overset{+2}{C}\overset{-2}{O} \rightarrow \overset{+4}{C}\overset{-2}{O_2}$	
4. Hydrogen (with heated metal oxides) (H_2)	oxidized to water	$\overset{0}{H_2} \rightarrow \overset{+1}{H_2}\overset{-2}{O}$	Water appears
5. Potassium iodide (KI)	oxidized to iodine	$\overset{-1}{I} \rightarrow \overset{0}{I_2}$	A brown colour appears
6. Carbon (with heated metal oxides) (C)	oxidized to carbon monoxide	$\overset{0}{C} \rightarrow \overset{+4}{C}\overset{-2}{O}$	

Oxidizing agents		*Equation*	*Changes observed*
1. Oxygen (heat with metals) (O_2)	reduced to oxides	$\overset{0}{O_2} \rightarrow \overset{-2}{O}{}^{2-}$	
2. Chlorine (combined with metals) (Cl_2)	reduced to chlorides	$\overset{0}{Cl_2} \rightarrow \overset{-1}{Cl}{}^{-}$	
3. Hydrogen peroxide (H_2O_2)	reduced to water	$\overset{+1}{H_2}\overset{-1}{O_2} \rightarrow \overset{+1}{H_2}\overset{-2}{O}$	
4. Concentrated nitric acid (HNO_3)	reduced to water, nitrogen dioxide or nitrogen monoxide	$\overset{+5}{N}\overset{-2}{O_3}{}^{-} \rightarrow \overset{+4}{N}\overset{-2}{O_2}$ $\overset{+5}{N}\overset{-2}{O_3}{}^{-} \rightarrow \overset{+2}{N}\overset{-2}{O}$	Brown gas evolved
5. Concentrated sulphuric acid (H_2SO_4)	reduced to sulphur dioxide	$\overset{+6}{S}\overset{-2}{O_4}{}^{2-} \rightarrow \overset{+4}{S}\overset{-2}{O_2}$	Sulphur dioxide characteristic smell
6. Acidified potassium manganate(VII) solution ($KMnO_4$)	reduced to colourless managanese(II) salts	$\overset{+7}{Mn}\overset{-2}{O_4}{}^{-} \rightarrow \overset{+2}{Mn}{}^{2+}$	Purple to colourless solution
7. Acidified potassium dichromate(VI) solution ($K_2Cr_2O_7$)	reduced to chromium(III) salts	$\overset{+6}{Cr_2}\overset{-2}{O_7}{}^{2-} \rightarrow \overset{+3}{Cr}{}^{3+}$	Orange to green solution

Note: Redox reactions require you to think clearly. It is worth the effort to master them as they are always popular with examiners.

Examination Questions

1. (*Associated Examining Board, June* 1980).

(*a*) *What do you understand by the term oxidation?*

For each of the following reactions state which substance is being oxidized and give a reason for your answer:

(i) $PbO + CO \rightarrow Pb + CO_2$

(ii) $2I^- + Br_2 \rightarrow I_2 + 2Br^-$

(iii) $2Fe^{3+} + H_2S \rightarrow 2Fe^{2+} + 2H^+ + S$

(iv) $Cu^{2+} + Zn \rightarrow Cu + Zn^{2+}$ (10)

(b) *When an electric current is passed between platinum electrodes immersed in aqueous copper*(II) *sulphate, what would you* see *happening at each electrode?*

If the direction of current flow is now reversed and an identical quantity of electricity is passed through the solution state, what would be the final observation? (Assume that the solution remains blue in colour throughout both experiments).

Write ionic equations for any reactions occurring at the electrodes and indicate whether oxidation or reduction has taken place. (10)

(c) *When the same electric current was passed for a fixed time through aqueous copper(II) sulphate and aqueous mercury(I) nitrate, $HgNO_3$, in separate vessels equipped with suitable electrodes, it was found that 1.0 g of mercury was deposited. What mass, in grams, of copper would also have been obtained?* (4)

Answer

(a) There are three ways of recognizing oxidation.

(1) The addition of oxygen to an element or compound.

e.g. $2Mg(s) + O_2(g) \rightarrow 2MgO(s)$

(2) The removal of hydrogen from a compound.

e.g. $Mg(s) + 2HCl(aq) \rightarrow MgCl_2(aq) + H_2(g)$

Here the hydrogen is being removed from the hydrochloric acid by the magnesium.

(3) The loss of electron(s) by an atom or ion.

e.g. $Mg \rightarrow Mg^{2+} + 2e^-$

Note: It is always a good idea to give examples.

(i) $\overset{+2\,-2}{PbO} + \overset{+2\,-2}{C\,O} \rightarrow \overset{0}{Pb} + \overset{+4\,-2}{C\,O_2}$

The carbon monoxide is gaining oxygen. So the carbon monoxide is being oxidized to carbon dioxide.

or $\overset{+2\,-2}{C\,O} \rightarrow \overset{+4\,-2}{C\,O_2}$

The oxidation number of carbon has increased from +2 in carbon monoxide to +4 in carbon dioxide. So the carbon is being oxidized.

(ii) $\overset{-1}{2I^-} + \overset{0}{Br_2} \rightarrow \overset{0}{I_2} + \overset{-1}{2Br^-}$

or $2I^- \rightarrow I_2 + 2e^-$

$Br_2 + 2e^- \rightarrow 2Br^-$

The iodide ions are losing electrons to become iodine. So the iodide ion is oxidized to iodine.

or

The oxidation number of the iodide ion has increased. So the iodide ion is being oxidized.

(iii) $\overset{+3}{2Fe^{3+}} + \overset{+1}{H_2}\overset{-2}{S} \rightarrow \overset{+2}{2Fe^{2+}} + \overset{+1}{2H^+} + \overset{0}{S}$

The oxidation number of sulphur in the sulphide ion has increased. So the sulphide ion has been oxidized to sulphur.

or

When a sulphide ion becomes a sulphur atom it loses electrons, which is oxidation. So the sulphide ion has been oxidized to sulphur.

(iv) $\overset{+2}{Cu^{2+}} + \overset{0}{Zn} \rightarrow \overset{0}{Cu} + \overset{+2}{Zn^{2+}}$

The oxidation number of zinc has increased. So the zinc metal has been oxidized to the zinc ion.

or

The zinc metal has lost electrons in becoming a zinc ion. So it has been oxidized to the zinc ion.

Note: You are only asked to state which substance has been oxidized, so no marks would be awarded if you had written about reduction as well.

(b) At the cathode you would see a colour change as the copper coated the grey electrode a pink-brown colour.

At the anode you would see bubbles of gas.

Note: The word *see* is emphasized. It would be easy to state what was happening at each electrode, not what you saw.

If the current flow was reversed the pink coating would leave the electrode, which was the first cathode. Simultaneously the 'new' cathode would become pink. Finally, when an identical quantity of electricity was passed the 'old' cathode would have no coating of copper; it would be grey.

Ionic equations

Cathode	$Cu^{2+} + 2e^- \rightarrow Cu(s)$	reduction
Anode	$OH^- \rightarrow OH + e^-$	oxidation
	$4OH \rightarrow 2H_2O + O_2$	

(c) From Faraday's laws:

1 F deposits 1 mole of a univalent ion.

2 F deposit 1 mole of a divalent ion.

Mercury is a univalent ion with an R.A.M. of 200 g (from data).

If 1 g mercury is deposited, this is $\frac{1}{200}$ mole

$= 5 \times 10^{-3}$ moles mercury.

Since the same amount of electricity was flowing this would deposit half this number of moles of copper (as it is divalent).

So 2.5×10^{-3} moles copper are deposited

1 mole of copper has an R.A.M. of 64 g

so number grams copper deposited $= 64 \times 2.5 \times 10^{-3}$ g

$= \underline{0.16 \text{ g copper}}$

2. (*Associated Examining Board, June 1976*)

(a) *By reference to the structures of the substances mentioned, briefly explain the following:*

(i) *solid sodium conducts electricity;*

(ii) *solid sodium chloride is a non-conductor of electricity but it will conduct when molten.* (9)

(b) *Scandium (Sc) is a trivalent metal of relative atomic mass 45. The same quantity of electricity was passed through two cells, liberating scandium in the first cell and 0.3 mole of sodium in the second. Calculate the mass of scandium liberated.* (6)

(c) *Describe how crude copper is purified by an electrolytic method. Indicate the reaction that takes place at each electrode and explain briefly what happens to the other metals present in the crude copper.* (9)

Answer

(a) (i) In solid sodium, sodium ions form a metallic lattice, as shown in the diagram below.

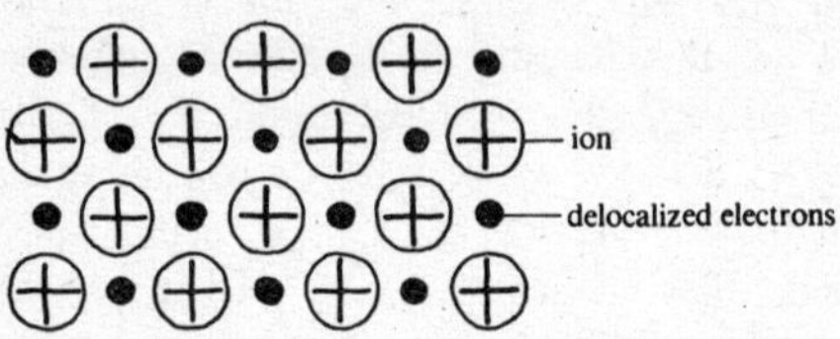

The electrons form a cloud around the positive ions so they are free to move and therefore can conduct electricity.

(ii) In solid sodium chloride the sodium and chloride ions arrange themselves in a rigid structure. The ions are held together by the attraction of their opposite charges, as shown below.

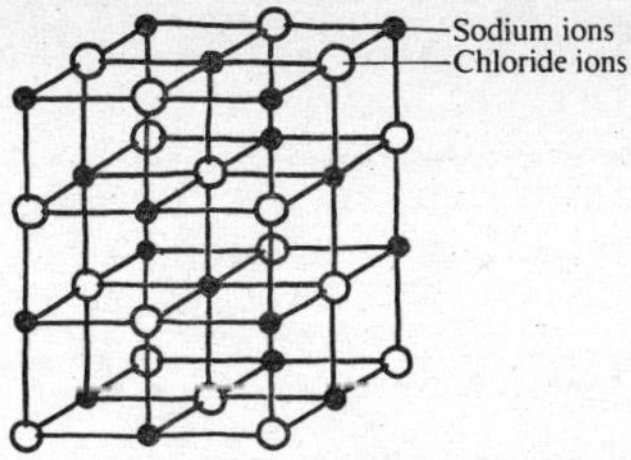

No electrons are free to move to conduct electricity. When sodium chloride is molten this crystal lattice breaks down and the ions are free to move and so conduct electricity.

(b) 1F will liberate 1 mole of sodium ions.

3 F will liberate 1 mole of scandium ions.

So if 0.3 mole of sodium is liberated $\frac{0.3}{3} = 0.1$ mole of scandium is liberated.

1 mole of scandium has a relative atomic mass of 45.

0.1 mole of scandium has a mass of 45×0.1

$= \underline{4.05\text{ g}}$

(c) The impure copper is made the anode of a cell, which has a pure copper rod as the cathode. The electrolyte is copper(II) sulphate solution.

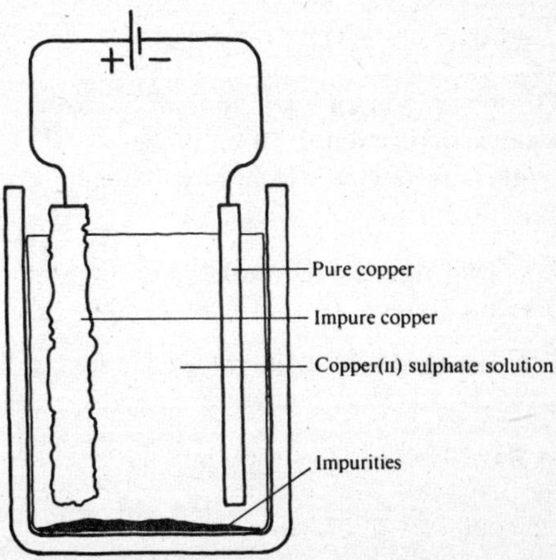

During electrolysis the impure copper leaves the anode and travels to the cathode. Impurities sink to the bottom of the container.

7. Acids, Bases and Salts

Acids and Bases

It is not easy to define an acid and a base as several definitions can be used.

1. Acids turn blue litmus paper red.
   Bases turn red litmus paper blue.
2. During the preparation of chemical salts, the hydrogen in an acid is replaced by a metal. An acid contains hydrogen, which can be replaced by a metal.

Unfortunately, this is not always true as hydrogen chloride gas (HCl) does not turn blue litmus paper red, except when it is dissolved in water. Thus water is necessary for a substance to act as an acid. In water the water molecule attracts the nucleus of the hydrogen atom (which is just a proton) from the covalently bonded hydrogen chloride. This leaves behind a chloride ion.

$$H_2O(l) + HCl(g) \rightarrow H_3O^+(aq) + Cl^-(aq)$$

The H_3O^+ ion is called a hydroxonium or oxonium ion. This causes blue litmus paper to turn red.

So acids are substances which have reacted with water to form hydroxonium ions.

$$H_2SO_4(l) + 2H_2O(l) \rightarrow 2H_3O^+(aq) + SO_4^{2-}(aq)$$
$$HNO_3(l) + H_2O(l) \rightarrow H_3O^+(aq) + NO_3^-(aq)$$

Note: Many textbooks write these equations as follows:

$$HCl \rightarrow H^+ + Cl^-$$
$$H_2SO_4 \rightarrow 2H^+ + SO_4^{=}$$

i.e., the water molecule is omitted, although the authors know it should be there. This can cause confusion as hydrogen chloride gas is covalently bonded, while hydrochloric acid is ionically bonded.

The Bronsted–Lowry Theory

This is the modern definition of acids. **Acids** are substances which donate protons to other molecules. A base is the opposite of an acid.

A base is a substance which accepts a proton, e.g. many metal hydroxides and oxides are basic as their hydroxide or oxide ions can accept protons. Ammonia gas is also a base.

(a) $\underset{\text{(from hydroxide)}}{OH^-(aq)} + \underset{\text{(from acid)}}{H^+(aq)} \rightarrow H_2O(l)$

(b) $NH_3 + H^+ \rightarrow NH_4^+$

An alkali is a base which is soluble in water, e.g. sodium hydroxide, potassium hydroxide and ammonia solution. Calcium hydroxide is sparingly soluble.

Neutralization

Since acids and bases are chemical opposites, when mixed they cancel each other out until the final solution is neither acidic nor basic but neutral. The products are a salt and water only, e.g. when hydrochloric acid is neutralized with sodium hydroxide, sodium chloride and water are formed.

$$HCl(aq) + NaOH(aq) \rightarrow NaCl(aq) + H_2O(l)$$

Properties of Acids

1. They turn blue litmus red.
2. They are corrosive (have a burning action).
3. They react with metals and metal oxides, which are higher than hydrogen in the electrochemical series, to form a salt.

e.g. $Mg(s) + 2HCl(aq) \rightarrow MgCl_2(aq) + H_2(g)$
$MgO(s) + H_2SO_4(aq) \rightarrow MgSO_4(aq) + H_2O(l)$

4. They neutralize bases and alkalis.

Properties of Bases (including Alkalis)

1. They turn red litmus blue.
2. They neutralize an acid.
3. Strong alkalis feel soapy because they react with the skin.

4. Solutions of alkalis will precipitate insoluble hydroxides of other metals from solutions of their salts. For example, when sodium hydroxide solution is added to copper(II) sulphate solution a blue precipitate of copper(II) hydroxide is seen.

$$CuSO_4(aq) + 2NaOH(aq) \rightarrow Cu(OH)_2(s) + Na_2SO_4(aq)$$

or

$$Cu^{2+}(aq) + 2OH^-(aq) \rightarrow Cu(OH)_2(s)$$

5. Strong alkalis react with zinc or aluminium to give hydrogen

$$2Al(s) + 2NaOH(aq) + 6H_2O(l) \rightarrow \underset{\text{sodium aluminate}}{2NaAl(OH)_4(aq)} + 3H_2(g)$$

6. When an ammonium compound is heated with a base ammonia is evolved (given off).

e.g. $Ca(OH)_2(s) + 2NH_4Cl(s) \rightarrow CaCl_2(s) + 2H_2O(l) + 2NH_3(g)$

or

$$OH^-(aq) + NH_4^+(aq) \rightarrow NH_3(g) + H_2O(l)$$

pH Scale

The pH scale measures the concentration of hydrogen ions (really as hydroxonium ions) in a solution. The scale normally used goes from pH = 0–14.

A Table of pH Values

pH value		*Examples*
0	↑	1 mole hydrochloric acid
1		0.1 mole hydrochloric acid
2	increasing	1 mole ethanoic acid
3	acidity	
4		
5		
6		
7	neutral	distilled water
8		
9	increasing	
10	basicity	
11		1.0 mole ammonia
12		
13	↓	0.1 mole sodium hydroxide
14		1 mole sodium hydroxide

Measurement of pH Values by Indicators

Indicators are dyes which change colour, depending on the acidity or alkalinity of the solution they are in. Different indicators change colours in different ranges of the pH scale.

Indicator	*pH Colour change*	*Colours*
Litmus	7	red ← 7 → blue
Methyl orange	3.4	red ← 3.4 → yellow
Phenolphthalein	9.8	colourless ← 9.8 → pink

Instead of using one indicator, a mixture of indicators may be used. This mixture will change colour through the whole range of pH 0–14 and is called Universal Indicator. This is used as a solution or as pH paper.

The Strength of Acids

Strong Acids

In dilute solutions of strong acids, the acids react completely when placed in water so that a large number of hydroxonium ions are produced. For example, 1 mole of hydrochloric acid will produce 1 mole of hydroxonium ions and 1 mole of chloride ions. So the acid is said to be completely ionized.

$$HCl(g) + H_2O(l) \rightarrow H_3O^+(aq) + Cl^-(aq)$$

Weak Acids

In dilute solutions of weak acids the acids do not react completely with water so 1 mole of ethanoic acid does *not* produce 1 mole of hydroxonium ions and 1 mole of ethanoate ions.

Concentrated Acids

1. In concentrated solutions of the strong acids, sulphuric acid and nitric acid, the acid molecules are unable to react with water to form many hydroxonium ions as so few water molecules are present. Since only a few hydroxonium ions are formed the concentrated acids are not very acidic and the oxidizing properties of these acids become important in their reactions.

2. In concentrated solutions of the strong acid, hydrochloric acid, there is about 60% of water, so a high proportion of hydroxonium ions are present. This concentrated acid is more active than dilute hydrochloric acid.

3. In concentrated solutions of weak acids even fewer hydroxonium ions are present than in a dilute solution of these acids, since fewer water molecules are present for the acid to react with.

Salts

A salt is prepared when the hydrogen in an acid is partly or completely replaced by a metal or ammonium ion.

Acids which contain more than one hydrogen atom can react to produce more than one type of salt, e.g. sulphuric acid H_2SO_4.
(a) a salt where only one hydrogen in the formula is replaced is called an acid salt (as one hydrogen is *still* present), e.g. sodium hydrogen-sulphate $NaHSO_4$
(b) a salt where the two hydrogen atoms are replaced is called a normal salt, e.g. Na_2SO_4.

Preparation of Salts

There are five different methods of preparing salts and you might be asked to describe the preparation of any named salt in detail.

1. *To neutralize an acid with an alkali* (or vice versa), e.g. hydrochloric acid and sodium hydroxide (or potassium hydroxide and ammonia solution).

A quantity of the acid is placed in an evaporating dish, and the alkali is added dropwise until the acid has been neutralized. This can be tested by placing a stirring rod in the liquid and then placing this on litmus paper. The solution is slowly evaporated over a water bath until most of the water has been driven off. The remaining solution is left to cool and the salt will crystallize out.

$$NaOH(aq) + HCl(aq) \rightarrow NaCl(aq) + H_2O(l)$$

2. *To react a basic oxide with an acid*, e.g. sulphuric acid and copper(II) oxide.

A quantity of acid is placed in a beaker and warmed gently; portions of copper(II) oxide are added while the acid is stirred. The addition of copper(II) oxide is discontinued when some of the solid remains undissolved, i.e. all the acid has reacted with the oxide. The solution is filtered to remove the excess copper(II) oxide and then the solution is heated over a water bath (as in Chapter 1) to obtain the crystals.

$$CuO(s) + H_2SO_4(aq) \rightarrow CuSO_4(aq) + H_2O(l)$$

3. *To react a metal with an acid*, e.g. sulphuric and zinc.

Note: You can *not* use this method if it involves the metals sodium or potassium as they react too vigorously with acids.

A quantity of acid is placed in a beaker and warmed gently. The zinc granules are added until no further effervescence is seen. This means that all the acid present has reacted. The solution is filtered to remove the excess zinc and the solution is then heated over a water bath as before.

$$Zn(s) + H_2SO_4(aq) \rightarrow ZnSO_4(aq) + H_2(g)$$

4. *To react a carbonate with an acid*, e.g. nitric acid and lead carbonate.

Note: Most carbonates, whether they are soluble or insoluble, react with acids to form salts.

A beaker containing nitric acid is gently warmed and the lead carbonate added until no further effervescence is seen. This means that all the acid present has reacted to form a salt. The solution is then filtered and evaporated to obtain crystals of lead nitrate.

$$PbCO_3(s) + 2HNO_3(aq) \rightarrow Pb(NO_3)_2(aq) + CO_2(g) + H_2O(l)$$

The above preparations have all produced soluble salts, which have been obtained from their solutions by evaporation. The following preparation is used for *insoluble* salts.

5. *To prepare a salt by precipitation (double decomposition)*, e.g. to prepare lead sulphate.

Solutions of a soluble lead salt and a soluble sulphate salt are prepared in separate containers. When these are mixed an insoluble salt is formed as a precipitate. This is separated by filtration; the salt, which is the residue on the filter paper, is washed and dried.

$$Pb(NO_3)_2(aq) + Na_2SO_4(aq) \rightarrow 2NaNO_3(aq) + PbSO_4(s)$$

Note: The difficulties arise in knowing which solutions to mix, so it is helpful to memorize the following table.

A table of the common soluble and insoluble salts

Soluble	*Insoluble*
1. All common salts of sodium, potassium and ammonium	
2. All common nitrates of metals	
3. All common chlorides	except silver, mercury, lead
4. All common sulphates	except barium, lead, calcium
5. Sodium, potassium and ammonium carbonates	all other common carbonates
6. Sodium, potassium, ammonium and calcium hydroxides	all other common hydroxides

Examination Question

From the short section of an Oxford paper (*Summer, 1978*).

(a) *Name* four different *salts which could be prepared using only the substances hydrochloric acid, nitric acid, sodium hydroxide and potassium hydroxide.*

(b) *Write the ionic equation common to all four reactions involved in the preparation of these salts.*

Answer

(a) Sodium chloride
Sodium nitrate
Potassium chloride
Potassium nitrate

(b) $H^+(aq) + OH^-(aq) \rightarrow H_2O(l)$

8. Chemical Changes

Types of Chemical Change (or Reaction)

You must be able to define these changes and describe examples of each type. Many examples can be used from other chapters of this book.

Combination takes place when two or more substances combine to form a single substance.

Examples

1. When iron and sulphur are heated together iron(II) sulphide is produced.

$Fe(s) + S(s) \rightarrow FeS(s)$

2. When magnesium ribbon is burned in oxygen, magnesium oxide is produced.

$2Mg(s) + O_2(g) \rightarrow 2MgO(s)$

Decomposition occurs when a compound splits up into simpler substances.

Examples

1. When calcium carbonate is heated it decomposes to calcium oxide and carbon dioxide.

$CaCO_3(s) \rightarrow CaO(s) + CO_2(g)$

2. When sodium nitrate is heated it decomposes to sodium nitrate and oxygen.

$2NaNO_3(s) \rightarrow 2NaNO_2(s) + O_2(g)$

Displacement occurs when one element (or group) takes the place of another element (or group) in a compound.

Examples

1. When a piece of magnesium ribbon is placed in copper(II) sulphate solution the copper is displaced by the magnesium and is seen as a brown deposit, while the blue solution becomes colourless. This displacement occurs because magnesium is more reactive than copper.

$$Mg(s) + CuSO_4(aq) \rightarrow MgSO_4(aq) + Cu(s)$$

> *Note:* You need to remember the reactivity series of metals to decide whether a specific displacement reaction will take place. A metal will only replace another metal from solution if it is higher in the reactivity series.

2. When chlorine is bubbled through potassium bromide solution the chlorine displaces the bromine and so a brown coloration of bromine is seen. This displacement occurs because chlorine is more reactive than bromine.

$$Cl_2(g) + 2KBr(aq) \rightarrow 2KCl(aq) + Br_2(l)$$

or

$$Cl_2(g) + 2Br^-(aq) \rightarrow 2Cl^-(aq) + Br_2(l)$$

> *Note:* You need to know the order of reactivity of the halogens to decide whether this sort of displacement reaction occurs (page 159).

Precipitation (or Double Decomposition) When two different solutions of soluble salts are mixed, then if one of the cations and one of the anions form an insoluble salt, precipitation or double decomposition occurs.

Examples

1. If a solution of barium chloride and a solution of copper(II) sulphate are mixed then a precipitate of barium sulphate will be seen.

$$BaCl_2(aq) + CuSO_4(aq) \rightarrow BaSO_4(s) + CuCl_2(aq)$$

or

$$Ba^{2+}(aq) + SO_4^{2-}(aq) \rightarrow BaSO_4(s)$$

The copper(II) and chloride ions are spectator ions.

2. If a solution of silver nitrate and a solution of sodium chloride are mixed then a precipitate of silver chloride is seen.

$$AgNO_3(aq) + NaCl(aq) \rightarrow AgCl(s) + NaNO_3(aq)$$

or

$$Ag^+(aq) + Cl^-(aq) \rightarrow AgCl(s)$$

Reversible Reactions

A reversible reaction is one that proceeds from left to right (as shown in an equation) *and* also from right to left (as shown in the same equation).

Examples

1. When blue copper(II) sulphate crystals are heated strongly they turn to a white powder and water is evolved. If this water is then added to the white powder blue copper(II) sulphate crystals are formed.

Stage 1: $CuSO_4{\cdot}5H_2O \rightarrow CuSO_4 + 5H_2O$
Stage 2: $CuSO_4 + 5H_2O \rightarrow CuSO_4{\cdot}5H_2O$

This can be written in a shortened form.

$$CuSO_4{\cdot}5H_2O \rightleftharpoons CuSO_4 + 5H_2O$$

↑
reversible sign

2. Nitrogen and hydrogen gases combine on heating to produce ammonia gas, while ammonia gas decomposes into nitrogen and hydrogen.

$$N_2(g) + 3H_2(g) \rightleftharpoons 2NH_3(g)$$

Energy Changes in Chemical Reactions

Most chemical reactions are accompanied by a definite heat change.

Exothermic reactions give out heat to their surroundings.
Endothermic reactions take in (absorb) heat from their surroundings.

Chemical reactions involve the breaking of bonds between atoms and then the making of new different bonds.

e.g. A—A + C—C → A—C + A—C

Energy is *needed* to break the bonds between A—A and C—C stage 1.

Energy is *released* when bonds are formed between A—C stage 2.

Since these amounts of energy will be different they will lead to an overall energy change. If the energy needed in stage 1 is more than the energy released in stage 2 then the overall reaction will be endothermic. If the energy needed in stage 1 is less than the energy released in stage 2 then the overall reaction will be exothermic.

These situations can be summarized by the following energy diagrams.

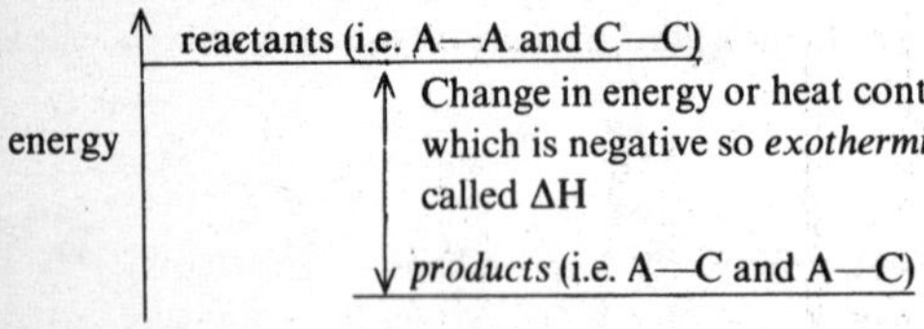

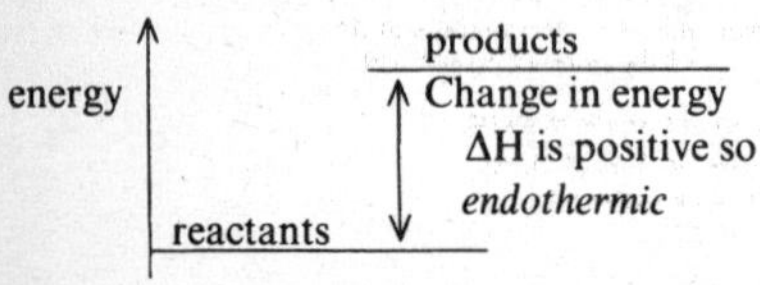

These energy changes are measured in kilojoules (kJ).

1000 joules = 1 kilojoule.

Some Different Types of Energy Changes

1. **The heat of reaction**

This is the heat change involved in a particular chemical reaction, so the reaction is always described.

e.g. $N_2(g) + 3H_2(g) \rightarrow 2NH_3(g) \qquad \Delta H = -92.4$ kJ.

This means that when 1 mole of nitrogen reacts with 3 moles of hydrogen to form 2 moles of ammonia 92.4 kJ of energy is given out.

2. **The heat of neutralization**

This is the heat change which occurs when 1 mole of water is formed when an acid is neutralized with an alkali.

e.g. $HCl(aq) + NaOH(aq) \rightarrow NaCl(aq) + H_2O(l)$

$$H_2SO_4(aq) + 2NaOH(aq) \rightarrow Na_2SO_4(aq) + 2H_2O(l)$$

Note: Beware of calculations involving sulphuric acid as 2 moles of water are formed.

Experiment to Determine the Heat of Neutralization

This is a simple experiment and the procedure is shown in the diagrams below.

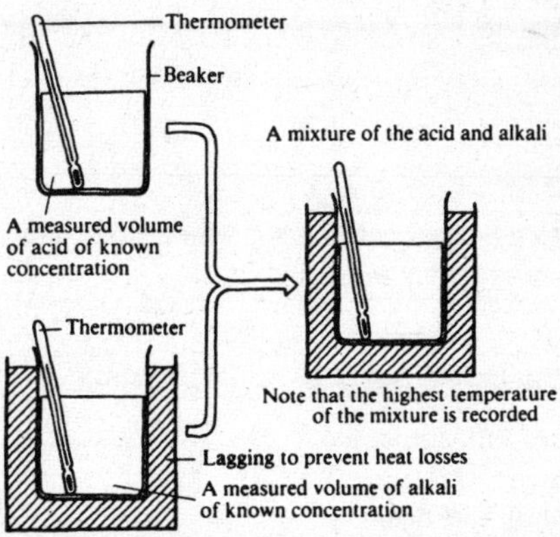

Example of a Calculation

100 cm^3 2 M hydrochloric acid was neutralized with 100 cm^3 2 M sodium hydroxide. The initial (starting) temperature was 20 °C and the final temperature 33.5 °C.

Assuming all the energy given out on neutralization was transferred to the mixture of the acid and alkali

Energy given out on neutralization = mass × specific heat capacity × temperature rise

Specific heat capacity for water = 4.2 J/gK
Temperature rise = 33.5 − 20 = 13.5 K
Volume of mixture = 100 cm^3 + 100 cm^3 = 200 cm^3
Mass of mixture (assuming this is water, so density = 1 g/cm^3) = 200 × 1 = 200 g
Energy given out on neutralization = 200 × 4.2 × 13.5
= 11 340 joules.

But 100 cm^3 2 moles hydrochloric acid contain $2 \times \frac{100}{1000} = 0.2$ mole.

From the definition of the heat of neutralization 1 mole of water needs to be formed, whereas in the experiment only 0.2 mole of water would be formed.

Therefore heat of neutralization = 11 340 J × 5
= 56 700 J = 56.7 kJ

The accurate value for neutralization of a strong acid with a strong base is 57.5 kJ.

Heat of Combustion

Heat of combustion is the heat change which takes place when 1 mole of a substance is completely burnt in oxygen.

Experiment to Determine the Heat of Combustion

This can be carried out simply by burning a known mass of an alcohol, e.g. ethanol. The heat produced is taken in by a known mass of water, whose initial and final temperatures are recorded. The final mass of the alcohol is also recorded.

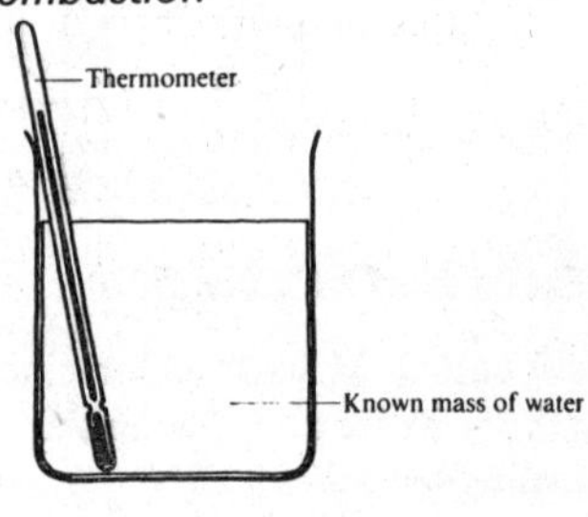

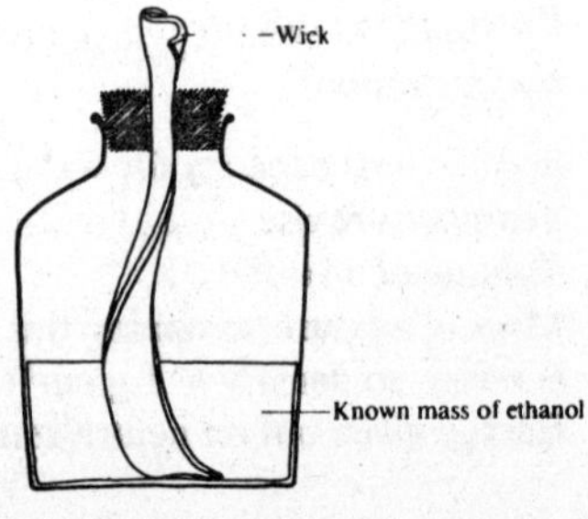

A diagram of the apparatus used to determine the heat of combustion

Example of a Calculation

Mass of bottle and ethanol before burning = 30.50 g
Mass of bottle and ethanol burning = 30.04 g
Mass of water = 198 g
Final temperature of the water = 34 °C
Initial temperature of the water = 19 °C
Specific heat capacity of water = 4.2 J/gK
Mass of ethanol burnt = 30.50 – 30.04 g = 0.46 g
Temperature rise of the water = 34 – 19 °C = 15 K

Assuming that all the energy given out when the ethanol is burnt is transferred to the water

$$\text{Energy given out} = \text{mass of water} \times \begin{matrix}\text{specific heat}\\ \text{capacity}\end{matrix} \times \begin{matrix}\text{temperature}\\ \text{rise}\end{matrix}$$

$$= 198 \times 4.2 \times 15$$
$$= 12\,474 \text{ joules}$$

But this amount of energy is obtained from burning 0.46 g ethanol.

$$\text{This is equivalent to } \frac{\text{mass ethanol}}{\text{R.M.M}}$$

R.M.M ethanol is 24 + 16 + 6 = 46.

$$= \frac{0.46}{46}$$

$$= 0.01 \text{ mole ethanol}$$

Since 0.01 mole of ethanol when burnt produces 12 474 J energy

$$\text{1 mole of ethanol when burnt produces } \frac{12\,474}{0.1} \text{ joules}$$

$$= 1\,247\,400 \text{ J} \quad \text{or} \quad \underline{1247.4 \text{ kJ}}$$

The accurate value for the heat of combustion of ethanol is 1371 kJ per mole.

Rates of Reaction

Reactions between chemicals occur at different speeds. Some are very fast and so cause explosions, others are slower, e.g. the rusting of iron (which occurs over a period of weeks).

The rate of reaction can be investigated by timing it from start to finish. In order to find out what factors affect this rate you alter one of the conditions and then re-time the reaction.

You can detect when a reaction is finished by measuring any of the following during the course of the reaction:

(a) the volume of any gas produced
(b) the decrease in mass of the reactant(s)
(c) the appearance of a coloured compound
(d) the disappearance of a coloured compound

The following factors affect the rate of a chemical reaction:

1. The concentration of reactants (or pressure if the reactants are gaseous).
2. The temperature of the reaction.
3. The surface area of the reactants.
4. The presence of catalysts.
5. Light affects a few chemical reactions.

1. *The concentration of reactants*

(a) The following experiment demonstrates the effect of concentration on the rate of a reaction. The following apparatus is set up. The plunger of the gas syringe will be pushed in at first.

A measured volume of hydrochloric acid and a known mass of calcium

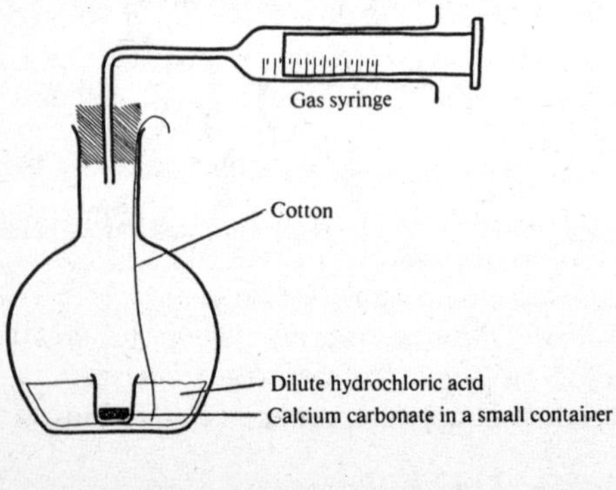

carbonate are used. When the flask is tilted the two substances react producing carbon dioxide.

The volume of the carbon dioxide is measured as it forces the plunger of the gas syringe out. The volume is read every minute.

This experiment would then be repeated using the same mass of calcium carbonate, the same volume of hydrochloric acid but at *different* concentrations.

(b) An alternative method for this experiment would be to place the substance in a beaker on a balance and the total mass could be determined every minute. This mass would decrease as the carbon dioxide was produced.

$$CaCO_3(s) + 2HCl(aq) \rightarrow CaCl_2(aq) + H_2O(l) + CO_2(g)$$

Results from these experiments can be plotted on graphs.

(a)

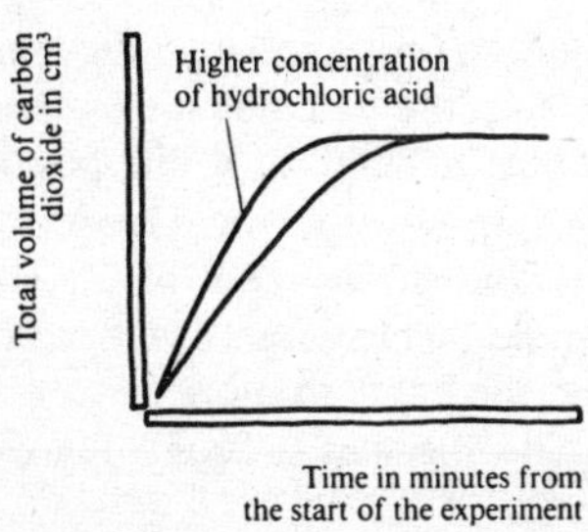

(b)

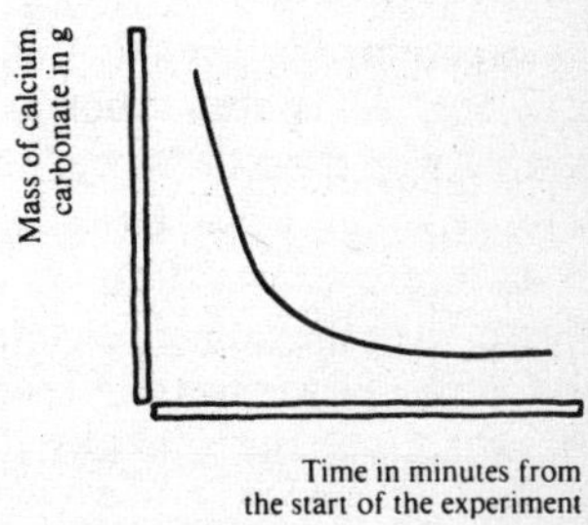

These experiments show that if the concentration of one of the reactants is increased, then the rate of reaction increases (and so the time taken to complete the reaction decreases). This can be explained as follows: When there are more molecules of either of the reacting substances present, then there is more chance that they will collide and so react.

2. *The temperature of the reaction*
Experiment 1(a) can be adapted so that the effect of temperature can be determined. The volume and concentration of hydrochloric acid and the mass of calcium carbonate would be the *same* in both experiments. The first experiment would be carried out at room temperature, the second would be carried out, while the flask was immersed in a water bath, at a known temperature. As before, a graph could be plotted.

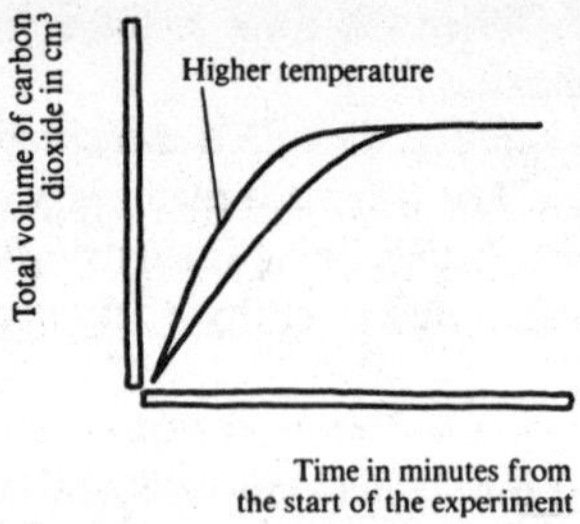

If the temperature of a reaction is increased, then the rate of reaction is increased (so the time taken to complete the reaction decreases). If the temperature of a reaction is increased, then the molecules involved in that reaction acquire more energy, so they move around faster and are more likely to collide with other molecules and so react.

3. *Surface area of the reactants*

Again experiment 1(a) could be adapted. In this experiment the temperature, volume and concentration of hydrochloric acid and mass of calcium carbonate would be the same, but either a lump, or a fine powder, of calcium carbonate would be used. The graph plotted would have the same form as in experiment 1(a), i.e. when the surface area of the solid is increased, then the rate of reaction would be increased. The fine powder would have a larger surface area than the lump, so more molecules will be in contact with the hydrochloric acid molecules and so be able to react with them.

4. *Catalysts*

Catalysts are substances which alter the rate of a chemical reaction (they usually speed it up) but remain chemically unchanged at the end of the reaction.

This effect can be demonstrated by measuring the time to collect a certain volume of gas when hydrogen peroxide decomposes in the presence and absence of manganese(IV) oxide. The apparatus used in experiment 1(a) can be used. The presence of a catalyst increases the rate of this reaction.

$$2H_2O_2(aq) \xrightarrow{\text{manganese(IV) oxide}} 2H_2O(l) + O_2(g)$$

Note: Catalysts are written over the arrow in an equation and not included on either side, since they are chemically unchanged.

5. *Light*

Light affects only a few reactions.

(a) It speeds up the process of photosynthesis.

(b) It causes a mixture of hydrogen and chlorine to explode.

(c) It causes precipitates of silver chloride, silver bromide and silver iodide to darken due to the reduction of silver ions to metallic silver.

Equilibrium

In a reversible reaction (p. 107) in which substances A and B react together to form C and D, when A and B are mixed no molecules of C and D are present; then A and B react to produce small amounts of C and D. Once C and D are formed they will react to form A and B, but since such small amounts of C and D are present, they will not form much A and B. So at first the concentrations of A and B are high and the rate of the forward reaction, i.e. $A + B \rightarrow C + D$, is rapid, while the concentration of C and D is small, so the rate of the backward reaction $C + D \rightarrow A + B$ is small.

As the reaction proceeds the rate of the forward reaction will fall, while the rate of the backward reaction and the concentrations of C and D increase, until finally, the rate of both reactions will be the same, when the concentrations of A, B, C and D in the mixture will be constant. However, both reactions will still be proceeding, but because they are proceeding at the same rate, no changes in concentrations will be detected and this is said to be a dynamic equilibrium.

> *Note:* At equilibrium the percentage of reactants and products are not necessarily equal, i.e. 50% reactants : 50% products; but they are constant, e.g. 20% reactants: 80% products.

Equilibrium Positions

Equilibrium positions can be changed by altering the conditions of a reaction. This can be done by changing:

(a) the concentration of one of the reactants
(b) the temperature
(c) the pressure

There is an important rule which predicts the effects of these changes.

Le Chatelier's Principle

This states that if a system is in equilibrium and a change is made to this system then the system alters so as to oppose the effect of the change.

Factors Affecting an Equilibrium

Altering Concentrations

1. e.g. $H_2(g) + I_2(g) \rightleftharpoons 2HI(g)$

Change: Remove $I_2(g)$

Effect: The concentration of iodine has been decreased and more hydrogen iodide will break up to give hydrogen and iodine. So the rate of the backward reaction will increase and the equilibrium is said to shift to the left.

2. e.g. $H_2O(l) \rightleftharpoons H_2O(g)$

Change: Remove $H_2O(g)$

Effect: More liquid will vaporize to increase the concentration of $H_2O(g)$, so the equilibrium shifts to the right.

Altering Pressure

1. e.g. $\underbrace{N_2(g) + 3H_2(g)}_{\text{4 moles of gas}} \rightleftharpoons \underbrace{2NH_3(g)}_{\text{2 moles of gas}}$

Change: Increase the pressure on this system. This will reduce the volume which will mean the molecules of the gases will be closer together.

Effect: To reduce this crowding of the molecules, more nitrogen and hydrogen molecules will react to produce ammonia as this will decrease the total number of molecules present, i.e. the equilibrium will shift to the right.

2. e.g. $2O_3(g) \rightleftharpoons 3O_2(g)$

Change: Increase the pressure.

Effect: As above example, but this time in order to reduce the crowding the equilibrium will shift to the left.

3. e.g. $H_2(g) + I_2(g) \rightleftharpoons 2HI(g)$

Change: Increase the pressure.

Effect: This will cause the molecules to move closer together, but since there are the same number of molecules on both sides of the equation there will be no shift in the equilibrium position.

4. e.g. $\underbrace{2SO_2(g) + O_2(g)}_{\text{3 moles of gas}} \rightleftharpoons \underbrace{2SO_3(g)}_{\text{2 moles of gas}}$

Change: Decrease the pressure, so the volume of the system will increase and the molecules will be further apart.

Effect: To increase the pressure the number of molecules needs to be increased, so the equilibrium shifts to the left.

Altering Temperature

1. e.g. $2SO_2(g) + O_2(g) \rightleftharpoons 2SO_3(g) \quad \Delta H = -189$ kJ (exothermic)

Change: Increase the temperature.

Effect: The system needs to lose heat to counteract the increase in temperature, so the equilibrium will shift to the left (as this reaction takes in heat, as it is the opposite of the forward reaction).

2. e.g. $H_2O(l) \rightleftharpoons H_2O(g) \quad \Delta H = +44$ kJ (endothermic)

Change: Increase the temperature.

Effect: The system needs to counteract the increase in temperature, which it will do if the equilibrium shifts to the right because this will take in heat.

3. e.g. $2Mg(s) + O_2(g) \rightleftharpoons 2MgO(s) \quad \Delta H = -1204$ kJ

Change: Decrease the temperature.

Effect: The decrease in temperature will be counteracted if the equilibrium shifts to the right.

> *Note:* These ideas of equilibria and how the position of equilibria are changed need to be understood, so that you can apply Le Chatelier's Principle to any reaction, especially the manufacture of ammonia (page 149) and concentrated sulphuric acid (page 157).

Examination Questions

1. (*London, June 1982*)

(a) *Describe how you would attempt to determine the heat of combustion of ethanol. As part of your answer you should state the measurement you would make and how you would use the results to calculate the heat of combustion in kJ mol*$^{-1}$.

The results of experiments to measure the heat evolved when mixtures of ethanol and propan-1-ol were completely burnt in a suitable apparatus are shown below.

Experiment	1	2	3	4	5	6
Number of moles of ethanol in mixture	0.010	0.008	0.006	0.004	0.002	0.000
Number of moles of propan-1-ol in mixture	0.000	0.002	0.004	0.006	0.008	0.010
Total number of moles in mixture	0.010	0.010	0.010	0.010	0.010	0.010
Heat evolved in kJ	13.65	14.95	16.25	17.50	18.80	20.10

(b) *Plot a graph of heat evolved (vertical axis) against number of moles of ethanol in each mixture.*

(c) (i) *Calculate the heat of combustion of ethanol in kJ mol*$^{-1}$.

(ii) *Write down the thermochemical equation for the complete combustion of ethanol, indicating the heat evolved.*

(d) *0.010 mole of a mixture of ethanol and propan-1-ol produced 15.60 kJ of heat on combustion.*

(i) *From your graph determine the number of moles of ethanol present in this mixture.*

(ii) *Calculate the mass of ethanol present in this mixture.* (25)

Answer

(a) A known mass of ethanol was burnt in air, so that the heat given out was transferred to a known mass of water. The apparatus was set up as follows:

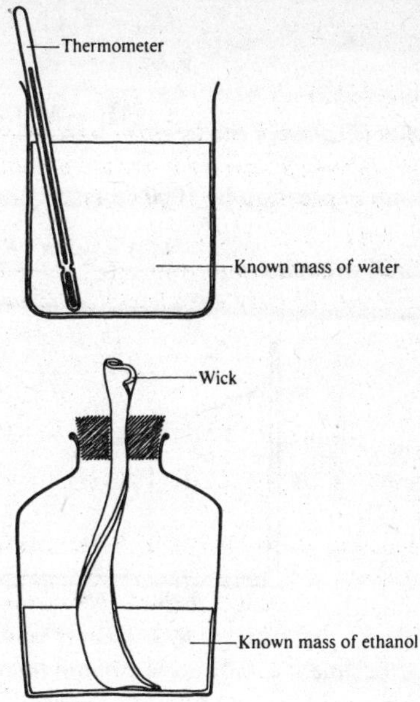

The following measurements would be taken.

Before combustion:	Temperature of the water in the tin can	T_1
	Mass of tin can + water	M_1
	Mass of tin can	M_2
	Mass of ethanol + bottle	X_1
After combustion:	Temperature of the water	T_2
	Mass of bottle + ethanol	X_2

Calculation

From the above measurements the mass of water, mass of ethanol burnt and temperature increase of the water can be found.

Assuming all the heat of combustion is transferred to the water then heat given to water = mass (water) × specific heat.

capacity (s.h.c.) (water) × temperature increase (water)

$$= (M_1 - M_2) \times \text{s.h.c.} \times (T_2 - T_1)$$

(s.h.c. = 4.2 J/gK)

Converting this to moles of ethanol $\frac{(X_1 - X_2)}{\text{R.M.M.} = 46}$

So $\frac{(X_1 - X_2)}{46}$ moles of ethanol provides $\frac{(M_1 - M_2) \times 4.2 \times (T_2 - T_1)}{1000}$ kJ

(Dividing the second expression by 1000 converts joules to kilojoules.)

$\therefore$ 1 mole of ethanol provides $\frac{(M_1 - M_2) \times 4.2 \times (T_2 - T_1)}{1000} \div \frac{(X_1 - X_2)}{46}$

(b)

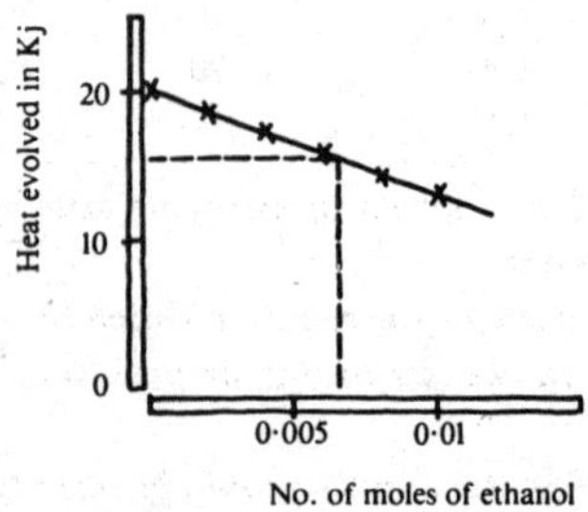

(c) (i) From experiment 1. 0.01 mole ethanol provides 13.65 kJ energy.

So 1 mole ethanol provides $\frac{13.65}{0.01}$

$= \underline{1365 \text{ kJ mol}^{-1} \text{ heat evolved}}$

(ii) $C_2H_5OH(l) + 3O_2(g) \rightarrow 2CO_2(g) + 3H_2O(l)$ $\Delta H = -1365 \text{ kJ mol}^{-1}$.

(d) (i) From the graph the mixture contains 0.0065 mole of ethanol.

(ii) 1 mole of ethanol has a mass of (24 + 6 + 16) 46 g.

So 0.0065 mole of ethanol has a mass of = 0.0065 × 46
= 0.2990 g
= 0.30 g (to two significant figures).

2. (*Associated Examining Board, June 1981*)

The table below is taken from a laboratory investigation into the rate of decomposition of hydrogen peroxide using a manganese(IV) oxide catalyst. For each set of initial conditions, the time taken to collect a fixed volume of gas was noted. In each experiment 50 cm³ of aqueous hydrogen peroxide and 1 g of catalyst were used.

Experiment	*Concentration of aqueous hydrogen peroxide in mol/dm³*	*Initial temperature in 0 °C*	*Form of the catalyst*	*Time in seconds to collect a fixed volume of gas*
A	0.1	20	Powder	200
B	0.1	30	Powder	115
C	0.1	40	Powder	60
D	0.2	20	Powder	100
E	0.3	20	Powder	65
F	0.4	20	Pellets	130
G	0.4	20	Powder	50

(a) *Draw a labelled diagram of an apparatus which could be used to perform this experiment.* (3)

(b) *Write an equation for the reaction which takes place when hydrogen peroxide decomposes and describe* one *simple test to identify the gas evolved.* (3)

(c) *Which experimental results should be used to draw a graph to show the relationship between concentration of reactant and rate of reaction? Explain briefly the reasons for the choice (Do* not *draw a graph).* (4)

(d) (i) *State and explain what happens to the rate of decomposition of the hydrogen peroxide when the concentration of its solution is increased.*

(ii) *Explain why the use of catalyst pellets instead of powder alters the rate of reaction (see experiments F and G).* (7)

(iii) *State how* one *other factor investigated in this experiment affects the rate of reaction.*

(e) *Define the term catalyst and describe briefly the essential steps of an experiment to prove that manganese(IV) oxide acts as a catalyst in this reaction.* (7)

Answer

(a)

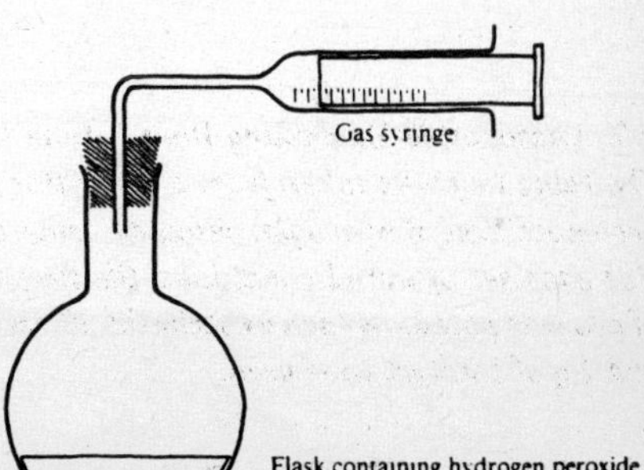

(b) $2H_2O_2 \rightarrow 2H_2O + O_2$

Oxygen relights a glowing spill.

(c) A, D, E, G.

These experiments should be used because the temperature and form of the catalyst are constant, so the effect of concentration is being investigated. These results show that as the concentration of hydrogen peroxide increases the time to collect a fixed volume of gas decreases.

(d) (i) The rate of decomposition of hydrogen peroxide increases when its concentration is increased. As the concentration increases there are more molecules of hydrogen peroxide present to decompose.

(ii) When pellets of catalyst are used they have a smaller surface area than the same mass of powdered catalyst, so there is less chance of contact with the hydrogen peroxide molecules and thus the rate of reaction is slower.

(iii) The temperature of the reaction affects its rate. This can be seen in experiments A, B, and C, where the concentrations of hydrogen peroxide and the form of the catalyst are the same. As the temperature is increased the rate of reaction also increases.

(e) A catalyst is a substance that alters the rate of a chemical reaction (usually increases it) but is left chemically unchanged at the end of this reaction.

In order to prove that manganese(IV) oxide acts as a catalyst experiment A could be carried out without the presence of manganese(IV) oxide. The time to collect the fixed volume of gas would be longer, showing that the rate of reaction was slower in the absence of a catalyst.

9. *Metals and their Compounds*

When learning inorganic chemistry it is easy to become confused by the vast amount of apparently unrelated facts, so it is important to see the underlying trends and learn the general properties of a particular group of elements or compounds. For example, if you are asked to describe the chemical properties of magnesium, think about the properties of metals in general (page 24) and then relate the properties of magnesium to its position in the reactivity series.

Extraction of Metals

Most of the metals in the activity series, except gold, silver and copper, are too reactive to be found as elements in the ground. They occur as compounds and are found in ores.

An ore is a compound of an element mixed with sand and rock.

Reactive metals form compounds which are stable and the more reactive the metal the stabler the compounds which it forms, so the more difficult it is to break up these compounds to obtain the elements. The following table shows the occurrence of the elements and their method of extraction from these compounds. The stabler the compound the more vigorous the process of extraction.

Element	*Occurrence*	*Extraction*
Potassium	Saltpetre (KNO_3) and K_2CO_3	Extraction by electrolysis
Sodium	Rock salt ($NaCl$)	
Calcium	Limestone, chalk, gypsum ($CaCO_3$)	
Magnesium	Magnesite ($MgCO_3$) and $MgCl_2$	
Aluminium	Bauxite (Al_2O_3)	

Element	*Occurrence*	*Extraction*	
Zinc	Zinc blende (Zns) and calamine ($ZnCO_3$)	ZnO	Reduced with carbon
Iron	Haematite (Fe_2O_3) and Magnetite (Fe_3O_4)	Fe_2O_3	Reduced with carbon
Lead	Galena (PbS)	PbO	Reduced with carbon
Copper	Copper pyrites ($CuFeS_2$) and copper	mined	
Silver	Silver	mined	

Note: Different examining boards require you to know about different extractions – so *check*. The following may be required:

The Extraction of Sodium and Potassium

These metals are extracted by electrolysis of the molten chlorides. The process for sodium occurs in the Down's cell. Calcium chloride is also added to lower the melting point of sodium chloride.

A diagram of the Down's cell

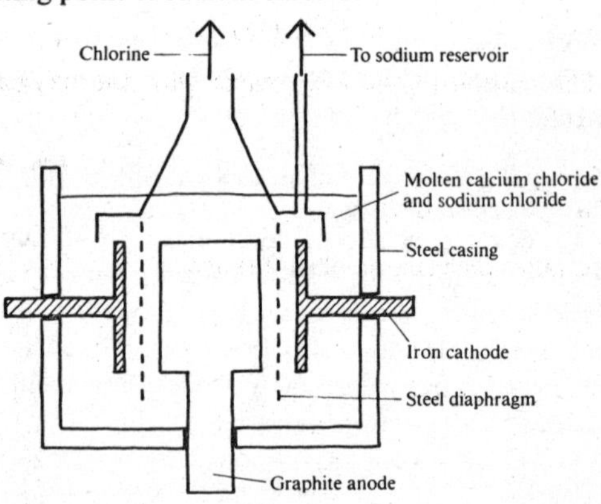

The following reactions occur:

At the cathode	$Na^+ + e^- \rightarrow Na$	(reduction)
At the anode	$Cl^- - e^- \rightarrow Cl$	(oxidation)
	$Cl + Cl \rightarrow Cl_2$	

The Extraction of Aluminium

Bauxite is purified before it is dissolved in cryolite (Na_3AlF_6) and electrolysed.

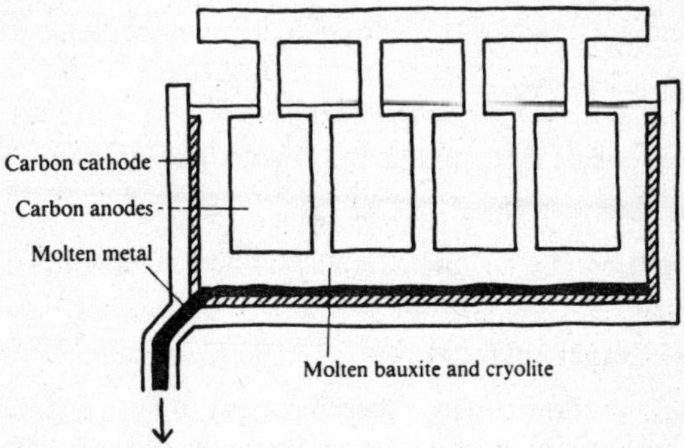

The following reactions occur:

At the cathode: $Al^{3+} + 3e^- \rightarrow Al$ (reduction)
At the anode: $O^{2-} - 2e^- \rightarrow O$ (oxidation)
$O + O \rightarrow O_2$

The carbon anode also reacts with the oxygen to produce carbon dioxide.

The Extraction of Iron

This takes place in the blast furnace.

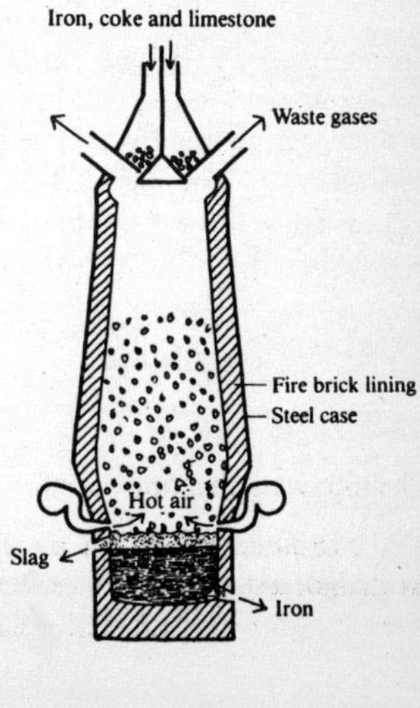

As the hot air moves up through the furnace the coke is oxidized to carbon dioxide.

$$C(s) + O_2(g) \rightarrow CO_2(g)$$

This carbon dioxide reacts with more coke to form carbon monoxide.

$$CO_2(g) + C(s) \rightarrow 2CO(g)$$

This carbon monoxide then reduces the iron(III) oxide to iron.

$$Fe_2O_3(s) + 3CO(g) \rightarrow 2Fe(s) + 3CO_2(g)$$

The limestone ($CaCO_3$) decomposes at this high temperature to form calcium oxide and carbon dioxide.

$$CaCO_3(s) \rightarrow CaO(s) + CO_2(g)$$

This then reacts with the earthy material present to form a slag, which is less dense than the molten iron and so floats on top of it. Both these liquids are removed at intervals.

$$CaO(s) + \underset{\text{sand}}{SiO_2(s)} \rightarrow \underset{\text{slag}}{CaSiO_3(s)}$$

The iron produced in the blast furnace is called 'pig iron'; its impurities are carbon, phosphorus and sulphur.

Conversion of Iron to Steel

Steel contains iron with up to 1.5% carbon. When the percentage of carbon is increased the steel will become harder.

Steel is prepared by heating pig iron in a blast of hot air. The various impurities are oxidized to their gaseous oxides or to solid oxides, which form a slag and so are removed. Finally, the required percentage of carbon is added.

Metallic Compounds

Carbonates

Preparation

1. Most carbonates are insoluble in water (except for those of potassium and sodium) and so are prepared by precipitation. A solution of soluble carbonate ions is mixed with a solution of the relevant metal ions.

The following table summarizes the important points about carbonates

Name	*Formula*	*Colour*	*Solubility in water*	*Effect on heating*	*Effect of acids*
Potassium carbonate	K_2CO_3	White	Soluble	Do not decompose	React to produce a salt, water and carbon dioxide
Sodium carbonate	Na_2CO_3	White			
Calcium carbonate	$CaCO_3$	White	Insoluble	Decomposes at high temperatures	
Magnesium carbonate	$MgCO_3$	White		Decompose to the oxide and carbon dioxide	
Aluminium carbonate	Does not exist				
Zinc carbonate	$ZnCO_3$	White			
Iron(II) carbonate	$FeCO_3$	Green			
Lead(II) carbonate	$PbCO_3$	White			
Copper(II) carbonate	$CuCO_3$	Green			

Example: To prepare copper(II) carbonate. Solutions of copper(II) sulphate and potassium carbonate are mixed and then the precipitate of copper(II) carbonate is separated by filtration and dried.

$$CuSO_4(aq) + K_2CO_3(aq) \rightarrow CuCO_3(s) + K_2SO_4(aq)$$

or

$$Cu^{2+}(aq) + CO_3^{2-}(aq) \rightarrow CuCO_3(s)$$

Test for Carbonates

Some hydrochloric acid is added to the solid carbonate. If a carbonate is present effervescence occurs and the carbon dioxide which is evolved turns lime water milky.

e.g. $CaCO_3(s) + 2HCl(aq) \rightarrow CaCl_2(aq) + H_2O(l) + CO_2(g)$

or

$$CO_3^{2-}(s) + 2H^+(aq) \rightarrow H_2O(l) + CO_2(g)$$

Metallic Chlorides

Preparation

1. These are hydrated salts (contain water) and can be prepared by the action of dilute hydrochloric acid on metals (except sodium and potassium), metallic oxides, metallic hydroxides and metallic carbonates, provided that the resulting chlorides are soluble.

e.g. $Mg(s) + 2HCl(aq) \rightarrow MgCl_2(aq) + H_2(g)$

2. The two insoluble chlorides are those of lead(II) and silver, so these must be prepared by precipitation.

e.g. $Pb^{2+}(aq) + 2Cl^-(aq) \rightarrow PbCl_2(s)$

Note: Lead(II) chloride is soluble in hot water, but insoluble in cold water.

3. By direct combination of the elements.

This method has to be used if anhydrous salts are to be prepared (salts without any water of crystallization). The apparatus on page 130 is used. Dry chlorine is passed over the heated metal, the metallic chloride is collected in a container which contains dry air.

e.g. $Fe(s) + 3Cl_2(g) \rightarrow 2FeCl_3(s)$

$$Al(s) + 3Cl_2(g) \rightarrow 2AlCl_3(s)$$

The following table summarizes the important points about chlorides

Chloride	*Formula*	*Colour*	*Solubility in water*	*Addition of acids*
Potassium chloride	KCl	White	Soluble	When concentrated sulphuric acid is added to the solid chloride on warming, fumes of hydrogen chloride gas are evolved (applies to all chlorides listed)
Sodium chloride	$NaCl$	White	Soluble	
Calcium chloride	$CaCl_2$	White	Soluble	
Magnesium chloride	$MgCl_2$	White	Soluble	
Aluminium chloride	$AlCl_3$	White	Soluble	
Zinc chloride	$ZnCl_2$	White	Soluble	
Iron(III) chloride	$FeCl_3$	Brown	Soluble	e.g. $MgCl_2(s) + H_2SO_4(l) \rightarrow MgSO_4(aq) + 2HCl(g)$
Lead(II) chloride	$PbCl_2$	White	Soluble in hot water only	
Copper(I) chloride	$CuCl$	White	Insoluble	
Copper(II) chloride	$CuCl_2$	Blue-Green	Soluble	
Silver chloride	$AgCl$	White	Insoluble	

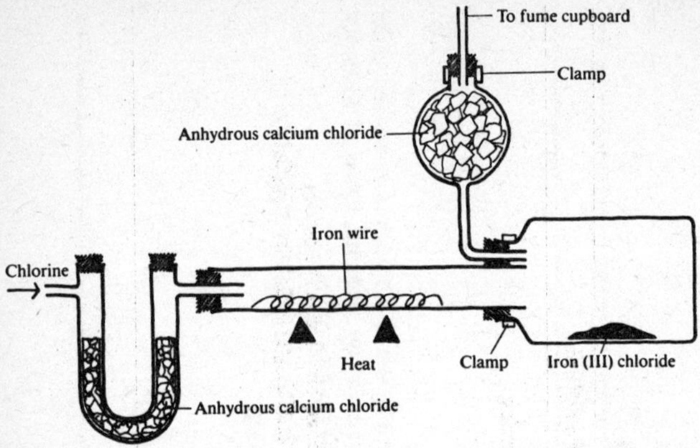

A diagram of the apparatus used to prepare anhydrous iron(III) chloride

Test for Chlorides

A few drops of dilute nitric acid are added to a solution of the chloride, then some silver nitrate solution is added. A white precipitate of silver chloride is seen.

$$Ag^+(aq) + Cl^-(aq) \rightarrow AgCl(s)$$

Metallic Hydroxides

Preparation

1. Hydroxides of sodium, potassium and calcium can be prepared by reacting the metals with water.

e.g. $Ca(s) + H_2O(l) \rightarrow Ca(OH)_2(aq) + H_2(g)$

2. Metallic hydroxides can be prepared by precipitation (except for those of potassium and sodium).

Example: To prepare lead(II) hydroxide a solution of a soluble lead(II) salt is mixed with a solution of a soluble hydroxide and a precipitate of lead(II) hydroxide is formed.

$$Pb^{2+}(aq) + 2OH^-(aq) \rightarrow Pb(OH)_2(s)$$

The difficulty is that excess hydroxide will dissolve most of the precipitates.

The following table summarizes the important points about hydroxides

Hydroxide	*Formula*	*Colour*	*Solubility in water*	*Action of heat*
Potassium hydroxide	KOH	White	Soluble	Nothing
Sodium hydroxide	$NaOH$	White	Soluble	
Calcium hydroxide	$Ca(OH)_2$	White	Slightly soluble	Decompose to give the oxide e.g. $Zn(OH)_2(s) \rightarrow ZnO(s) + H_2O(l)$
Magnesium hydroxide	$Mg(OH)_2$	White	Insoluble	
Aluminium hydroxide	$Al(OH)_3$	White	Insoluble	
Zinc hydroxide	$Zn(OH)_2$	White	Insoluble	
Iron(II) hydroxide	$Fe(OH)_2$	Green	Insoluble	
Iron(III) hydroxide	$Fe(OH)_3$	Brown	Insoluble	
Copper(II) hydroxide	$Cu(OH)_2$	Blue	Insoluble	

Metal ion in solution	*Sodium hydroxide (aq) (or potassium hydroxide)*		*Ammonia solution*	
	Addition	*Excess*	*Addition*	*Excess*
Ca^{2+} or $^{+}Mg^{2+}$	White precipitate	Insoluble	White precipitate	Insoluble
Fe^{2+}	Green precipitate	Insoluble	Green precipitate	Insoluble
Fe^{3+}	Red-brown precipitate	Insoluble	Red-brown precipitate	Insoluble
Al^{3+}	White precipitate	Soluble	White precipitate	Insoluble
Pb^{2+}	White precipitate	Soluble	White precipitate	Insoluble
Cu^{2+}	Blue precipitate	Insoluble	Blue precipitate	Soluble
Zn^{2+}	White precipitate	Soluble	White precipitate	Soluble

Notes:

1. Metallic hydroxides are bases and also alkalis if they are soluble in water.

2. The hydroxides of aluminium, iron(II), copper(II) and zinc are precipitated by ammonia solution, sodium hydroxide and potassium hydroxide; addition of excess alkali may redissolve the precipitate as some of the compounds are amphoteric. These reactions are important practical tests for the presence of these metal ions. The table opposite shows the effect of alkalis on these metal ions.

Lead, zinc and aluminium hydroxides dissolve in excess sodium hydroxide as plumbates, zincates and aluminates respectively are formed because these metals are amphoteric (page 136).

e.g. $2NaOH(aq) + Zn(OH)_2(s) \rightarrow \underset{\text{sodium zincate}}{Na_2ZnO_2(aq)} + 2H_2O(l)$

Copper and zinc hydroxides dissolve in excess ammonium hydroxide solution as they form complexes.

e.g. $Cu(OH)_2(s) + 4NH_3(aq) \rightarrow \underset{\text{tetraamminecopper(II) ion}}{[Cu(NH_3)_4]^{2+}} + 2OH^-(aq)$

Note: These reactions are often referred to on examination papers. You need to know *why* the metal hydroxide redissolves, but you are not expected to learn these difficult equations.

Metallic Nitrates

Preparation

1. By neutralization of an acid with an alkali.

e.g. $KOH(aq) + HNO_3(aq) \rightarrow KNO_3(aq) + H_2O(l)$

2. By the reaction of dilute nitric acid with a metal or metal oxide.

e.g. $Mg(s) + 2HNO_3(aq) \rightarrow Mg(NO_3)_2(aq) + H_2(g)$

or

$MgO(s) + 2HNO_3(aq) \rightarrow Mg(NO_3)_2(aq) + H_2O(l)$

This is not a suitable method to prepare:

The following table summarizes the important points about nitrates

Nitrate	*Formula*	*Colour*	*Solubility in water*	*Action of heat*
Potassium nitrate	KNO_3	White	Soluble	Decompose to give the nitrite and oxygen
Sodium	$NaNO_3$	White	Soluble	
Calcium	$Ca(NO_3)_2$	White	Soluble	Decompose to give the oxide, nitrogen dioxide and oxygen
Magnesium	$Mg(NO_3)_2$	White	Soluble	
Aluminium	$Al(NO_3)_3$	White	Soluble	
Zinc	$Zn(NO_3)_2$	White	Soluble	
Iron(II)	$Fe(NO_3)_2$	Found only in solutions	Soluble	
Iron(III)	$Fe(NO_3)_3$		Soluble	
Lead(II)	$Pb(NO_3)_2$	White	Soluble	
Copper(II)	$Cu(NO_3)_2$	Blue	Soluble	

(a) aluminium nitrate as aluminium does not react with this acid.
(b) potassium nitrate or sodium nitrate as the reaction of sodium or potassium metal with an acid is too dangerous.

Note: There may be difficulties in using dilute nitric acid, as it is an oxidizing agent; so if the metal, or metal compound, has two valencies then the compound with the metal in the higher valency state will be produced.

Test for Nitrates

1. A freshly made solution of iron(II) sulphate is added to a solution of the nitrate. Concentrated sulphuric acid is then poured slowly down the side of the test tube so that it forms a layer below the aqueous layer. If a brown ring appears between the two layers then a nitrate is present.

2. Sodium hydroxide solution is added to a solution of the nitrate and then a little Devarda's alloy is added. If ammonia is evolved on warming then a nitrate is present.

Metallic Oxides

Preparation

1. Heating the metal in air or oxygen. This is not always satisfactory as some metals are covered with a thin layer of their oxide and so do not react, while other metals, e.g. sodium and potassium, are not widely available.

2. Heating a nitrate. This is not always possible because potassium nitrate and sodium nitrate decompose on heating to give the respective nitrites, while the nitrates of mercury and silver decompose to give the respective metals.

e.g. $2Cu(NO_3)_2(s) \rightarrow 2CuO(s) + 4NO_2(g) + O_2(g)$

3. Heating a carbonate. The only carbonates which do not decompose on heating are those of sodium and potassium, while carbonates of aluminium and iron(III) do not exist.

e.g. $PbCO_3(s) \rightarrow PbO(s) + CO_2(g)$

4. Heating a hydroxide. This is possible for metal hydroxides when the metals are between calcium and copper in the reactivity series. The hydroxides of potassium and sodium do not decompose on heating.

e.g. $Zn(OH)_2(s) \rightarrow ZnO(s) + H_2O(l)$

5. Reacting the metal with another oxide. This is only possible if the free metal is higher in the activity series than the one present in the oxide.

e.g. $Fe_2O_3(s) + 2Al(s) \rightarrow Al_2O_3(s) + 2Fe(s)$

Most of these oxides are basic and react with acids to produce salts and water.

e.g. $MgO(s) + 2HCl(aq) \rightarrow MgCl_2(aq) + H_2O(l)$

Oxides are of four types:

1. Basic oxides
Basic oxides are metallic oxides which react with an acid to produce a salt and water only. If they are soluble in water they form an alkaline solution, e.g. sodium oxide or calcium oxide.

2. Acidic oxides
Acidic oxides are non-metallic oxides which react with water to produce acids, e.g. carbon dioxide and sulphur dioxide.

3. Amphoteric oxides
Amphoteric oxides are metallic oxides which show both basic and acid properties, e.g. aluminium oxide and zinc oxide.

4. Neutral oxides
Neutral oxides are non-metallic oxides which show neither basic nor acidic properties, e.g. carbon monoxide and nitrogen oxide.

Metallic Sulphates

Preparation

1. Soluble sulphates can be prepared by the action of dilute sulphuric acid on a metal, metal oxide, hydroxide or carbonate.

e.g. $Mg(s) + H_2SO_4(aq) \rightarrow MgSO_4(aq) + H_2(g)$

2. Insoluble sulphates, that is those of calcium, barium and lead, can be prepared by precipitation. A solution of a soluble sulphate and a solution of the metal are mixed and a precipitate is formed.

e.g. $Ca(NO_3)_2(aq) + Na_2SO_4(aq) \rightarrow CaSO_4(s) + 2NaNO_3(aq)$

or

$$Ca^{2+}(aq) + SO_4^{2-}(aq) \rightarrow CaSO_4(s)$$

The following table summarizes the important points about oxides

Oxide	*Formula*	*Colour*	*Important reactions*	*Reduction to the metal*
Potassium oxide	K_2O	White	With water reacts to form the hydroxide	Oxides can not be reduced to metals with hydrogen
Sodium oxide	Na_2O	White		
Calcium oxide	CaO	White	Reacts vigorously with water, hydroxide and steam formed $CaO(s) + H_2O(l) \rightarrow Ca(OH)_2(s)$	
Magnesium oxide	MgO	White	Amphoteric (zinc oxide yellow when hot)	
Aluminium oxide	Al_2O_3	White		
Zinc oxide	ZnO	White		
Iron(II) oxide	FeO	Black		Oxides reduced to the metal by passing hydrogen or carbon monoxide over the heated metal or heating oxide with carbon
Iron(III) oxide	Fe_2O_3	Red		
Iron tetraoxide	Fe_3O_4	Black	Prepared by heating iron in steam $3Fe(s) + 4H_2O(g) \rightarrow Fe_3O_4(s) + 4H_2(g)$	
Lead(II) oxide	PbO	Yellow	Amphoteric	
Copper(II) oxide	CuO	Black		

The following table summarizes the important points about sulphates

Sulphate	*Formula*	*Colour*	*Solubility in water*	
Potassium sulphate	K_2SO_4	White	Soluble	usually contain water of crystallization, which is easily lost on heating
Sodium sulphate	Na_2SO_4	White	Soluble	
Calcium sulphate	$CaSO_4$	White	Insoluble	
Magnesium sulphate	$MgSO_4$	White	Soluble	
Aluminium sulphate	$Al_2(SO_4)_3$	White	Soluble	
Zinc sulphate	$ZnSO_4$	White	Soluble	
Iron(II) sulphate	$FeSO_4$	Green	Soluble	
Lead(II) sulphate	$PbSO_4$	White	Insoluble	
Copper(II) sulphate	$CuSO_4$	Blue	Soluble	

Test for Sulphates

A small amount of dilute hydrochloric acid is added to a solution of the sulphate followed by a barium chloride solution. A white precipitate is seen

$$Ba^{2+}(aq) + SO_4^{2-}(aq) \rightarrow BaSO_4(s)$$

Remaining Important Points about Metals

Sodium and Potassium

Metals

1. Very reactive, as they only need to lose one electron to become a stable, inert gas structure.
2. React so readily with water and oxygen that they are stored under oil.
3. React dangerously with acids.
4. Soft metals with low densities.
5. Flame tests: Sodium – yellow, Potassium – lilac.

Compounds

1. All soluble in water.
2. All white.
3. All form ionic compounds.

Magnesium, Calcium and Zinc Compounds

Metals

1. Less reactive than group 1 metals as they need to lose two electrons from their outer shell to attain a stable, inert gas structure.
2. React with water and oxygen, but heat may be necessary.
3. React with acids, hydrogen evolved.
4. Hard metals.
5. Flame tests: Calcium – brick-red, Barium – apple-green.

Compounds

1. All white.
2. All ionic compounds.
3. Solubility varies.

Aluminium

Metal

1. This metal is covered with a thin persistent layer of its oxide which often makes it unreactive.
2. Reacts with water and oxygen on heating (if the oxide layer is removed).
3. Reacts with dilute hydrochloric acid on heating.
4. A low density metal.
5. Does not corrode, so it is often used in alloys to make saucepans, aircraft bodies and electricity cables.

An alloy is a substance made up of two or more metals.

Compounds

1. The aluminium atom needs to lose three electrons in order to form an ion. This is not always possible, so some of its compounds are covalent.
2. Usually white in colour.

Iron

Metal

1. This metal has a valency of +2 or +3 so it is a special type of metal called a transition metal.

2. Reacts slowly with acids.

3. When iron or steel is in contact with water and air over a period of time rusting occurs. The iron reacts with the water and air to produce mainly iron(III) oxide on the surface of the metal. This is the disadvantage of using iron and steel, so steps must be taken to prevent this process: the surface of the metal is covered to prevent any contact with the air or water, e.g. by painting, greasing, coating with plastic or galvanizing.

Galvanizing is the coating of iron or steel with zinc to protect it. The zinc reacts with the air to form zinc oxide, which is unreactive.

Alternatively, the iron is connected to a small piece of a more reactive metal. This more reactive metal then reacts with air and water and gradually dissolves away, which leaves the iron unchanged. This piece of reactive metal is known as a sacrificial anode.

> *Note:* You should be able to describe an experiment which shows the conditions that are necessary for rusting.

Compounds

1. Iron can form iron(II) and iron(III) compounds. Iron(II) salts are easily oxidized in air to iron(III) salts, e.g. a fresh aqueous solution of iron(II) sulphate goes brown very quickly.

2. Iron(II) salts are prepared by the action of the appropriate acid on iron; these can be easily oxidized to iron(III) salts

Tests to Distinguish Between Iron(II) and Iron(III) Salts

1. When a solution of an iron(II) salt is mixed with sodium hydroxide a green precipitate of iron(II) hydroxide is seen.

2. When a solution of an iron(III) salt is mixed with sodium hydroxide a red-brown precipitate of iron(III) hydroxide is seen.

3. Iron(II) compounds are usually green. Iron(III) compounds are usually a dark yellow or brown.

Copper

Metal

1. Another transition metal.
2. An excellent conductor of heat and electricity.
3. Used in copper piping and electrical wiring.
4. Used in alloys with tin.
5. Flame test green-blue.

Compounds

1. Forms copper(I) and copper(II) compounds but you are only concerned with copper(II) compounds.

2. Coloured substances (copper(II) only).

Test for Copper(II) Ions

When dilute ammonia solution is added to a solution of copper(II) ions a pale blue precipitate of copper(II) hydroxide is seen; this redissolves to form a deep blue solution (page 133).

Examination Question

There are many examination questions on these topics, they may be on the extraction of a particular metal or relating the activity of metals and compounds to their position in the reactivity series.

(*Associated Examining Board, June 1976*)

(a) *Crude iron is produced in a blast furnace from a mixture of iron, coke and limestone.*

(i) *Give the common name and formula of one iron ore used.* (2)

(ii) *What happens chemically to the coke?* (3)

(iii) *Give the equation for one reaction by which iron ore is converted to iron.* (1)

(iv) *Why is limestone used? What happens to it?* (4)

(v) *What are the essential differences between the composition of crude iron and that of steel?* (4)

(b) *State, without further description, one reaction in each case by which you could:*

(i) *Obtain a solution containing iron(II) ions (Fe^{2+}) from metallic iron;*

(ii) *convert this solution to one containing iron(III) ions (Fe^{3+}).*

Briefly describe a chemical test to confirm that the change in (ii) has taken place. (9)

Answer

(a) (i) Haematite Fe_2O_3 *or* Magnetite Fe_3O_4.

(ii) The coke is oxidized to carbon dioxide, which reacts with more carbon to form carbon monoxide.

$$C(s) + O_2(g) \rightarrow CO_2(g)$$

$$C(s) + CO_2(g) \rightarrow 2CO(g)$$

This carbon monoxide then reduces the iron(III) oxide to iron.

(iii) $Fe_2O_3(s) + 3CO(g) \rightarrow 2Fe(s) + 3CO_2(g)$

(iv) Limestone decomposes to form carbon dioxide and calcium oxide. The latter then reacts with the earthy material present to form a slag.

$$CaCO_3(s) \rightarrow CaO(s) + CO_2(g)$$

$$CaO(s) + SiO_2(s) \rightarrow CaSiO_3(s)$$

(v) Crude iron contains mainly iron with impurities of carbon, phosphorus and sulphur. Steel is a mixture of iron and up to 1.5% carbon. There are no impurities of phosphorus and sulphur.

(b) (i) React iron with dilute sulphuric acid.

$$Fe(s) + H_2SO_4(aq) \rightarrow FeSO_4(aq) + H_2(g)$$

(ii) Bubble chlorine through a solution of iron(II) ions.

$$2FeCl_2(aq) + Cl_2(g) \rightarrow 2FeCl_3(aq)$$

(An oxidizing agent is required to oxidize iron(II) ions to iron(III) ions.)

When sodium hydroxide solution is added dropwise to a solution of Fe(III) ions, a red-brown precipitate will be seen. This is insoluble on addition of further sodium hydroxide solution.

10. Non-Metals and their Compounds

Carbon and its Compounds

Carbon

Occurrence

Carbon occurs in the form of diamond and graphite, so it exists in two allotropic forms.

Allotropes are different forms of the same element, which can exist in the same state, i.e. carbon has two forms in solid state – diamond and graphite.

A comparison of the physical properties of diamond and graphite is shown below.

Graphite	*Diamond*
1. Density 2.25 g/cm^3	Density 3.53 g/cm^3
2. Black	Colourless, transparent, high refractive index
3. Very soft, marks paper	Hardest natural substance known
4. Good conduction of heat and electricity	Does not conduct heat and electricity
5. High melting and boiling points	High melting and boiling points

Chemical Properties

Carbon is not very reactive and always forms covalent bonds as it needs to share four electrons in order to reach an inert gas structure.

1. When heated in air, or oxygen, carbon dioxide is produced.

$$C(s) + O_2(g) \rightarrow CO_2(g)$$

2. When heated with oxides of unreactive metals, it reduces them to the metals.

e.g. $PbO(s) + C(s) \rightarrow Pb(s) + CO(g)$

3. When carbon is heated to white heat it reacts with steam.

$C(s) + H_2O(g) \rightarrow CO(g) + H_2(g)$

Carbon Dioxide

The Laboratory Preparation

Marble chips ($CaCO_3$) and dilute hydrochloric acid are mixed in a flask. Effervescence occurs and the carbon dioxide produced passes through a delivery tube and then is collected by displacement of water or by downward delivery (see the diagrams below).

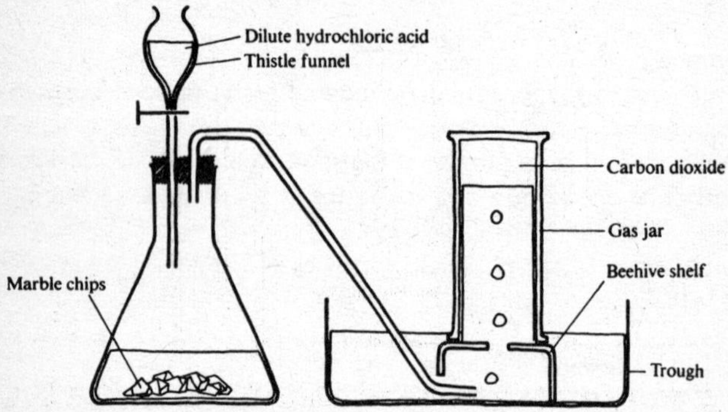

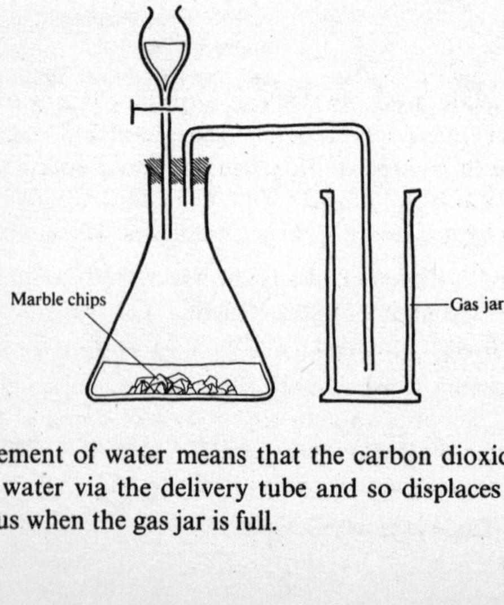

Displacement of water means that the carbon dioxide enters the full gas jar of water via the delivery tube and so displaces the water. Thus it is obvious when the gas jar is full.

Note: This method cannot be used if the gas required is soluble, e.g. hydrogen chloride.

Downward delivery is only suitable if the gas collected is denser than air because then the gas collects at the bottom of the gas jar and so pushes out the air. This method is unsuitable if the gas is lighter than air, e.g. hydrogen, as it would move upwards out of the open gas jar.

If the gas needs to be dry then it can be passed through concentrated sulphuric acid or anhydrous calcium chloride (see the diagram below).

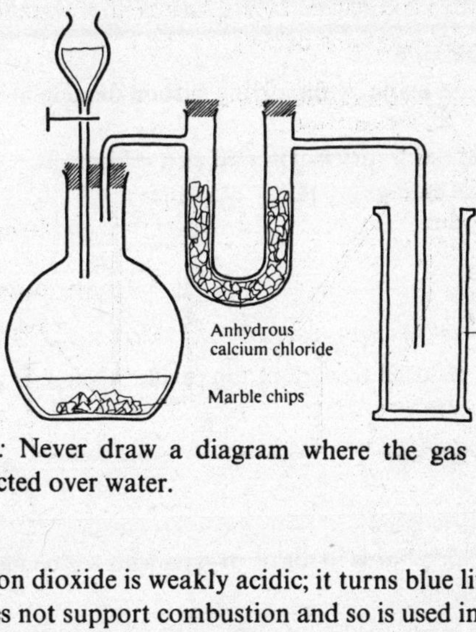

Note: Never draw a diagram where the gas is dried and then collected over water.

Properties

1. Carbon dioxide is weakly acidic; it turns blue litmus red.
2. It does not support combustion and so is used in fire extinguishers.
3. It reacts with sodium hydroxide to produce sodium hydrogen-carbonate. So if a mixture of gases containing carbon dioxide is passed through sodium hydroxide the carbon dioxide will be removed.

$$2NaOH(aq) + CO_2(g) \rightarrow Na_2CO_3(aq) + H_2O(l)$$
$$Na_2CO_3(aq) + H_2O(l) + CO_2(g) \rightarrow 2NaHCO_3(s)$$

4. When burning magnesium ribbon is plunged into a gas jar of carbon dioxide, black specks of carbon are seen. The magnesium turns to a white ash. This demonstrates that carbon dioxide contains carbon and oxygen. The latter must have been present as it has combined with magnesium to form magnesium oxide (the white ash).

$$CO_2(g) + 2Mg(s) \rightarrow 2MgO(s) + C(s)$$

Test foı Carbon Dioxide

When carbon dioxide is bubbled through lime water a white precipitate of calcium carbonate is produced.

$$Ca(OH)_2(aq) + CO_2(g) \rightarrow CaCO_3(s) + H_2O(l)$$

If further carbon dioxide is passed into the liquid then calcium hydrogencarbonate is formed and the precipitate disappears.

$$CaCO_3(s) + H_2O(l) + CO_2(g) \rightarrow Ca(HCO_3)_2(aq)$$

Uses of Carbon Dioxide

1. Fizzy drinks are made by dissolving carbon dioxide in water under pressure.
2. Solid carbon dioxide (dry ice) is used as a refrigerant.
3. It is used in fire extinguishers.

Carbon Monoxide

Preparation

Carbon dioxide is reduced to carbon monoxide when it is passed over red-hot charcoal.

$$C(s) + CO_2(g) \rightarrow 2CO(g)$$

Properties

1. Carbon monoxide burns in air or oxygen with a blue flame; carbon dioxide is produced.

$$2CO(g) + O_2(g) \rightarrow 2CO_2(g)$$

> *Note:* Compare this reaction with carbon dioxide, which does not burn.

2. It is a good reducing agent, e.g. in blast furnaces, iron(III) oxide is reduced to iron (page 126).
3. It is a neutral oxide.
4. It is odourless and colourless, but very toxic as it forms a cherry-red compound with the blood, so preventing the normal reaction of the blood with oxygen.

Nitrogen and its Compounds

Nitrogen (*See also Chapter 11 on Air*)

Preparation

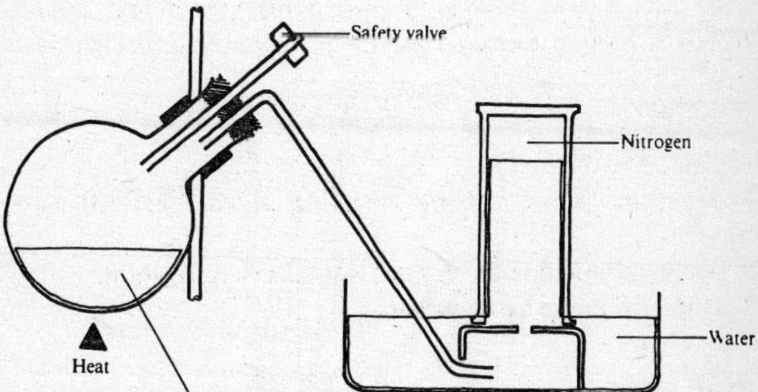

On heating a solution of sodium nitrite and ammonium chloride ammonium nitrite is produced, which decomposes to produce nitrogen which is collected over water.

$$NH_4NO_2(aq) \rightarrow N_2(g) + 2H_2O(l)$$

Properties

Nitrogen is an unreactive gas. No positive tests identify it, it does not smell, does not support combustion and does not change lime water.

Nitrogen Dioxide

Preparation

When lead nitrate is heated it decomposes, producing nitrogen dioxide. This is liquefied by cooling it in an ice–salt mixture.

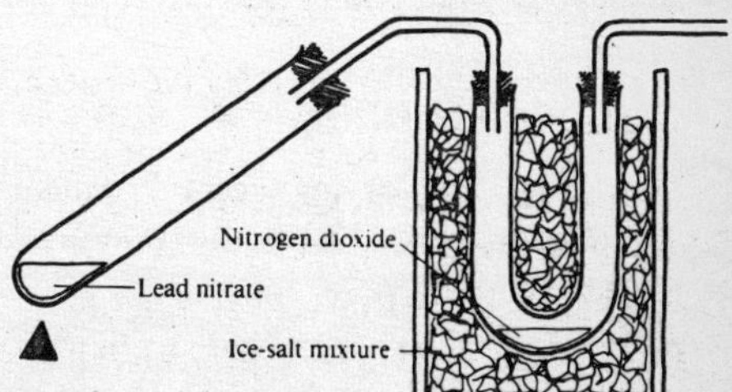

$$2Pb(NO_3)_2(s) \rightarrow 2PbO(s) + 4NO_2(g) + O_2(g)$$

Properties

1. A reddish-brown gas with an irritating smell.
2. It forms nitrous acid and nitric acid when passed into water.

$$2NO_2(g) + H_2O(l) \rightarrow HNO_3(aq) + HNO_2(aq)$$

Ammonia

Preparation

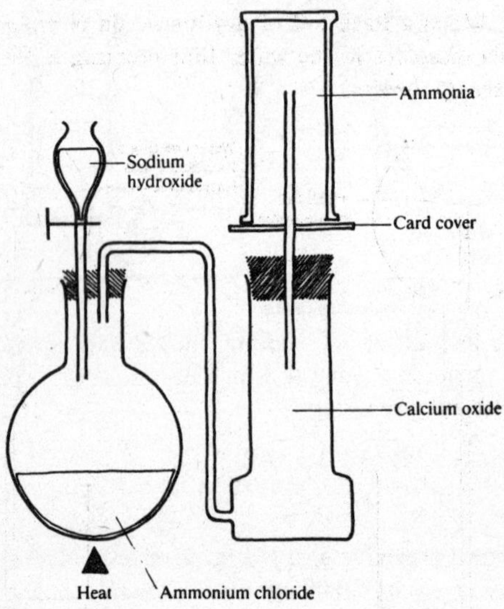

On heating ammonium chloride and sodium hydroxide ammonia is produced.

$$NH_4Cl(s) + NaOH(aq) \rightarrow NaCl(aq) + H_2O(l) + NH_3(g)$$

Note: The drying agent is calcium oxide, which is unusual. Ammonia reacts with the two normal drying agents as follows:

$$H_2SO_4(l) + 2NH_3(g) \rightarrow (NH_4)_2SO_4(s)$$
$$CaCl_2(s) + 4NH_3(g) \rightarrow CaCl_2 \cdot 4NH_3(s)$$

Ammonia is less dense than air, so it is collected by upward delivery.

Manufacture of Ammonia (the Haber Process)

Nitrogen and hydrogen are combined directly at a pressure of 200–500 atmospheres in the presence of a catalyst of finely divided iron at a temperature of 450 °C.

$$N_2(g) + 3H_2(g) \leftrightharpoons 2NH_3(g)$$

Properties

1. Ammonia is very soluble in water, as demonstrated by the fountain experiment. When a flask full of dry ammonia is opened under water, the ammonia dissolves in the water thus creating a partial vacuum, so the water rises up the flask.

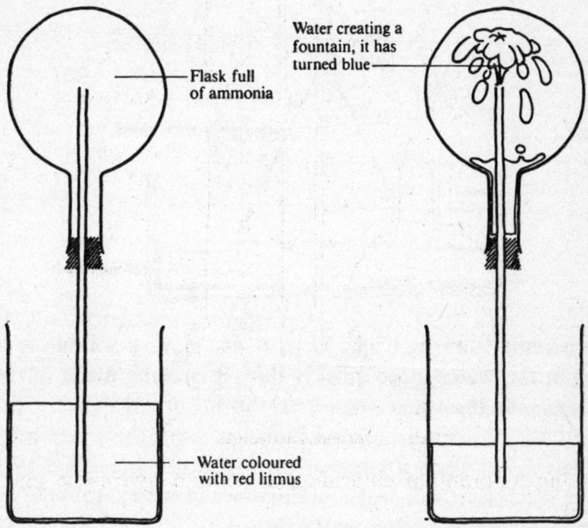

2. When ammonia is passed over hot copper(II) oxide the copper oxide is reduced to copper while the ammonia is oxidized to nitrogen.

$$2NH_3(g) + 3CuO(s) \rightarrow 3Cu(s) + 3H_2O(l) + N_2(g)$$

Tests for Ammonia

1. Ammonia turns red litmus paper blue.
2. When ammonia comes in contact with hydrogen chloride, dense white fumes of ammonium chloride are formed.

Uses of Ammonia

1. In the manufacture of nylon, rayon and nitric acid.
2. As a refrigerant.

Ammonia Solution

This is obtained by passing ammonia gas into water using the following apparatus:

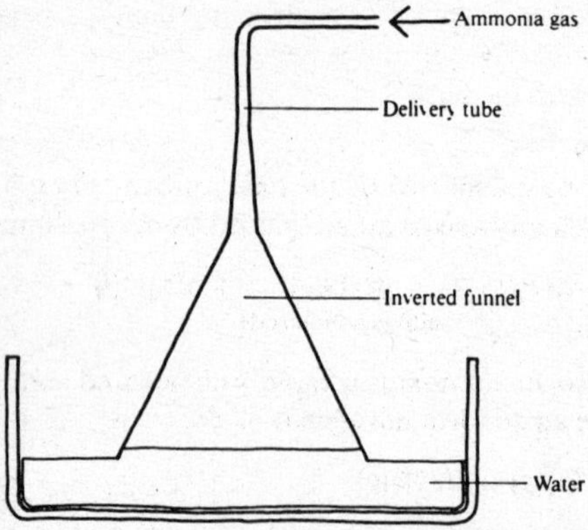

This prevents 'sucking-back', i.e. if a gas is very soluble it may be absorbed in the water more quickly than it is being made in the flask. This means that the water would rise up a normal delivery tube and enter the flask. When an inverted funnel is used, the water may begin to suck back, but since a large volume of water is needed to fill this funnel, the water level will drop and thus air will enter the funnel resulting in the liquid dropping back from the funnel.

Properties

1. Ammonia solution is a weak alkali so it neutralizes acids to give ammonium salts,
2. It precipitates metal hydroxides from their solutions.

Ammonium Salts

1. These are soluble in water.
2. When heated with alkalis, ammonia is produced. (This is a test for these salts.)
3. When heated, ammonium salts decompose.

e.g. $NH_4Cl(s) \rightarrow NH_3(g) + HCl(g)$
$(NH_4)_2CO_3(s) \rightarrow CO_2(g) + 2NH_3(g) + H_2O(l)$

Nitric Acid

Manufacture

Nitric acid is manufactured by the oxidation of ammonia.

1. Ammonia and excess air are passed over a red-hot catalyst.

$$4NH_3(g) + 5O_2(g) \rightarrow \underset{\text{nitrogen monoxide}}{4NO(g)} + 6H_2O(l)$$

2. The nitrogen monoxide is rapidly cooled and combines with further oxygen in the air to form nitrogen dioxide.

$$2NO(g) + O_2(g) \rightarrow 2NO_2(g)$$

3. The nitrogen dioxide is then absorbed in hot water in the presence of more air.

$$2H_2O(l) + 4NO_2(g) + O_2(g) \rightarrow 4HNO_3(aq)$$

Properties

Nitric acid is a colourless liquid which turns yellow in the presence of light as it decomposes to form nitrogen dioxide.

Its properties can be divided into two categories: properties of a typical strong acid (page 99) and properties of an oxidizing agent.

Even when dilute nitric acid can act as an oxidizing agent these reactions may be complicated. When nitric acid oxidizes another substance it is usually reduced to nitrogen dioxide (brown fumes) and water. It can oxidize:

copper to copper(II) nitrate
sulphur to sulphuric acid
carbon to carbon dioxide

Uses of Nitric Acid

1. To manufacture dyes, fertilizers and explosives.
2. As an oxidizing agent in the manufacture of nylon and Terylene.
3. In etching and refining precious metals.

The Nitrogen Cycle

About four-fifths of the air is made up of nitrogen; this fraction remains constant because the rate of removal of nitrogen must equal the rate of addition of nitrogen. The sequence of reactions involved in these processes is known as the 'nitrogen cycle' and can be represented as follows:

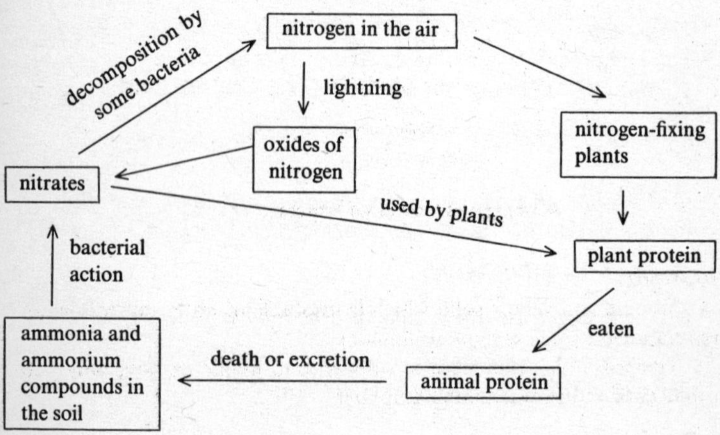

Sulphur and its Compounds

Sulphur

Sulphur is found uncombined, or as hydrogen sulphide in petroleum gases.

Extraction

Sulphur is extracted from under the ground by the Frasch process. An iron tube about 160 metres long containing three small concentric tubes is sunk into the ground. Steam and air, under pressure, are blown into the sulphur layer. This melts this layer and liquid sulphur is pumped up to the surface.

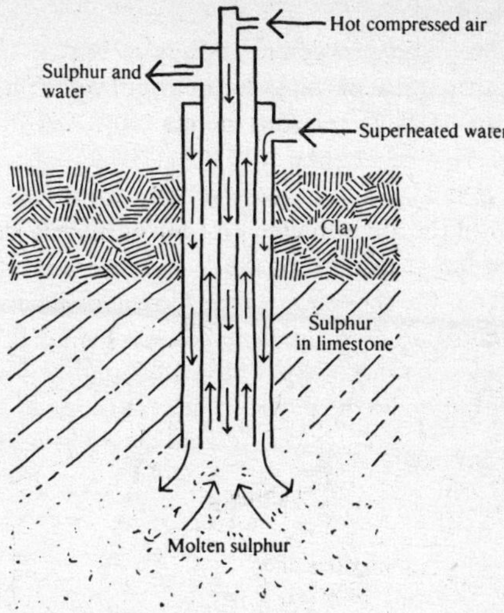

A diagram of the Frasch process

Properties

1. Sulphur is a yellow solid which is insoluble in water but soluble in organic solvents (e.g. carbon disulphide).

2. There are two allotropes of sulphur but, unlike carbon, only one form occurs naturally (rhombic sulphur).

A comparison of the two allotropes of sulphur

Rhombic (octahedral)	*Monoclinic (prismatic)*
Density 2.08 g/cm³	Density 1.98 g/cm³
Melting point 114 °C	119 °C
Stable at temperatures below 96°C	Unstable at temperatures below 96 °C. Reverts to the rhombic form
Both contain S_8 molecules	
S_8 molecules more tightly packed	

Preparation of the Allotropes of Sulphur

1. *Monoclinic.* Some powdered sulphur is heated gently in a large evaporating dish until it melts, then on cooling a solid crust forms on the surface. Two holes are pierced in this crust and the liquid sulphur is poured off, leaving needle-like crystals on the underside of this crust.

2. *Rhombic.* Some sulphur is dissolved in carbon disulphide in a test-tube. This solution is then filtered to remove any undissolved sulphur and the solution left to evaporate.

Sulphur Molecules

Sulphur molecules consist of eight atoms of sulphur joined together by strong covalent bonds, so the molecule has the shape of a 'puckered' ring.

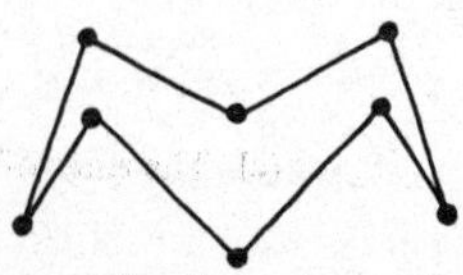

The forces between the molecules are weak (called Van der Waal's forces) and so they are easily broken by heating: therefore sulphur has a low melting point.

The Effect of Heating Sulphur

The following changes are physical changes. When sulphur is heated gently (a) it first melts to a brown liquid (b). On further heating this runny liquid becomes thicker (more viscous) until finally it changes to an even thicker nearly black liquid (c, d, e). At the boiling point it suddenly becomes runny again; if this is poured into water, plastic sulphur is formed (f).

Uses of Sulphur

1. In making vulcanized rubber.
2. In the manufacture of sulphuric acid.
3. In making insecticides and fungicides.

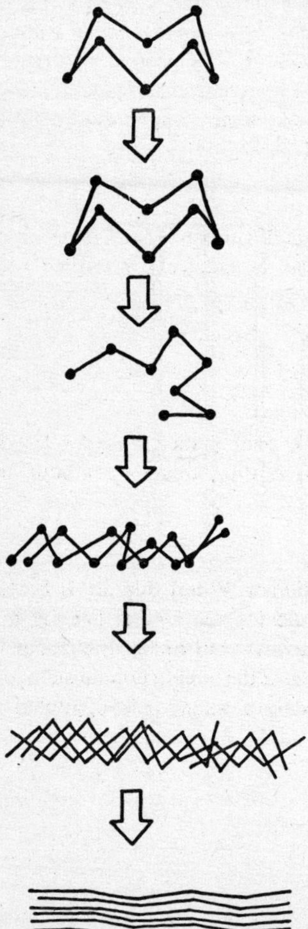

(a) Many molecules held together by weak intermolecular forces

(b) The melting point, when the molecules are not held together by intermolecular forces

(c) The rings of S_8 molecules break

(d) Open rings become entangled

(e) Finally all the open rings are entangled

(f) Separate stretched rings

Sulphur Dioxide

Preparation

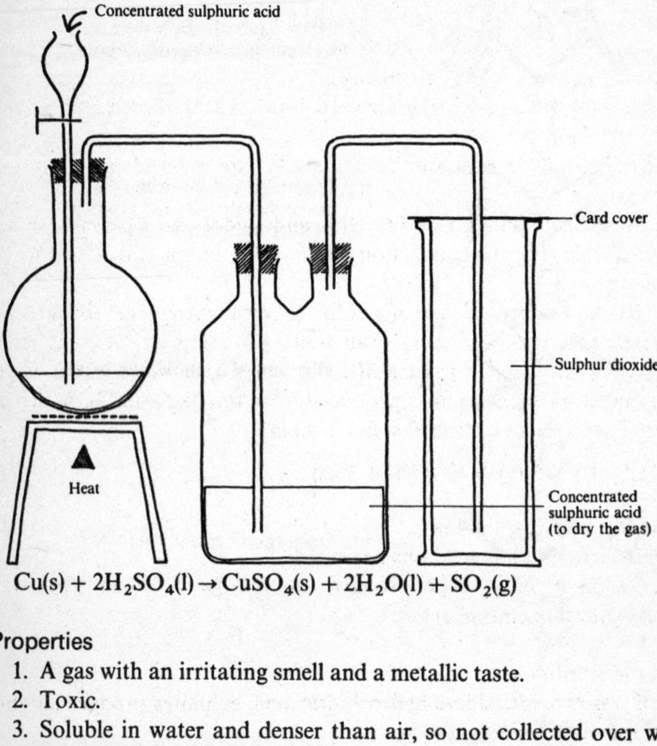

$$Cu(s) + 2H_2SO_4(l) \rightarrow CuSO_4(s) + 2H_2O(l) + SO_2(g)$$

Properties

1. A gas with an irritating smell and a metallic taste.
2. Toxic.
3. Soluble in water and denser than air, so not collected over water but by downward delivery.
4. In the presence of water, sulphur dioxide acts as a reducing agent. It dissolves in water to form sulphurous acid.

$$SO_2(g) + H_2O(l) \rightarrow H_2SO_3(aq)$$

When water is not present sulphur dioxide does *not* have a reducing action.

Sulphurous acid ionizes as follows:

$$H_2SO_3 \rightarrow 2H^+ + \underset{\text{sulphite ion}}{SO_3^{2-}}$$

This sulphite ion is oxidized to the sulphate ion (SO_4^{2-}). So if sulphur dioxide is bubbled into the following solutions they are reduced.
(a) Acidified potassium dichromate(VI) solution (orange) is turned green as chromium(III) ions are formed as well as sulphate ions.
(b) Acidified potassium manganate(VII) solution (purple) becomes colourless as manganese(II) ions are formed.
(c) Bromine water (orange) is turned colourless as the bromine is reduced to bromide ions.
(d) Iron(III) ions in solution (brown colour) are reduced to iron(II) ions (light green).

5. Moist sulphur dioxide bleaches some wool and dyes, straws and flowers. This is a reducing action as the sulphite ion is oxidized to the sulphate ion.

6. Sulphur dioxide acts as an oxidizing agent when it is in the presence of a stronger reducing agent than itself. For example, if a gas jar of sulphur dioxide and a gas jar of hydrogen sulphide are mixed in the presence of water, sulphur is produced from the oxidation of hydrogen sulphide and the reduction of sulphur dioxide.

$$2H_2S(g) + SO_2(g) \rightarrow 2H_2O(l) + 3S(s)$$

Tests for Sulphur Dioxide

1. It turns damp blue litmus paper red.
2. It turns filter paper soaked in orange acidified potassium dichromate(VI) solution green.

Test for Sulphites

When warmed with dilute hydrochloric acid, sulphites produce sulphur dioxide (sulphates do not).

Sulphuric Acid

Manufacture (Contact Process)

1. Sulphur is burnt in air to produce sulphur dioxide.

$$S(s) + O_2(g) \rightarrow SO_2(g)$$

2. Sulphur dioxide and air are then passed over a catalyst of vanadium(V) oxide at 450–500 °C to produce sulphur trioxide.

$$2SO_2(g) + O_2(g) \rightarrow 2SO_3(g)$$

3. Sulphur trioxide cannot be passed directly into water. It reacts so violently that a mist of sulphuric acid droplets would fill the surrounding air; therefore it is passed into concentrated sulphuric acid. It dissolves, forming 'oleum'.

$$SO_3(g) + H_2SO_4(l) \rightarrow H_2S_2O_7(l)$$

4. The oleum is then diluted carefully with water to produce concentrated sulphuric acid.

$$H_2S_2O_7(l) + H_2O(l) \rightarrow 2H_2SO_4(l)$$

Properties

These can be divided into two types: those of a strong acid, and those of an oxidizing agent.

(a) Strong acid

(i) Dilute sulphuric acid is a strong acid which forms two series of salts (page 102).

(ii) Like all strong acids, it is almost completely ionized in solution.

(iii) It acts as a typical acid (page 99).

(b) Concentrated acid

(i) Hot concentrated sulphuric acid acts as an oxidizing agent. It can oxidize copper, carbon, and sulphur while it is reduced to sulphur dioxide.

$$Cu(s) + 2H_2SO_4(l) \rightarrow CuSO_4(aq) + 2H_2O(l) + SO_2(g)$$
$$S(s) + 2H_2SO_4(l) \rightarrow 2H_2O(l) + 2SO_2(g)$$
$$C(s) + 2H_2SO_4(l) \rightarrow 2H_2O(l) + 2SO_2(g) + CO_2(g)$$

(You are not required to memorize these equations.)

(ii) It acts as a drying agent. Gases are bubbled through it before collection. It is not suitable for drying any gases, which react with it, e.g. ammonia and hydrogen sulphide.

(iii) It acts as a dehydrating agent. This means that it removes the elements of water from compounds. When added to blue hydrated crystals of copper(II) sulphate a white powder is produced.

$$\underset{\text{blue crystals}}{CuSO_4\cdot 5H_2O} \xrightarrow{H_2SO_4(l)} \underset{\text{anhydrous copper(II) sulphate}}{CuSO_4} + 5H_2O(g)$$

When added to sugar, the sugar chars, steam is evolved and the whole process gives out heat.

(iv) It is used as a catalyst in ester formation (page 88).

(v) When mixed with salts of nitric acid or hydrochloric acid it displaces them from their salts.

e.g. $NaCl(s) + H_2SO_4(l) \rightarrow NaHSO_4 + HCl(g)$

$KNO_3(s) + H_2SO_4(l) \rightarrow KHSO_4(s) + HNO_3(g)$

Uses of Sulphuric Acid

It is used to manufacture paints, dyes, drugs, soaps and fertilizers.

The Halogens

The halogens consist of the following elements:

Element	*Symbol*	*Mass number*	*Electronic structure*	*Physical state at room temperature*	*Colour*
Fluorine	F	19	2,7	Gas	Pale yellow
Chlorine	Cl	35.5	2,8,7	Gas	Yellow-green
Bromine	Br	80	2,8,18,7	Liquid	Red-brown
Iodine	I	127	2,8,18,18,7	Solid	Black-purple

Note: Questions on these elements seem to concentrate on the comparison of their properties. Fluorine is not used in practical work as it is *very* active.

The Reactivity of the Halogens

As the atomic number of the halogens increases their reactivity decreases. Consider the structures of the following:

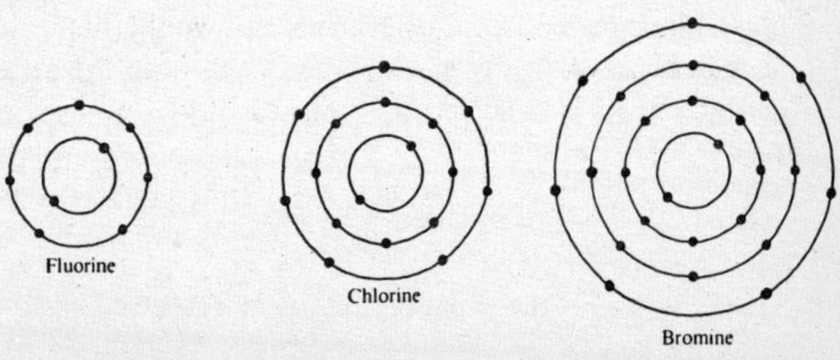

A diagram of the electronic structure of three halogens

Since these elements need to gain only one electron to attain an inert gas structure, the fluorine atom will be most likely to attract an electron as it is so small. The attracting power of the nucleus is strongest, as it does not have to act over such a large distance as that of chlorine or bromine.

Chlorine

Manufacture

Chlorine is obtained industrially by the electrolysis of sodium chloride (page 124).

Preparation

Chlorine can be prepared by the oxidation of concentrated hydrochloric acid, e.g. with potassium manganate(VII) (potassium permanganate).

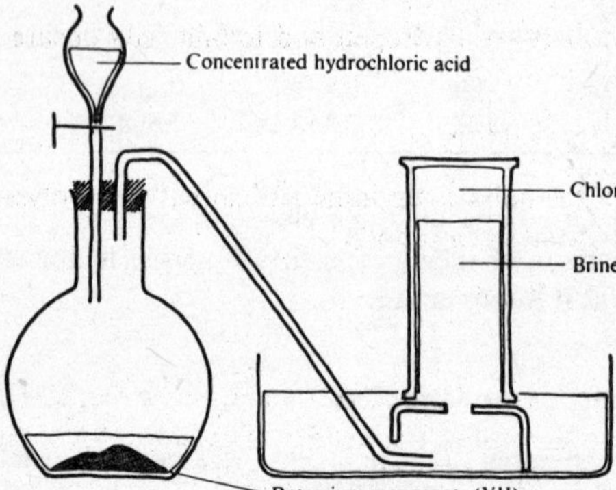

Note: Chlorine is collected over brine, as it would dissolve in water and then break down, releasing chlorine gas into the atmosphere. Alternatively, it is collected by downward delivery as it is denser than air.

Properties of the Halogens

The following properties are shown by all the halogens. However, reactions involving chlorine will occur more easily and violently than those occurring with iodine.

1. Halogens react directly with heated metals.

e.g. $2Fe(s) + 3Cl_2(g) \rightarrow 2FeCl_3(s)$

$$Fe(s) + I_2 \xrightarrow{\text{catalyst}} FeI_2(s)$$

Iron(II) iodide is unstable.

2. They react with hydrogen. The reaction between chlorine and hydrogen is explosive in sunlight.

$$Cl_2(g) + H_2(g) \rightarrow 2HCl(g)$$

The reaction between hydrogen and iodine only occurs on heating and is reversible.

$$I_2(g) + H_2(g) \rightleftharpoons 2HI(g)$$

3. Salts of the halides are ionic and so will electrolyse. The following reaction will occur at the anode

$$X^- \text{ (halide)} \rightarrow X + e^-$$
$$X + X \rightarrow X_2$$

i.e. the halogen is oxidized. The iodide ion is oxidized the most easily and the fluoride ion the least easily. Therefore if a solution containing potassium bromide and potassium iodide is subjected to electrolysis the iodide ions are discharged first.

4. Chlorine and bromine are soluble in water

$$H_2O(l) + Cl_2(g) \rightarrow HCl(aq) + \underbrace{HOCl(aq)}_{\text{chloric(I)acid}} = \text{chlorine water}$$

$$H_2O(l) + Br_2(l) \rightarrow HBr(aq) + \underbrace{HOBr(aq)}_{\text{bromic(I)acid}} = \text{bromine water}$$

Iodine is insoluble in water.

5. Halogens are absorbed by cold dilute alkalis

e.g. $Cl_2(g) + 2NaOH(aq) \rightarrow \underbrace{NaOCl(aq)}_{\text{sodium chlorate(I)}} + NaCl(aq) + H_2O(l)$

while if bubbled into hot concentrated potassium hydroxide solution a mixture of potassium chloride and potassium chlorate(v) is obtained.

$$Cl_2(g) + 6KOH(aq) \rightarrow 5KCl(aq) + KClO_3(aq) + 3H_2O(l)$$

6. The halogens are strong oxidizing agents.

(a) When gas jars of chlorine and hydrogen sulphide are mixed, a yellow precipitate of sulphur is seen. The chlorine is oxidized to hydrogen chloride while the hydrogen sulphide is reduced to sulphur.

$$Cl_2 + H_2S \rightarrow 2HCl + S(s)$$
or
$$Cl_2 + S^{2-} \rightarrow 2Cl^- + S(s)$$

(b) When chlorine is bubbled through a solution of iron(II) chloride the colour of the solution will change from pale green to yellow. The iron(II) chloride has been oxidized to iron(III) chloride, while the chlorine has been reduced to the chloride ion.

$$2FeCl_2(aq) + Cl_2(g) \rightarrow 2FeCl_3(aq)$$

(c) When chlorine is bubbled through water containing dissolved sulphur dioxide then dilute sulphuric acid is produced as the sulphite ion is oxidized to the sulphate ion.

7. *Displacement reactions.* If a more reactive halogen is passed into a solution containing a less reactive halogen, then the former will displace this halogen from the solution (this causes a colour change).

Halogen	*Solutions*		
	Potassium chloride	*Potassium bromide*	*Potassium iodide*
1. Chlorine	No reaction	Bromine displaced An orange-brown colour seen $2Br^- + Cl_2 \rightarrow 2Cl^- + Br_2$	Iodine displaced A darker colour appears $2I^-(aq) + Cl_2(g) \rightarrow 2Cl^-(aq) + I_2(aq)$
2. Bromine	No reaction	No reaction	Iodine displaced A dark colour appears
3. Iodine	No reaction	No reaction	No reaction

8. Chlorine acts as a bleaching agent in the presence of moisture, e.g. litmus paper and inks are bleached. Bromine is a weaker bleaching agent, while iodine has no such action.

Tests for Halogens

1. As gases.

Chlorine is a yellow-green gas. It turns damp blue litmus paper red then bleaches it.

Bromine vapour is red-brown with a choking smell.

Iodine vapour is purple.

2. As ions.

(a) A few drops of nitric acid are added to a solution of the halide. This is followed by a few drops of silver nitrate solution.

A white precipitate, soluble in ammonia solution = chloride present.

A cream precipitate, slightly soluble in ammonia solution = bromide present.

A yellow precipitate, insoluble in ammonia solution = iodide present.

(b) A solution of the halide is made and chlorine water added.

No coloration = chloride present.

Orange-brown coloration: on shaking with dichloromethane, then standing, the lower organic layer will be orange-brown = bromide present.

Brown coloration: on shaking with dichloromethane, then standing, the lower organic layer will have a violet coloration = iodide present.

Hydrogen Halides

Hydrogen chloride (HCl), hydrogen bromide (HBr) and hydrogen iodide (HI).

Preparation

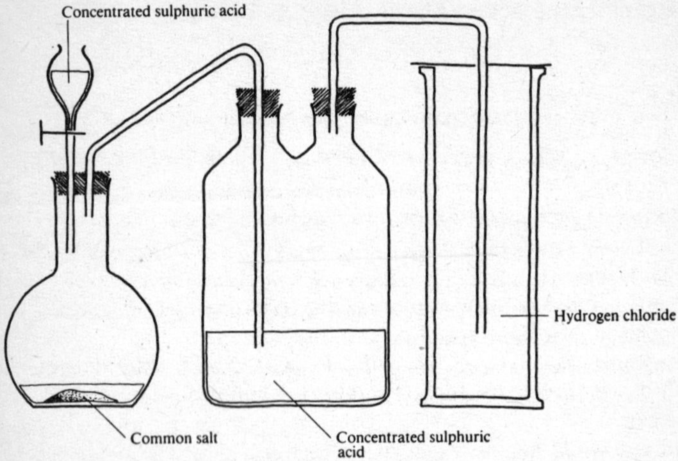

$$H_2SO_4(l) + NaCl(s) \rightarrow NaHSO_4(s) + HCl(g)$$

Note: The gas is collected by downward delivery as hydrogen chloride is denser than air. The preparations of the other halides are unimportant.

Properties

The least stable hydrogen halide is hydrogen iodide. The remaining hydrogen halides have similar properties, so only hydrogen chloride will be considered.

1. It has an irritating smell.
2. It is very soluble in water so a solution is made by using an inverted funnel (page 150).
3. It only acts as an acid when dissolved in water as hydroxonium ions are formed. Hydrogen chloride dissolved in methylbenzene (an organic solvent) is a covalent compound.
4. Hydrochloric acid is a strong acid but the concentrated acid has no oxidizing or dehydrating properties (compare with sulphuric acid and nitric acid). It behaves as a typical acid (page 99).

Test for Hydrogen Chloride Gas

1. It turns damp blue litmus paper red, it produces misty fumes in damp air.

2. It produces dense white fumes of ammonium chloride in the presence of ammonia.

Examination Question

There are many examination questions set on non-metals.

(*Oxford, Autumn 1978*)

(a) *Describe the production of sulphuric acid in industry.* (*Details of plant are* not *required.*) (9)

(b) *Give examples of the use of sulphuric acid as* (i) *an oxidizing agent,* (ii) *a dehydrating agent,* (iii) *a catalyst,* (iv) *an electrolyte in everyday usage.*

(*In your answers state whether the acid is dilute or concentrated, and for* (i) *and* (ii) *give equations to illustrate your answers.*) (4, 4, 3, 2)

(c) *State and explain the change which occurs when concentrated sulphuric acid is left in an open beaker.* (3)

Answer

(a) Sulphur is burnt in air to produce sulphur dioxide.

$$S(s) + O_2(g) \rightarrow SO_2(g)$$

Sulphur dioxide and air are then passed over a catalyst of vanadium(V) oxide at 450–500 °C to produce sulphur trioxide.

$$2SO_2(g) + O_2(g) \rightarrow 2SO_3(g)$$

Sulphur trioxide is passed into concentrated sulphuric acid to produce oleum. This is then diluted with water to produce concentrated sulphuric acid.

$$SO_3(g) + H_2SO_4(l) \rightarrow H_2S_2O_7(l)$$

$$H_2S_2O_7(l) + H_2O(l) \rightarrow 2H_2SO_4(l)$$

(b) (i) Hot concentrated sulphuric acid acts as an oxidizing agent. It oxidizes copper to copper(II) sulphate while it is reduced to sulphur dioxide and water.

$$Cu(s) + 2H_2SO_4(l) \rightarrow CuSO_4(aq) + SO_2(g) + 2H_2O(l)$$

(ii) Concentrated sulphuric acid also acts as a dehydrating agent. When it is added to sugar, charring is seen, steam is evolved and the whole process gives out heat.

$$C_{12}H_{22}O_{11} \xrightarrow[-H_2O]{H_2SO_4} 12C$$

(iii) When an organic acid and an alcohol are heated in the presence of concentrated sulphuric acid an ester is produced. The acid is acting as a catalyst.

$$CH_3COOH + C_2H_5OH \xrightarrow{H_2SO_4} CH_3COOC_2H_5 + H_2O$$

ethanoic acid — ethanol — ethyl ethanoate

(iv) Concentrated sulphuric acid is the electrolyte in car batteries.

(c) When concentrated sulphuric acid is left in an open beaker, it absorbs water vapour from the atmosphere and so the liquid increases in volume and the acid becomes dilute.

11. *Air, Oxygen, Hydrogen and Water*

Air

Air is a mixture of gases. It contains about 20% oxygen and 80% nitrogen by volume. The following gases are present in small amounts:

carbon dioxide
the noble gases (argon, neon)
water vapour

Impurities are also present; they are sulphur dioxide, hydrogen sulphide and methane.

Experiment to Show that Air is a Mixture of Gases

Several different experiments could be set up to demonstrate that air is a mixture of gases. The following is just one example:

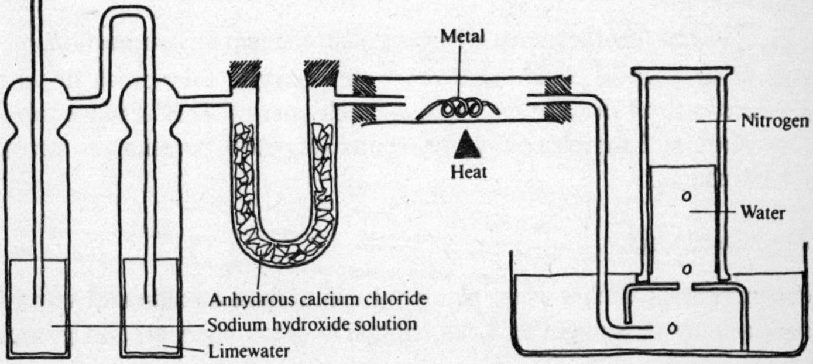

When the plunger of the syringe is pushed in, the air is forced through the system. Carbon dioxide is removed by the sodium hydroxide solution;

this is checked with lime water. Water vapour is removed by anhydrous calcium chloride. Oxygen is removed as it combines with the heated metal and finally the nitrogen is collected by displacement of water.

The Liquefaction and Fractional Distillation of Air

Nitrogen and oxygen have widespread uses, so it is necessary to produce them on a large scale. This is carried out by extracting them from air by the following stages:

1. Air is made into a liquid (liquefied) by compressing it to about 200 atmospheres of pressure.
2. This liquid is then evaporated: the liquid with the lower boiling point will vaporize first and so it is separated from the mixture. Nitrogen has a boiling point of 77 K (−196 °C) so it is vaporized first.
3. The oxygen then vaporizes at 90 K (−183 °C).

This process is fractional distillation.

Combustion (burning)

Combustion is the combination of a substance with oxygen to produce a chemical change (heat and/or light are often emitted). Combustion can be demonstrated by:

1. Observing a change in appearance of an element when heated in air.
2. Determining the increase in mass of an element on combustion.
3. Hydrocarbon compounds react with oxygen; they break down to produce carbon dioxide, water and much energy. This is made use of in our homes. Examples of hydrocarbons are petrol, paraffin and natural gas (methane).

Photosynthesis

Photosynthesis occurs when plants take in carbon dioxide and water in the presence of sunlight and chlorophyll (a green pigment) and produce carbohydrates.

$$6CO_2(g) + 6H_2O(l) \xrightarrow[\text{energy}]{\text{chlorophyll}} C_6H_{12}O_6(aq) + 6O_2(g)$$

Internal Respiration

This is the process by which living organisms obtain their energy. Carbohydrates combine with oxygen (combustion) and break down releasing water, carbon dioxide and energy.

$$C_6H_{12}O_6 + 6O_2 \rightarrow 6CO_2(g) + 6H_2O(l) + \text{energy}$$

Nitrogen and Carbon Dioxide (see Chapter 10)

Oxygen

Preparation

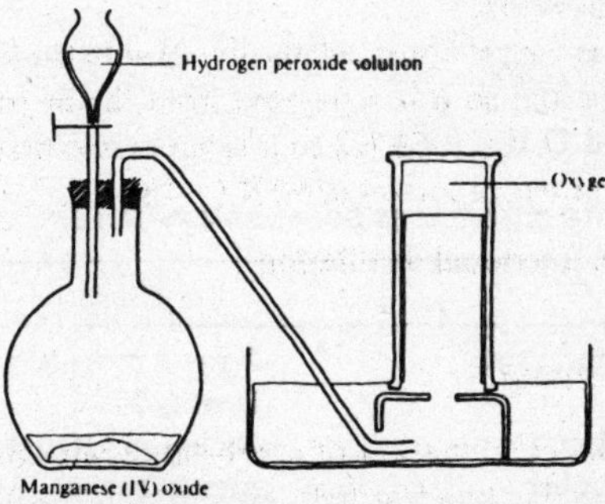

Hydrogen peroxide solution is added dropwise to manganese(IV) oxide. The oxygen produced is collected over water. Manganese(IV) oxide is acting as a catalyst.

$$2H_2O_2(l) \rightarrow 2H_2O(l) + O_2(g)$$

Properties

1. A colourless odourless gas.
2. It has the same density as air.
3. When a metal is heated in oxygen oxides are formed.

e.g. $2Mg(s) + O_2(g) \rightarrow 2MgO(s)$

The metals at the bottom of the electrochemical series do not oxidize easily.

4. When carbon is burnt in oxygen carbon dioxide is produced

$$C(s) + O_2(g) \rightarrow CO_2(g)$$

Test for Oxygen

It relights a glowing spill.

Uses of Oxygen

1. Used in blast furnaces to enrich the blast of hot air.
2. Used in the cutting and welding of metals as an oxyacetylene flame.
3. Used to aid breathing, whenever the supply of oxygen in the air is insufficient, e.g. at high altitudes, deep sea diving, and for patients who are ill with respiratory diseases.

Allotropes of Oxygen

Oxygen (O_2) and Ozone (O_3)

A summary of the differences between oxygen and ozone

Oxygen	*Ozone*
A gas at room temperature	A gas at room temperature
Density 16	Density 24
Heating has no effect	On heating $2O_3(g) \rightarrow 3O_2(g)$
Does not attack rubber	Attacks rubber
Does not liberate iodine from potassium iodide solution	Liberates iodine from potassium iodide solution
Oxidizing agent	Vigorous oxidizing agent

Hydrogen

Preparation

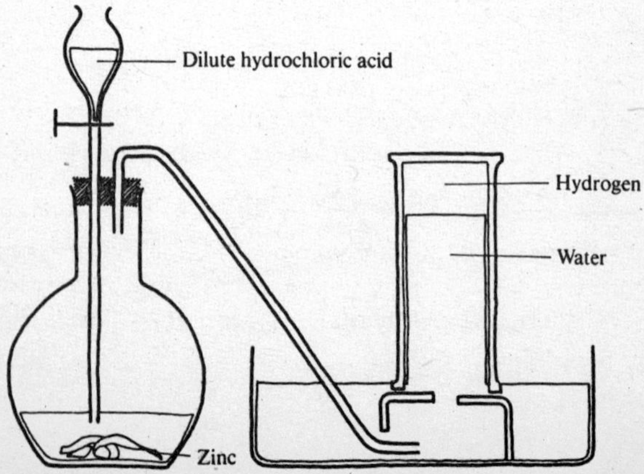

The apparatus is set up as shown in the diagram. The hydrogen is collected by displacement of water.

$Zn(s) + 2HCl(aq) \rightarrow ZnCl_2(aq) + H_2(g)$

2. When methane and steam are passed over a nickel catalyst, at 800 °C and 300 atmospheres pressure, hydrogen is produced.

$CH_4(g) + H_2O(g) \rightarrow CO(g) + 3H_2(g)$

3. When steam is passed over heated iron, hydrogen is produced.

$3Fe(s) + 4H_2O(g) \rightleftharpoons Fe_3O_4(s) + 4H_2(g)$

Properties

1. A colourless, odourless, tasteless gas.
2. Density less than air.
3. Highly inflammable.
4. Reacts with Group 1 and Group 2 metals to form hydrides.

$2Na(s) + H_2(g) \rightarrow 2NaH(s)$

5. Hydrogen reacts with nitrogen to form ammonia.

$3H_2(g) + N_2(g) \rightleftharpoons 2NH_3(g)$

6. It burns in air or oxygen, forming water.
7. It reacts with the halogens to form hydrogen halides.

e.g. $H_2(g) + Cl_2(g) \rightarrow 2HCl(g)$

8. Hydrogen reduces heated metallic oxides, which are below hydrogen in the electrochemical series, to the metal.

e.g. $Fe_2O_3(s) + 3H_2(g) \rightarrow 2Fe(s) + 3H_2O(l)$

This is carried out using the following apparatus.

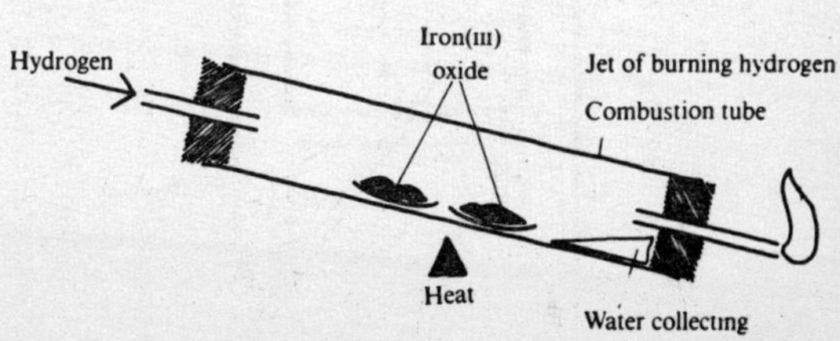

The combustion tube slopes so that the water formed does not run back into the hot part of the tube, which would crack it.

Test for Hydrogen

In the presence of hydrogen a burning spill burns with a 'pop'.

Uses of Hydrogen

1. Manufacture of ammonia.
2. Manufacture of methanol (page 185).

$CO(g) + 2H_2(g) \rightarrow CH_3OH(l)$

3. Used in the hardening of oils in the manufacture of margarine.
4. Used in rocket fuels.

Water

Water is found in seas, lakes and rivers, as well as in humans, the air and plants. So its preparation is unimportant.

The composition of water can be demonstrated by electrolysis. A voltameter is filled with water containing some dilute sulphuric acid. On electrolysis, gases are seen in the two side arms; these can be tested.

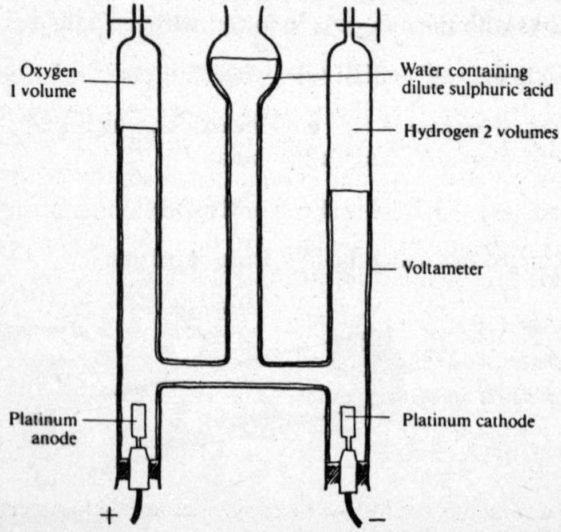

Properties

1. Melting point 0 °C. Boiling point 100 °C.
2. A colourless liquid which is a good solvent for ionic compounds.
3. Some metals displace hydrogen from water, e.g. sodium and calcium.

$$2Na(s) + H_2O(l) \rightarrow 2NaOH(aq) + H_2(g)$$

4. Some non-metallic oxides react with water to form acids.

e.g. $CO_2(g) + H_2O(l) \rightarrow H_2CO_3(aq)$
carbonic acid

$$SO_3(g) + H_2O(l) \rightarrow H_2SO_4(aq)$$

5. Carbon, as white-hot coke, reacts with steam to form water gas.

$$C(s) + H_2O(g) \rightarrow CO(g) + H_2(g)$$

6. Chlorine dissolves in water to form chloric(I) acid.

The following definitions are connected with water.

A Hydrated Substance

When water is combined with a substance to form one product only in such a way that the water molecules are bonded to that substance, then the substance is said to be hydrated.

Water of Crystallization

When crystalline salts contain water, which is chemically bonded within their crystal structure, then this water is known as the water of crystallization. The crystals are said to be hydrated, e.g. $CuSO_4 \cdot 5H_2O$.

When the water of crystallization is removed, the product is said to be anhydrous, e.g. blue hydrated copper(II) sulphate crystals lose their water of crystallization on heating and become a white powder. When water is added to this powder it turns blue again.

$$CuSO_4 \cdot 5H_2O \rightleftharpoons CuSO_4 + 5H_2O$$

blue hydrated copper(II) sulphate — white anhydrous copper(II) sulphate

Note: $CuSO_4 \cdot 5H_2O$
↑
This dot means the following molecules are water of crystallization

Experiment to Determine the Water of Crystallization (*page 66*)

Efflorescent Compounds

When a compound loses all or some of the water of crystallization on exposure to the air, this compound is said to effloresce. For example, when crystals of sodium carbonate decahydrate are exposed to the atmosphere they lose water and become a white powder, which is sodium carbonate monohydrate.

$$Na_2CO_3 \cdot 10H_2O \rightarrow Na_2CO_3 \cdot H_2O + 9H_2O$$

Deliquescent Compounds

These compounds absorb water on exposure to the atmosphere; they eventually dissolve in it to form a solution, e.g. sodium hydroxide, calcium chloride, and magnesium chloride.

Hygroscopic Compounds

These compounds absorb water on exposure to the atmosphere but they do not dissolve in the water to form a solution, e.g. copper(II) oxide and concentrated sulphuric acid.

Hard Water

There are two types of hardness: (a) temporary hardness, (b) permanent hardness.

Hard water contains dissolved solids and does not lather easily with soap.

Temporary Hardness

This is caused by the presence of calcium hydrogencarbonate and can be removed by boiling when a deposit of insoluble calcium carbonate is formed.

$$Ca(HCO_3)_2(aq) \rightarrow CaCO_3(s) + CO_2(g) + H_2O(l)$$

Permanent Hardness

This is caused by the presence of calcium sulphate (also magnesium sulphate) and cannot be removed by boiling. It is removed by adding washing soda crystals to the water when a precipitate of calcium carbonate is formed.

$CaSO_4(aq) + Na_2CO_3(aq) \rightarrow Na_2SO_4(aq) + CaCO_3(s)$

It can also be removed by a water softener where the calcium and magnesium ions are removed by a complex substance (hydrated sodium and aluminium silicate) or by resins.

Examination Questions

1. (*Oxford, Summer, 1980*)

(a) *Describe the purpose and the chemistry involved in the following three stages of an experiment. A sample of air is successively passed through:*

(i) *Sodium hydroxide solution*

(ii) *Calcium hydroxide solution*

(iii) *A strongly heated tube packed loosely with copper turnings and the remaining gas is then collected.* (9)

(b) *What volume of air, 20% oxygen, would be required for the complete combustion of 10 dm^3 of propane, C_3H_8? (All volumes are measured at the same temperature and pressure.)* (4)

(c) (i) *Explain what is meant by the term 'hard water'.*

(ii) *Give the names and formulae of one compound which causes temporary hardness of water and one which causes permanent hardness.* (4)

(iii) *Explain why the terms 'temporary' and 'permanent' are used to describe hardness in water.* (5)

Answer

(a) (i) Sodium hydroxide solution reacts with carbon dioxide and so removes it from the air.

$2NaOH(aq) + CO_2(g) \rightarrow Na_2CO_3(aq) + H_2O(l)$

(ii) The calcium hydroxide solution will show whether there is any carbon dioxide left in the air as a white precipitate will be seen.

$CO_2(g) + Ca(OH)_2(aq) \rightarrow CaCO_3(g) + H_2O(l)$

(iii) The oxygen in the remaining mixture will combine with the copper to form copper(II) oxide.

$2Cu(s) + O_2(g) \rightarrow 2CuO(s)$

Nitrogen is left.

(b) $C_3H_8 \quad + 5O_2 \quad \rightarrow 3CO_2 + 4H_2O$
so 1 volume + 5 volumes
$\therefore$ 10 dm^3 + 50 dm^3

Thus 50 dm^3 oxygen will be required to react with 10 dm^3 propane. But air contains 20% oxygen. Therefore if 50 dm^3 of oxygen is required, this is present in $5 \times 50 =$ 250 dm^3 air.

(c) (i) Hard water contains dissolved solids and does not form a lather easily with soap.

(ii) Temporary hardness can be caused by calcium hydrogen-carbonate $Ca(HCO_3)_2$. Permanent hardness can be caused by calcium sulphate $CaSO_4$.

(iii) Temporary hardness can be removed by boiling when a deposit of insoluble calcium carbonate is formed.

$$Ca(HCO_3)_2(aq) \rightarrow CaCO_3(s) + CO_2(g) + H_2O(l)$$

Permanent hardness cannot be removed so easily, i.e. it cannot be removed by boiling. It can be removed by addition of washing soda.

$$CaSO_4(aq) + \underset{\text{washing soda}}{Na_2CO_3(aq)} \rightarrow Na_2SO_4(aq) + CaCO_3(s)$$

12. *Organic Chemistry*

Organic chemistry is the study of carbon compounds. Carbon is an unusual element in that it forms chains or rings of its atoms. These chains and rings may be included in the same molecule, thus complicated structures can be formed. Organic compounds also contain hydrogen and may contain nitrogen, oxygen, sulphur or chlorine.

Some compounds contain carbon, but not in chains or rings. These compounds are regarded as *inorganic* substances, e.g. carbon monoxide, carbon dioxide and carbonates.

Hydrocarbons

Hydrocarbons are compounds which contain hydrogen and carbon only. They are divided into the following groups: alkanes; alkenes; alkynes.

Alkanes

General Formula C_nH_{2n+2}
When n = 1, formula = CH_4 which is called methane.

Saturated Compounds
Alkanes are saturated compounds, that is, every carbon atom in the chain has as many hydrogen atoms bonded to it as possible.

A table of some alkanes

Name	*Formula*	*State at room temperature*	
Methane	CH_4	Gas	Boiling point and melting point increase ↓
Ethane	C_2H_6	Gas	
Propane	C_3H_8	Gas	
Butane	C_4H_{10}	Gas	
Pentane	C_5H_{12}	Liquid	
Hexane	C_6H_{14}	Liquid	

A Homologous Series

When a group of compounds is related to each other, then this group of compounds is called a homologous series. Such a series shows the following:

1. The members of the series can be represented by a general formula.
2. Each member varies from the next by a CH_2 group.
3. The same methods of preparation can be used for any member of the group.
4. The physical properties change gradually along the series, e.g. in the alkanes the boiling point and melting point both increase as the number of carbon atoms increase.
5. The chemical properties are similar, although some compounds will react more vigorously.

e.g. homologous series are alkanes, alkenes, alcohols and acids.

A homologous series is a group of organic compounds which have the same general formula and similar chemical properties.

In organic compounds covalent bonding occurs. For the structure of methane (page 41). The next member of the series is ethane.

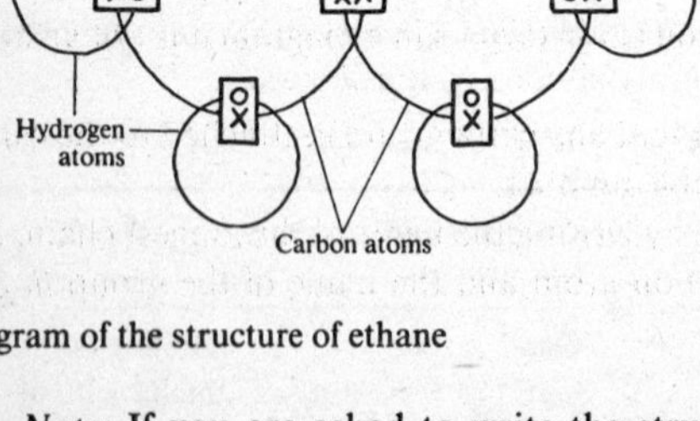

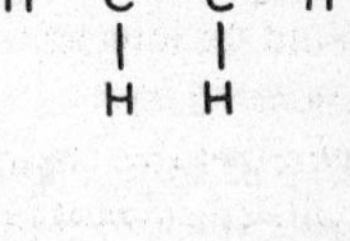

A diagram of the structure of ethane

> *Note:* If you are asked to write the structural formula of ethane you would draw (b) above. The only problem with this representation is that the alkane molecule appears flat, whereas methane is tetrahedral.

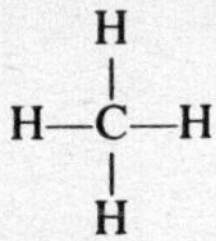

methane
appearing flat

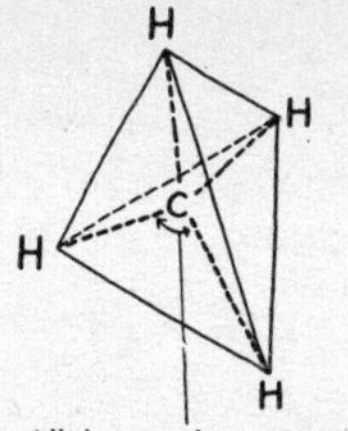

All these angles are equal

Isomerism and the Naming of Compounds

When the number of carbon atoms in a compound increases then it is possible to arrange the same number of carbon atoms in different ways, so that different structures occur.

Isomerism is the occurrence of two or more compounds with the same molecular formula, but a different arrangement of atoms within their molecules.

Isomers of C_4H_{10}

(a) 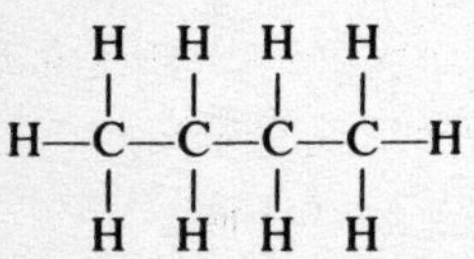

butane

(b) 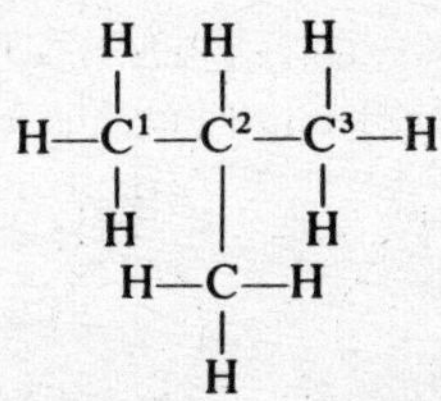

In order to distinguish between these two compounds, the following procedure is followed:

1. Find the longest carbon chain (even if in a diagram it is not arranged in a straight line).
2. Number this chain so that any extra group is attached to the carbon atom with the lowest possible number.
3. Name the compound by writing the name of the longest chain, then put the number of the carbon atom and the name of the group *in front* of the name.

(b) = 2-methylpropane.

Note: CH_3 group = methyl group
C_2H_5 group = ethyl group
C_3H_7 group = propyl group
} these are known as alkyl groups

Isomerism of $C_2H_4Cl_2$

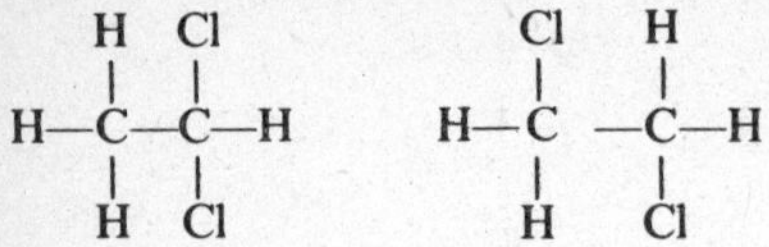

1,1-dichloroethane 1,2-dichloroethane

The Oil Industry

Crude oil is a mixture of hydrocarbons; their chain length varies from C_1 to C_{50}. The amount of each hydrocarbon present varies and depends on the source of this crude oil. The process of fractional distillation is used to separate crude oil into different groups of substances.

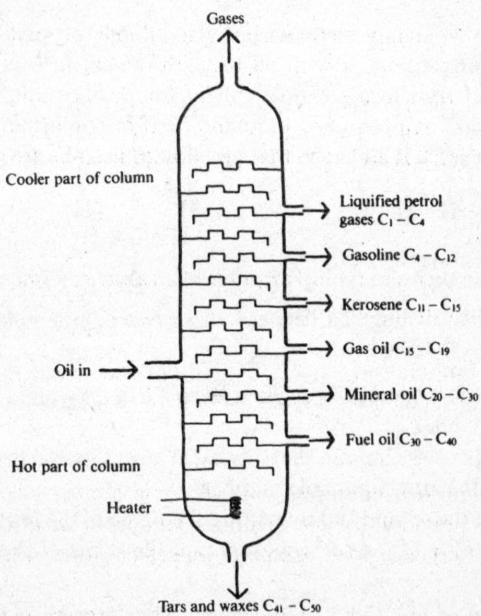

A diagram of a fractionating column to separate crude oil

The lighter fractions (groups) of the hydrocarbons are more volatile and so are removed at different heights in the fractionating column. Each fraction has a special name and consists of carbon chains of a certain length. Unfortunately this process does not produce enough of the lighter fractions of the oil, so the following process is used.

Catalytic Cracking

Heavier fractions of the oil are heated in the presence of catalysts. This breaks the bonds between the carbon atoms in a molecule, producing lighter molecules. This produces saturated and unsaturated compounds.

e.g. at 12 atmospheres and 520 °C

$$C_{17}H_{36}(l) \rightarrow C_8H_{18}(g) + 3C_2H_4(g) + C_3H_6(g)$$

Natural Gas

This contains mainly methane but also ethane, propane and butane. It is found either alone or with oil beneath the earth. It is pumped to the surface and then to a treatment plant for purification, so that natural gas (methane) is produced. Methane itself is colourless and odourless, therefore a smell is added so that any domestic leaks are detectable.

Methane

Methane is taken as a typical example of an alkane. Remember, its properties can apply to any alkane.

Industrial Preparation

See preparation of natural gas.

Properties

1. A colourless, odourless gas, which is almost insoluble in water. Methane is not very reactive as it does *not* decolorize acidified potassium manganate(VII) solution, bromine water, chlorine water, chlorine or bromine.

2. Burns in air with a blue flame. This process gives out heat (is exothermic).

$$CH_4(g) + 2O_2(g) \rightarrow CO_2(g) + 2H_2O(l)$$

3. Methane reacts explosively with chlorine in the presence of sunlight. The chlorine replaces the hydrogen atoms one by one (substitution reaction).

$$CH_4(g) + Cl_2(g) \rightarrow CH_3Cl(g) + HCl(g)$$

$$CH_3Cl(g) + Cl_2(g) \rightarrow CH_2Cl_2(l) + HCl(g)$$

$$CH_2Cl_2(g) + Cl_2(g) \rightarrow CHCl_3(l) + HCl(g)$$

$$CHCl_3(l) + Cl_2(g) \rightarrow CCl_4(l) + HCl(g)$$

A Substitution Reaction

This occurs when an organic molecule reacts with an element or compound (X–X or X–Y). X replaces an atom in the organic compound (usually hydrogen) which combines with the other X or Y.

Alkenes

General Formula C_nH_{2n}

e.g.

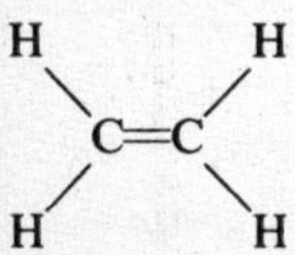

ethene

or $C_2H_4 \rightarrow$

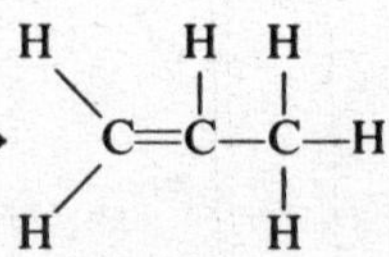

propene

or C_3H_6

The ending -ene means that one carbon to carbon double bond is present in the compound.

Ethene

Ethene is taken as a typical example of an alkene. Ethene is more reactive than ethane as it undergoes addition reactions.

An Addition Reaction

This occurs, in organic chemistry, when two or more molecules combine to form a single compound. This is because an unsaturated bond is broken and a more saturated, or saturated, bond is formed.

Unsaturated Compounds

An unsaturated compound is an organic compound whose molecule contains at least one double or triple bond.

e.g. ethene

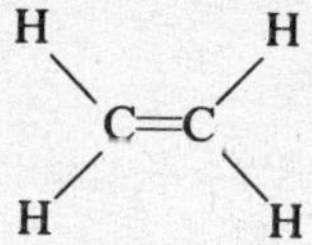

or

ethyne

H—C≡C—H

Laboratory Preparation of Ethene

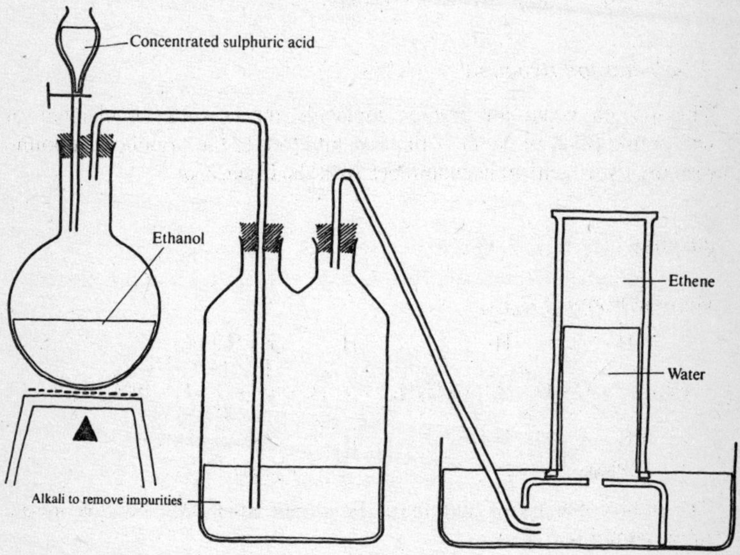

When concentrated sulphuric acid and ethanol are heated together the sulphuric acid acts as a dehydrating agent.

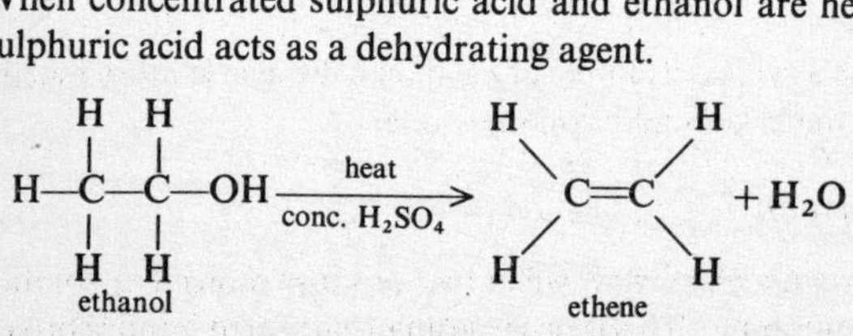

or

$$C_2H_5OH \xrightarrow[\text{conc. } H_2SO_4]{\text{heat}} C_2H_4$$

Properties

1. Ethene is a colourless, odourless gas which is almost insoluble in water.

2. Ethene burns with a smoky yellow flame.

$$C_2H_4(g) + 3O_2(g) \rightarrow 2CO_2(g) + 2H_2O(g)$$

3. When chlorine, bromine, chlorine water or bromine water are added to ethene they are rapidly decolorized.

e.g.

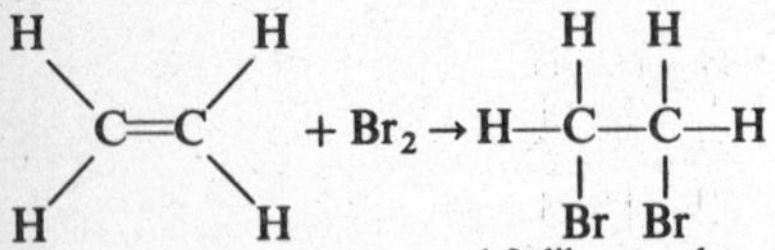

1,2-dibromoethane

or

$$C_2H_4 + Br_2 \rightarrow C_2H_4Br_2$$

4. When acidified potassium manganate(VII) solution is added to ethene it is rapidly decolorized.

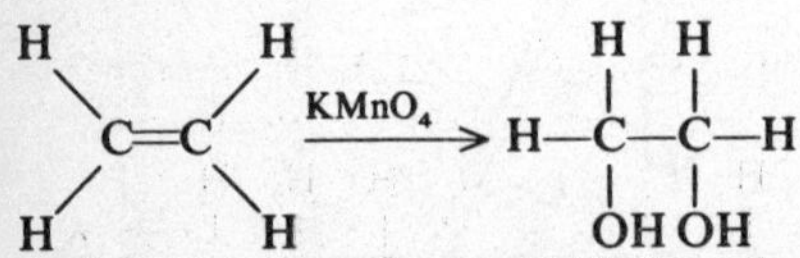

1,2-dihydroxyethane

5. When ethene and hydrogen are passed over a nickel catalyst at 200 °C ethane is produced.

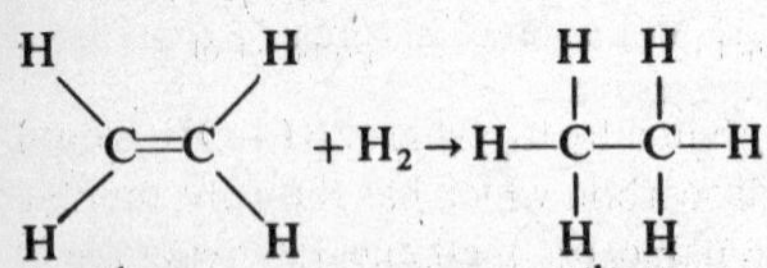

ethene ethane

Polymerization

This is the building up of a chain of molecules from a basic unit called a monomer.

A monomer is a small molecule which can be linked with other identical molecules to form a polymer.

Addition Polymerization

This is the linking together of unsaturated monomers to form a single large molecule.

e.g.

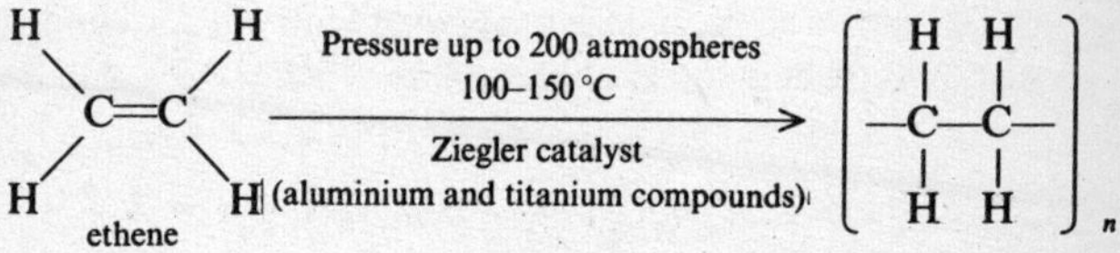

or

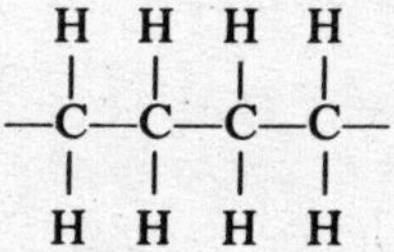

This polymer is called polythene. Another monomer is propene, which polymerizes to form polypropylene.

Alcohols

General Formula $C_nH_{2n+1}OH$

e.g.

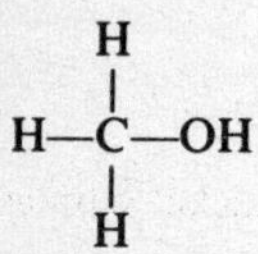

or CH_3OH

methanol

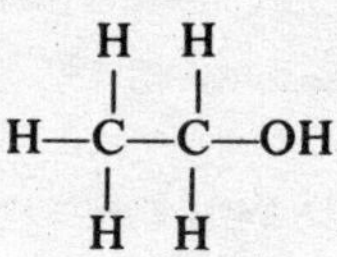

or C_2H_5OH

ethanol

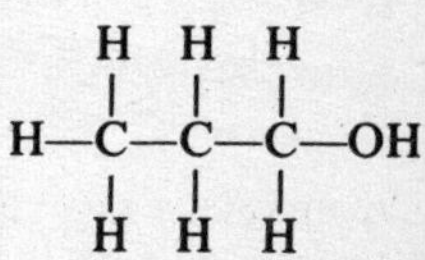

or C_3H_7OH

propan-1-ol

These are compounds which contain a hydroxyl group (–OH group). They are named by finding the hydrocarbon which has the same number of carbon atoms, writing down the name, e.g. methane, removing the 'e' and adding 'ol'.

Ethanol

Ethanol is taken as a typical example of an alcohol. Its preparation and properties are important.

Preparation

Ethanol is prepared by the fermentation of sugar. **Fermentation** occurs when a chemical change is produced in an organic substance by the action of a living organism, as a result of enzyme action. Sugar molecules are broken down into simpler molecules, this is catalysed by the enzymes present in yeast. A sugar and yeast solution is kept in a warm place for several days in a flask, which is plugged with cotton wool. This allows the carbon dioxide to escape. The solution is filtered, poured into a flask and the ethanol present is obtained by distillation.

$$C_6H_{12}O_6(aq) \rightarrow 2C_2H_5OH(aq) + 2CO_2(g)$$

Properties

These are really properties of the hydroxy group. The rest of the molecule is unreactive as it is a saturated hydrocarbon.

1. Alcohols are liquids which mix with water. They are colourless and volatile.
2. Ethanol burns easily, producing carbon dioxide and water.

$$C_2H_5OH(l) + 3O_2 \rightarrow 2CO_2(g) + 3H_2O(l)$$

3. Ethanol reacts with a small piece of sodium, producing hydrogen and sodium ethoxide.

$$2C_2H_5OH(l) + 2Na(s) \rightarrow 2C_2H_5ONa(s) + H_2(g)$$

4. Ethanol reacts with phosphorus pentachloride, producing hydrogen chloride gas.

$$C_2H_5OH(l) + PCl_5(l) \rightarrow \underset{\text{chloroethane}}{C_2H_5Cl(g)} + POCl_3(l) + HCl(g)$$

5. Ethanol can be oxidized with acidified potassium dichromate(VI) solution to form ethanal, while further oxidation produces ethanoic acid. A colour change from orange to green would be seen.

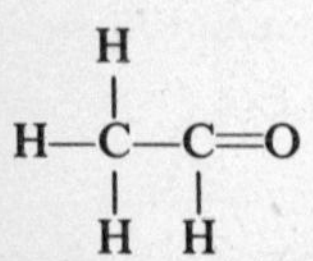

ethanal

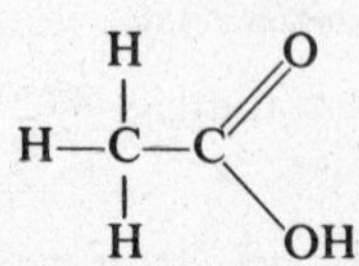

ethanoic acid

6. Ethanol reacts with carboxylic acids to form esters (see under carboxylic acids).

Carboxylic Acids

General Formula $C_nH_{2n+1}COOH$

e.g. 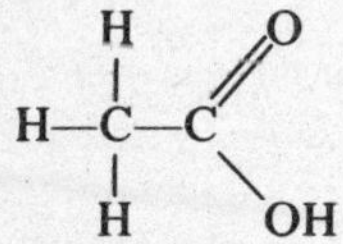 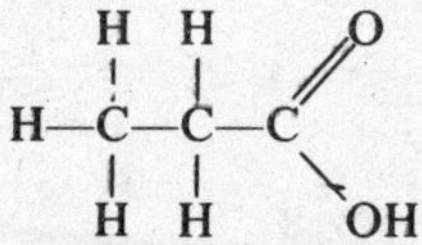

or CH_3COOH or C_2H_5COOH

ethanoic acid propanoic acid

These are compounds which contain a carboxylic acid group (−COOH). They are named by finding the hydrocarbon which has the same number of carbon atoms, writing down the name, e.g. ethane, removing the 'e' and adding 'oic acid'.

Ethanoic Acid

Ethanoic acid is taken as a typical example of a carboxylic acid.

Preparation

Ethanol is oxidized to ethanoic acid by acidified potassium dichromate(VI) solution.

$$C_2H_5OH(l) \xrightarrow[\text{acidified } K_2Cr_2O_7(aq)]{[O] \text{ from}} CH_3COOH(l)$$

Properties

1. It is a liquid which has a strong smell; it occurs in vinegar. Glacial (strong) ethanoic acid freezes at 17 °C so it is seen as a solid below this temperature.

2. It is a weak acid, it turns blue litmus red and has the properties of a typical acid (page 99). When it reacts with an alkali to form a salt, this salt is called an ethanoate.

$$CH_3COOH(l) + NaOH(aq) \rightarrow \underset{\text{sodium ethanoate}}{CH_3COONa(aq)} + H_2O(l)$$

3. It reacts with phosphorus pentachloride; hydrogen chloride fumes are produced.

$$CH_3COOH(l) + PCl_5(l) \rightarrow CH_3COCl(l) + HCl(g) + POCl_3(l)$$

4. When ethanoic acid is heated with ethanol in the presence of concentrated sulphuric acid, which acts as a catalyst, an ester is formed. This is a sweet-smelling liquid.

e.g.

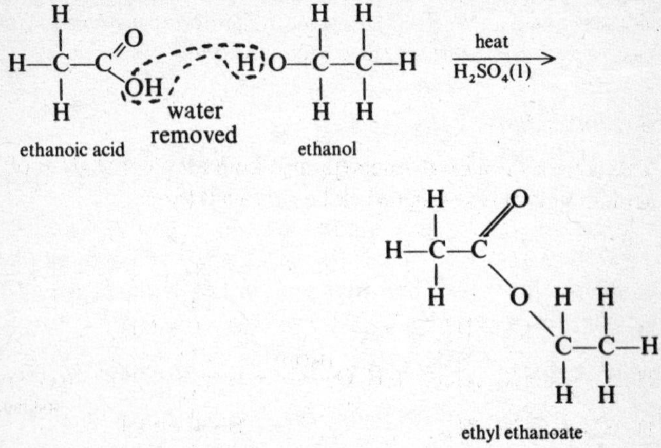

or

$$CH_3COOH + C_2H_5OH \rightarrow CH_3COOC_2H_5 + H_2O$$

To name esters you find the acid which has been used, e.g. ethanoic acid, then remove the 'ic acid' and add 'ate', so ethanoate. Then you add the name of the group which has replaced the hydrogen C_2H_5 = ethyl group. So the ester is ethyl ethanoate.

Esterification

This is the production of an ester by heating an alcohol with a carboxylic acid (organic acid). Esterification is a reversible reaction,

$$CH_3COOH(l) + C_2H_5OH(l) \rightleftharpoons CH_3COOC_2H_5(l) + H_2O(l)$$

So esters can be broken up by the addition of water (and a dilute acid). This is called the hydrolysis of an ester.

Hydrolysis

Hydrolysis is the chemical decomposition of a substance in the presence of water. The substance and the water break up to form new substances.

Fats, Oils and Soaps

Esters are found in animal fats and vegetable oils. If these esters are heated with concentrated sodium hydroxide solution the alcohol and the sodium salt of the acid are formed. This is the main substance in soap. This special case of ester hydrolysis is called saponification.

Saponification

This is the hydrolysis of esters (formed from the alcohol glycerol) to form sodium salts of long-chained carboxylic acids (soap).

e.g.

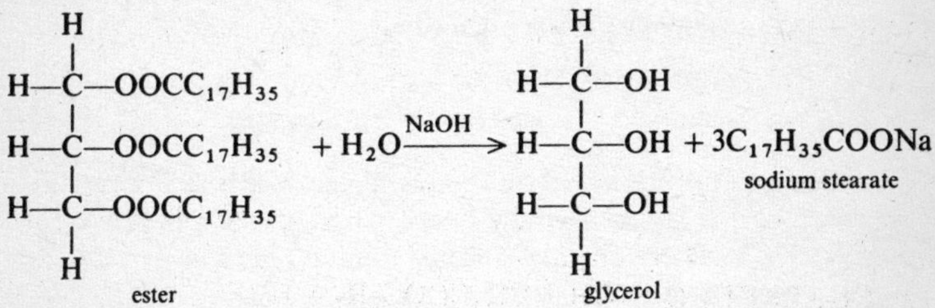

Polyesters

Condensation polymerization is the linking together of a large number of molecules by a reaction in which a product and water are formed. These polymers contain two different kinds of monomer molecules, e.g. an acid and an alcohol form a complex ester and water. The complex esters react with each other to form long-chained compounds which are called polyesters.

Examination Questions

1. (*Associated Examining Board, June 1976*)
This is a typical example of a question on definitions.
Select four *of the following processes and describe how an example of each one chosen is carried out either in the laboratory or on an industrial scale:* (a) *esterification*
(b) *fermentation*
(c) *polymerization*

(d) *pyrolysis (or 'cracking')*
(e) *saponification.*

Details of apparatus or industrial plant are not required, but you should give a clear statement of the essential reaction conditions and the names of the principal products formed. (24)

Answer
I have answered each question for completeness but you are only required to answer *four*.

(a) *Esterification*
This is the production of an ester obtained by heating an alcohol with a carboxylic acid in the presence of a catalyst.

e.g. $\underset{\text{ethanoic acid}}{CH_3COOH(l)} + \underset{\text{ethanol}}{C_2H_5OH(l)} \rightarrow \underset{\text{ethyl ethanoate}}{CH_3COOC_2H_5(l)} + H_2O$

Glacial ethanoic acid is mixed with excess ethanol in a flask. Concentrated sulphuric acid is added carefully to the mixture, which is then heated under reflux for fifteen minutes. The apparatus is then rearranged so that the ester is collected by distillation.

(b) *Fermentation*
This occurs when a chemical change is produced in an organic substance by the action of a living organism, as a result of an enzyme action.

e.g. $\underset{\text{sugar solution}}{C_6H_{12}O_6(aq)} \rightarrow 2C_2H_5OH(aq) + 2CO_2(g)$

The sugar solution and the yeast are placed in a stoppered flask and left in a warm place for several days. This allows the enzymes to break down the sugar. This suspension is then filtered to remove the solids before the filtrate is placed in a flask and the alcohol is collected by distillation.

(c) *Polymerization*
This is the building up of a chain of molecules from a monomer. A monomer is a small molecule, which can be linked with itself to form a long-chained compound. To form polythene, ethene is heated under a pressure of up to 200 atmospheres at 100–150°C in the presence of a Ziegler catalyst.

$$n(C_2H_4) \rightarrow (C_2H_4)_n$$

(d) *Pyrolysis* (cracking)

This is the decomposition of a chemical substance by heat, but it usually refers to the breaking up of the heavier fractions in oil to produce lighter fractions. If this takes place in the presence of a catalyst then it is known as catalytic cracking.

The fraction which is undergoing cracking is heated in the presence of a catalyst, for example, aluminium oxide. The products are then separated by fractional distillation.

e.g.

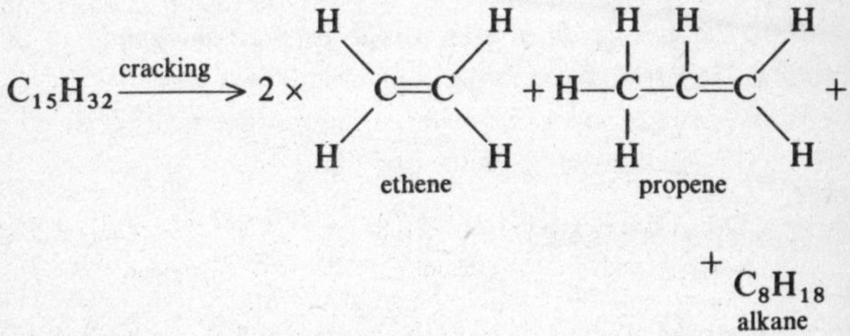

This process produces unsaturated hydrocarbons.

(e) *Saponification*

This is the hydrolysis of an ester of glycerol and a long-chain fatty acid to produce a soap.

e.g. fat or oil + sodium hydroxide solution → soap + glycerol

E.g. olive oil, potassium hydroxide and ethanol are refluxed together until a portion of this liquid when removed does not form an oil when added to water. The mixture is then distilled to remove the ethanol. Then the solution is added to sodium chloride solution so that the soap is precipitated.

2. (*Oxford, Autumn 1978*)

An organic compound X has the molecular formula $C_4H_8O_2$. Study the following information about X.

(i) *X is immiscible with water but when heated for about half an hour with aqueous sodium hydroxide, under reflux, an homogeneous liquid is produced.*

(ii) *The products of the reaction in* (i) *have the molecular formulae*

$C_2H_3O_2Na$ (an ionic substance) and C_2H_6O (a covalent but water soluble substance).

(iii) *X is a sweet-smelling liquid.*

(a) *Identify X. Name it and write out its structural formula.* (3,3)

(b) *What is the percentage by mass of carbon in X?* (3)

(c) *Write the equation for the reaction between X and aqueous sodium hydroxide. Name the products.* (2,2)

(d) *For each of the products from this reaction, give two properties you would expect it to have.* (4)

(e) *Describe briefly how you would prepare a sample of X in the laboratory. How would you know your sample was pure?* (6,2)

Answer

(a) X = ethyl ethanoate

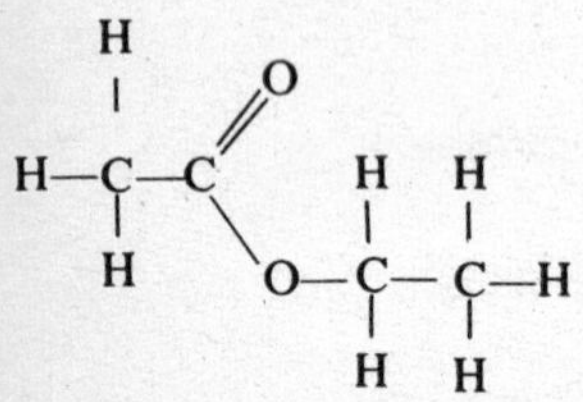

(b) $X = C_4H_8O_2$ $\%\ \text{carbon} = \dfrac{\text{mass carbon present}}{\text{R.M.M}} \times 100$

$$= \frac{48}{(48 + 8 + 32)} \times 100$$

$$= \frac{48}{88}\ \frac{6}{11}$$

$$\frac{6}{11} \times 100$$

$= \underline{54.2\%\ \text{of carbon is present in } X.}$

(c) $CH_3COOC_2H_5 + NaOH \rightarrow CH_3COONa + C_2H_5OH$

X (under $CH_3COOC_2H_5$); sodium ethanoate (under CH_3COONa); ethanol (under C_2H_5OH)

(d) When sodium ethanoate is acidified with sulphuric acid ethanoic acid is produced. This would turn blue litmus red and react with a metal carbonate to produce carbon dioxide, so effervescence would be seen.

Ethanol would change the colour of acidified potassium dichromate(VI) solution from orange to green. Ethanol reacts with a small piece of sodium producing hydrogen, so effervescence would be seen.

(e) A mixture of glacial ethanoic acid and excess ethanol is placed in a flask. Concentrated sulphuric acid is added carefully and the mixture is refluxed for fifteen minutes. The condenser is then rearranged so that the ester distils over into a flask.

To test the purity of the ester you would determine its boiling point and then compare it with the boiling point of the pure ester in a reference book. Pure samples of the same ester have the same boiling point.

Glossary 1
Identification Tests

Identification of Gases

Name	*Test*	*Result if positive*
1. Ammonia	(a) Test with damp red litmus paper	Blue
	(b) Test with stopper from concentrated hydrochloric acid bottle	White fumes
2. Carbon dioxide	Test with lime water	Turns 'milky'
3. Chlorine	Test with damp blue litmus paper	Red, then bleached
4. Hydrogen	Test with burning spill	'Pop' heard
5. Hydrogen chloride	Bubble through silver nitrate acidified with dil. nitric acid	White precipitate
6. Hydrogen sulphide	Test with filter paper soaked in lead acetate solution	Dark stain appears on paper
7. Nitrogen	No test available	
8. Oxygen	Test with glowing spill	Relights
9. Sulphur dioxide	Test with filter paper soaked in acidified potassium dichromate(VI) solution	Changes from orange to green

Identification of Metal Ions

Flame Test

Metal ion	*Colour of flame*
Barium	Apple-green
Calcium	Brick-red
Copper	Green-blue
Sodium	Yellow
Potassium	Lilac

Tests for Ions in Solution

Metal ion in solution	*Sodium hydroxide solution*		*Ammonia solution*	
	Addition	*Excess*	*Addition*	*Excess*
Ca^{2+} or Mg^{2+}	White precipitate	Insoluble	White precipitate	Insoluble
Fe^{2+}	Green precipitate	Insoluble	Green precipitate	Insoluble
Fe^{3+}	Red-brown precipitate	Insoluble	Red-brown precipitate	Insoluble
Al^{3+}	White precipitate	Soluble	White precipitate	Insoluble
Pb^{2+}	White precipitate	Soluble	White precipitate	Insoluble
Cu^{2+}	Blue precipitate	Insoluble	Blue precipitate	Soluble
Zn^{2+}	White precipitate	Soluble	White precipitate	Soluble

Identification of Anions

Anion	*Test*	*Result if positive*
1. Carbonate	Add dilute hydrochloric acid	Effervescence; lime water turns 'milky'
2. Halides (in solution)	Add nitric acid then silver nitrate solution	
Bromides		Cream precipitate slightly soluble in ammonia solution
Chlorides		White precipitate – soluble in ammonia solution
Iodides		Yellow precipitate – insoluble in ammonia solution
3. Nitrates (in solution)	Add iron(II) sulphate solution then concentrated sulphuric acid	A brown ring is seen
4. Sulphates (in solution)	Add dilute hydrochloric acid then barium chloride solution	White precipitate

Glossary 2
Questions on Practical Work

Volumetric Analysis

This is the analysis of a substance (often dissolved in a liquid) using another liquid. The volumes of these liquids are measured.

Titrations

One solution of known concentration is reacted with a second solution of unknown concentration (but known volume) so that the concentration of this second solution can be found.

Volumetric Calculations

The following are typical examples of titration calculations.

1. Part of a question (*Oxford, Summer 1978*).

(a) *When a solution of hydrochloric acid was titrated against 0.90 M sodium hydroxide solution, 23.0 cm³ of acid was needed to neutralize 25.0 cm³ of the alkali.*

Calculate:

(i) *The number of moles of alkali used in the titration.*
(ii) *The number of moles of acid used in the titration.*
(iii) *The number of moles of acid in 1.00 dm³ of solution.*
(iv) *The concentration of the acid in g/dm³.*

Answer

(i) (From the definition of a molar solution, page 71)

1000 cm^3 sodium hydroxide solution provides 0.90 mole NaOH

$$1\ cm^3 \text{ sodium hydroxide solution provides } \frac{0.90 \text{ mole}}{1000} \text{ NaOH}$$

$$25\ cm^3 \text{ sodium hydroxide solution provides } \frac{0.90 \times 25 \text{ moles}}{1000} \text{ NaOH}$$

$$= \underline{0.0225 \text{ mole}}$$

(ii) The equation for the reaction is

$HCl + NaOH \rightarrow NaCl + H_2O$

From the equation 1 mole of HCl reacts with 1 mole of NaOH.

If 0.0225 mole of NaOH is present, then it will react with 0.0225 mole of HCl.

(iii) 23 cm^3 hydrochloric acid contains 0.0225 mole HCl

1 cm^3 hydrochloric acid contains $\frac{0.0225 \text{ mole}}{23}$ HCl

1000 cm^3 hydrochloric acid contains $\frac{0.0225 \times 1000 \text{ moles}}{23}$ HCl

$= 0.978$ M HCL

(iv) 1 mole of hydrochloric acid has a mass of $35.5 + 1 = 36.5$ g

0.978 mole of hydrochloric acid has a mass of 36.5×0.978 mole

$= 35.7$ g/dm^3

2. Part of a question (*Oxford, Autumn 1978*).

(a) *2.50 g of pure calcium carbonate were completely dissolved in 100 cm^3 of 1.00 M nitric acid.*

(i) *Write an equation for the reaction.* (2)

(ii) *Calculate the number of moles of nitric acid which have reacted.* (3)

(iii) *How many moles of nitric acid remain?* (2)

(iv) *25.0 cm^3 of a solution of potassium hydroxide were needed to neutralize the unused nitric acid. What was the concentration of the potassium hydroxide solution in moles per dm^3?* (3)

(v) *If 0.5 M of sodium carbonate solution had been used instead of potassium hydroxide, what volume of solution would have been needed for complete neutralization?* (3)

Answer

(i) $CaCO_3 + 2HNO_3 \rightarrow Ca(NO_3)_2 + H_2O + CO_2$

(ii) From the equation 1 mole of $CaCO_3$ reacts with 2 moles of HNO_3.

1 mole of $CaCO_3$ has a mass of

	1 × Ca	40
	1 × C	12
	3 × O	48
		100 g

So 100 g $CaCO_3$ reacts with 2 moles HNO_3

$\therefore$ 1 g $CaCO_3$ reacts with $\frac{2}{100}$ mole HNO_3

So 2.5 g $CaCO_3$ reacts with $\frac{2}{100} \times 2.5$ moles

$= \underline{0.05 \text{ mole } HNO_3}$

(iii) 1000 cm^3 nitric acid contain 1.0 mole HNO_3
100 cm^3 nitric acid contain 0.1 mole HNO_3

So if 0.05 mole HNO_3 has reacted with the calcium carbonate then $0.1 - 0.05$ mole = $\underline{0.05 \text{ mole } HNO_3}$ remain

(iv) $KOH + HNO_3 \rightarrow KNO_3 + H_2O$

From the equation 1 mole of KOH reacts with 1 mole of HNO_3.

So 0.05 mole nitric acid reacts with 0.05 mole potassium hydroxide, which is present in 25.0 cm^3

25 cm^3 potassium hydroxide contains 0.05 mole KOH

1 cm^3 potassium hydroxide contains $\frac{0.05}{25}$ mole KOH

1000 cm^3 potassium hydroxide contain $\frac{0.05 \times 100}{25}$ mole KOH

$= \underline{2 \text{ M KOH}}$

(v) $2HNO_3 + Na_2CO_3 \rightarrow 2NaNO_3 + H_2O + CO_2$

From the equation 2 moles of HNO_3 react with 1 mole of Na_2CO_3.

So 0.05 mole nitric acid requires 0.025 mole sodium carbonate.

But 1000 cm^3 sodium carbonate solution provides 0.5 mole Na_2CO_3

1 cm^3 sodium carbonate solution provides $\frac{0.5}{1000}$ mole Na_2CO_3

x cm^3 sodium carbonate solution provides 0.025 mole.

Therefore $\frac{0.5x}{1000} = 0.025$ mole

$= \frac{0.025 \times 1000}{0.5}$

$= \underline{50 \text{ cm}^3 \text{ of } 0.5 \text{ M } Na_2CO_3}$

Questions on Identification of Compounds

These questions require you to solve a problem, but having succeeded there is not much to write down!

1. (*Oxford, Summer 1978*)

A deep blue crystalline solid A decomposed on heating to give a mixture of three vapours: a brown gas B; a colourless gas C, which rekindles a glowing splint; and a third substance D. The solid residue E was black and dissolved in dilute sulphuric acid to give a blue solution of F. When aqueous ammonia was added to the solution of F, a light blue precipitate G first appeared, but this dissolved in excess aqueous ammonia to give a deep blue solution of a substance H.

(a) *Name substances A, B, C, D, E, F, G and H.*

(b) *Write equations for the reactions which have taken place.*

(c) *Using two reactions not mentioned above, state how you would test for the ions in A.*

Answer

Note: You are not asked to explain your answers, so the reasoning behind the answers is given for information *only.*

(a) 1. Blue compounds suggest a copper compound.
2. A brown gas is nitrogen dioxide.
3. Oxygen rekindles a glowing splint.
4. Third substance probably water vapour.
5. Nitrates give off nitrogen dioxide on heating.
6. Black compounds are unusual and are often carbon or copper(II) oxide.
7. Copper(II) oxide would react with sulphuric acid to form a salt.
8. Ammonia solution is used to identify copper ions.

A = Copper(II) nitrate.
B = Nitrogen dioxide.
C = Oxygen.
D = Water vapour.
E = Copper(II) oxide.
F = Copper(II) sulphate solution.
G = Copper(II) hydroxide.
H = Tetraammine copper(II) ion.

(b) $2Cu(NO_3)_2 \cdot xH_2O \rightarrow 2CuO + 4NO_2 + O_2 + xH_2O$

Note: I do not think you would be expected to know the value of x.

$CuO + H_2SO_4 \rightarrow CuSO_4 + H_2O$
$CuSO_4 + 2NH_3 + 2H_2O \rightarrow Cu(OH)_2 + (NH_4)_2SO_4$
$Cu^{2+} + 4NH_3 \rightarrow [Cu(NH_3)_4]^{2+}$

(c) Copper ions can be detected by a flame test, which would be a blue-green colour.

The nitrate ion can be detected by adding a freshly prepared solution of iron(II) sulphate to a solution of A, then pouring concentrated sulphuric acid carefully down the side of the test tube. A brown ring would be seen at the junction of the layers.

2. Most of one question (*Oxford, Autumn 1978*)

A colourless salt S dissolved in warm aqueous sodium hydroxide solution with the liberation of a very soluble alkaline gas A. The solution which remained reacted with excess dilute hydrochloric acid and barium chloride solution to produce a white precipitate B. A solution of A in water, when added to copper(II) sulphate solution gave a light blue precipitate C, soluble in excess of solution A to give a deep blue solution D. The gas A reduced copper(II) oxide to form a brown solid E and two other products F and G were formed.

(a) *Identify A, B, C, D, E, F, G and the salt S.* (8)
(b) *Write equations for the reactions involved.* (10)
(c) *How would you use an aqueous solution of A to distinguish between silver chloride and silver iodide?* (2)

Answer

Note: Again, the reasoning is included for your information *only*.

1. Ammonium salts dissolve in sodium hydroxide solution; ammonia is evolved on warming.
2. Barium chloride tests for the presence of sulphates.
3. Blue precipitates are due to copper hydroxide.
4. A soluble copper complex is formed.
5. Reduction of copper(II) oxide will give copper.

(a) S = Ammonium sulphate.
A = Ammonia.
B = Barium sulphate.

C = Copper(II) hydroxide.
D = Tetraammine copper(II) ion.
E = Copper.
F = Water.
G = Nitrogen.

(b) $(NH_4)_2SO_4 + 2NaOH \rightarrow Na_2SO_4 + 2NH_3 + 2H_2O$
or
$NH_4^+ + OH^- \rightarrow NH_3 + H_2O$

$(NH_4)_2SO_4 + BaCl_2 \rightarrow BaSO_4 + 2NH_4Cl$
or
$SO_4^{2-} + Ba^{2+} \rightarrow BaSO_4$

$CuSO_4 + 2NH_3 + 2H_2O \rightarrow Cu(OH)_2 + (NH_4)_2SO_4$
or
$Cu^{2+} + 2OH^- \rightarrow Cu(OH)_2$

$Cu^{2+} + 4NH_3 \rightarrow [Cu(NH_3)_4]^{2+}$
$3CuO + 2NH_3 \rightarrow 3Cu + N_2 + 3H_2O$

(c) When A is added to silver chloride a soluble complex is formed. No such complex is formed between A and silver iodide, so the solid remains.

Glossary 3
Definitions

Acidic oxides
Acidic oxides are non-metallic oxides which react with water to produce acids.

Acids
Acids are substances which donate protons to other molecules.

Addition polymerization
This is the linking together of unsaturated monomers to form a single large molecule.

Addition reactions
These occur, in organic chemistry, when two or more molecules combine to form a single compound. This is because an unsaturated bond is broken and a more saturated, or saturated, bond is formed.

Alkalis
An alkali is a base, which is soluble in water.

Allotropy
When an element can exist in more than one form, in the same state, it is said to show allotropy.

Alloy
An alloy is a substance made up of two or more metals.

Amphoteric oxides
Amphoteric oxides are metallic oxides which show both basic and acidic properties.

Anion
An anion is a negatively charged ion, which is attracted to the anode during electrolysis.

Anode
The anode is the positive electrode.

Atom
An atom is the smallest particle into which an element can be divided without losing the properties of an element.

Atomic number
The atomic number of an atom is the number of protons in the nucleus of that atom.

Avogadro's Constant (Avogadro's Number)
6.02×10^{23} atoms of carbon are found in 12 g of carbon. This number is known as Avogadro's Constant.

Avogadro's Law
Equal volumes of all gases, under the same conditions of temperature and pressure, contain the same number of molecules.

Bases
A base is a substance which accepts a proton.

Basic oxides
Basic oxides are metallic oxides which react with an acid to produce a salt and water only.

Boiling point
This is the temperature at which a liquid turns to a vapour at normal atmospheric pressure.

Boyle's Law
The volume of a fixed mass of gas is inversely proportional to the pressure, if the temperature remains constant.

$$\text{Pressure} \propto \frac{1}{\text{volume}}$$

or $P_1V_1 = P_2V_2$

Brownian motion (or movement)
Brownian motion is the random movement of minute pieces of solid caused by their irregular bombardment from the surrounding, invisible, gas or liquid molecules.

Catalysts
Catalysts are substances which alter the rate of a chemical reaction (they usually speed it up) but remain chemically unchanged at the end of the reaction.

Cathode
The cathode is the negative electrode.

Cation
A cation is a positively charged ion, which is attracted to the cathode during electrolysis.

Charles' Law
The volume of a fixed mass of gas is directly proportional to its temperature, on the Kelvin scale, if the pressure remains constant.

$$V \propto T \text{ (in K)}$$

Chemical changes
A chemical change is a change which forms a new substance or substances and which is not easily reversed by a physical process.

Combination
Combination takes place when two or more substances combine to form a single substance; heat and/or light are often emitted.

Combustion
Combustion is the combination of a substance with oxygen to produce a chemical change.

Compounds
A compound is a substance, made up of two or more elements, which are joined together and so cannot be separated by a physical process.

Condensation
Condensation occurs when a vapour cools down and becomes a liquid.

Condensation polymerization
Condensation polymerization is the linking together of a large number of molecules by a reaction in which a polymer and a small molecule are formed. These polymers contain two different kinds of monomer molecules.

Cracking (Pyrolysis)
Cracking is the breaking up of the heavier fractions of oil so that lighter molecules are formed.

Decomposition
Decomposition occurs when a compound splits up into simpler substances.

Deliquescent compounds
Deliquescent compounds absorb water on exposure to the atmosphere; they eventually dissolve in it to form a solution.

Diffusion
Diffusion is the spreading of one sort of particle through another. Particles move from a region of high concentration to a region of low concentration.

Displacement
Displacement occurs when one element (or group) takes the place of another element (or group) in a compound.

Efflorescent compounds
When a compound loses all or some of its water of crystallization on exposure to the air this compound is said to effloresce.

Electrodes
Electrodes are metal or carbon rods where the current enters or leaves the electrolyte.

Electrolysis
Electrolysis occurs when an electric current is passed through a solution, or a molten substance, and a chemical change takes place.

Electrolyte
An electrolyte is a solution, or molten substance, which conducts an electric current and is decomposed by it.

Element
An element is a substance which cannot be split up chemically into anything simpler. It is made up of atoms which all have the same atomic number.

Endothermic reactions
Endothermic reactions take in (absorb) heat from their surroundings.

Esterification
Esterification is the production of an ester by heating an alcohol with a carboxylic acid.

Evaporation
Evaporation occurs when the surface molecules of a liquid change to vapour molecules below the boiling point of the liquid.

Exothermic reactions
Exothermic reactions give out heat to their surroundings.

Faraday's First Law
The mass of a substance produced in electrolysis is proportional to the quantity of electricity passing through the electrolyte.

Faraday's Second Law
When the same quantity of electricity is passed through solutions of different electrolytes the number of moles of the elements deposited are inversely proportional to the charges on the ions of the elements.

Fermentation
Fermentation occurs when a chemical change is produced in an organic substance by the action of a living organism, as a result of an enzyme action.

Galvanizing
Galvanizing is the coating of iron or steel with zinc to protect it.

Gas equation

$$\frac{P_1V_1}{T_1} = \frac{P_2V_2}{T_2}$$

Gay-Lussac's Law

When gases react together they do so in volumes which are related to each other simply and to the product if gaseous.

Graham's Law of Diffusion

The rate of diffusion of a gas at constant temperature and pressure is inversely proportional to the square root of its density.

Heat of combustion

This is the heat change which takes place when one mole of a substance is completely burnt in oxygen.

Heat of neutralization

This is the heat change which occurs when one mole of water is formed when an acid is neutralized by an alkali.

Heat of reaction

This is the heat change involved in a particular chemical reaction, so the reaction is always described.

Homologous series

A homologous series is a group of organic compounds which have the same general formula and similar chemical properties.

Hydrated substances

When water is combined with a substance to form one product only in such a way that the water molecules are bonded to the substance, then the substance is said to be hydrated.

Hydrolysis

Hydrolysis is the chemical decomposition of a substance in the presence of water; that is, the substance and the water break up to form new substances.

Hygroscopic substances
These compounds absorb water on exposure to the atmosphere, but they do not dissolve in the water to form a solution.

Ion
An ion is a charged atom or molecule. It does not contain an equal number of protons and electrons.

Isomerism
Isomerism is the occurrence of two or more compounds with the same molecular formula, but a different arrangement of atoms within their molecules.

Isotopes
Isotopes are atoms of the same element, which contain different numbers of neutrons; that is, they have the same atomic numbers but different mass numbers.

Law of Conservation of Mass
Matter is neither created nor destroyed in a chemical reaction.

Law of Constant Composition (or definite proportions)
All pure samples of the same chemical compound contain the same elements combined together in the same proportions by mass.

Law of Multiple Proportions
When two elements A and B combine together to form more than one compound, the different masses of A, which combine with a fixed mass of B, are in a simple ratio.

Le Chatelier's Principle
This states that if a system is in equilibrium and a change is made to this system, then the system alters so as to oppose this change.

Mass number
The mass number of an atom is the sum of the number of protons and the number of neutrons in the nucleus of that atom.

Melting point
This is the temperature at which a solid turns to a liquid.

Mixtures
A mixture consists of two or more different substances which are not chemically combined, so they can be separated by physical processes.

Molar solution
A molar solution of a compound contains one mole of the compound in one cubic decimetre of the solution.

Molar volume of a gas
One mole of any gas occupies a volume of 22.4 dm^3 at s.t.p.

Mole
The mole is the amount of any substance that contains 6.02×10^{23} particles of that substance.

Molecule
A molecule is a group of atoms which are bonded together and which can exist as a separate unit.

Monomer
A monomer is a small molecule which can be linked with other identical molecules to form a polymer.

Neutral oxides
Neutral oxides are non-metallic oxides which show neither basic nor acidic properties.

Ore
An ore is a compound of an element mixed with earth and rock.

Oxidation
Oxidation occurs when:

1. Oxygen is added to an element or compound
2. Hydrogen is removed from a compound
3. Electrons are lost from an atom or ion.

Oxidizing agents
An oxidizing agent is a substance which causes oxidation of another substance.

Photosynthesis

Photosynthesis occurs when plants take in carbon dioxide and water in the presence of sunlight and chlorophyll and produce carbohydrates.

Physical changes

A physical change is a reversible reaction where no new substance is formed but the chemical merely changes its state.

Polymerization

Polymerization is the building up of a chain of molecules from basic units called monomers.

Precipitation

When two different solutions of soluble salts are mixed, then if one of the cations and one of the anions form an insoluble salt, precipitation occurs.

Reducing agents

A reducing agent is a substance which causes reduction of another substance.

Reduction

Reduction occurs when:

1. A compound loses oxygen
2. Hydrogen is added to an element or compound
3. Electrons are added to an atom or ion.

Relative atomic mass (R.A.M.) or A_r

The R.A.M. of an element is the 'average' mass of an atom of the element compared with that of an atom of $^{12}_{6}C$, the mass of which is taken as 12 units.

Relative molecular mass (R.M.M.) or M_r

The R.M.M. of a molecule is the 'average' mass of a molecule of an element or compound compared with that of the mass of $^{12}_{6}C$.

Reversible reactions

A reversible reaction is one that proceeds from left to right (as shown in an equation) and also from right to left (as shown in the same equation).

Salts
A salt is prepared when the hydrogen in an acid is partly or completely replaced by a metal or ammonium ion.

Saponification
This is the hydrolysis of esters (formed from the alcohol glycerol) to form sodium salts of long-chained carboxylic acids (soap).

Saturated compounds
Saturated compounds are organic compounds where every carbon atom in the chain has as many single bonds as possible.

Solutions
A solution is formed when a solid, liquid or gas is mixed with a liquid to give a clear solution.

Standard solutions
A standard solution is a solution of known concentration.

Sublimation
Sublimation occurs when a solid does not melt but turns directly into a gas; or a gas cools and turns directly into a solid.

Substitution
Substitution occurs when an organic molecule reacts with an element or compound (X–X or X–Y), X replaces an atom in the organic compound (usually hydrogen) which combines with the other X or Y.

Suspensions
A suspension is formed if two substances are mixed and the resulting mixture is not clear; that is the substances are present in different states.

Unsaturated compounds
An unsaturated compound is an organic compound whose molecule contains at least one double or triple bond.

Valency
This is the combining power of an element.

Penguin Examination Bestsellers

Jane Austen/Pride and Prejudice
H. E. Bates/Fair Stood the Wind for France
Charlotte Brontë/Jane Eyre
Emily Brontë/Wuthering Heights
Charles Dickens/Great Expectations
Gerald Durrell/My Family and Other Animals
George Eliot/Silas Marner
Oliver Goldsmith/The Vicar of Wakefield
Graham Greene/Brighton Rock
Graham Greene/The Power and the Glory
Thomas Hardy/Far from the Madding Crowd
Thomas Hardy/The Mayor of Casterbridge
L. P. Hartley/The Go-Between
Barry Hines/A Kestrel for a Knave
Geoffrey Household/Rogue Male

Penguin Passnotes

Carefully tailored to the requirements of the main examination boards (for O-level or CSE exams), Penguin Passnotes are an invaluable companion to your studies.

Covering a wide range of English literature texts as well as many other subjects, Penguin Passnotes include:

English Literature

A Man for All Seasons
Chaucer: General Prologue
Cider With Rosie
Great Expectations
Jane Eyre
Pride and Prejudice
Silas Marner
The Mayor of Casterbridge
The Woman in White
To Kill a Mockingbird
Wuthering Heights

Shakespeare

As You Like It
Henry IV, Part I
Julius Caesar
Macbeth
The Merchant of Venice
Twelfth Night
Romeo and Juliet

Subject Areas

Biology
Chemistry
Economics
English Language
French
Geography
Modern World History
Physics
Human Biology
Mathematics
Modern Mathematics

The New Pelican Guide to English Literature

Edited by Boris Ford

Authoritative, stimulating and accessible, the original seven-volume *Pelican Guide to English Literature* has earned itself a distinguished reputation. Now enlarged to nine titles this popular series has been wholly revised and updated.

What this work sets out to offer is a guide to the history and traditions of English literature, a contour-map of the literary scene. Each volume includes these standard features:

(i) An account of the social context of literature in each period.
(ii) A general survey of the literature itself.
(iii) A series of critical essays on individual writers and their works – each written by an authority in their field.
(iv) Full appendices including short author biographies, listings of standard editions of authors' works, critical commentaries and titles for further study and reference.

The *Guide* consists of the following volumes:

1. Medieval Literature:
   Part One: Chaucer and the Alliterative Tradition
   Part Two: The European Inheritance
2. The Age of Shakespeare
3. From Donne to Marvell
4. From Dryden to Johnson
5. From Blake to Byron
6. From Dickens to Hardy
7. From James to Eliot
8. The Present

'The best and most lively general survey of English literature available to schools, students and general readers' – *The Times Educational Supplement*

PENGUIN REFERENCE BOOKS

☐ ***The Penguin Map of the World*** £2.95

Clear, colourful, crammed with information and fully up-to-date, this is a useful map to stick on your wall at home, at school or in the office.

☐ ***The Penguin Map of Europe*** £2.95

Covers all land eastwards to the Urals, southwards to North Africa and up to Syria, Iraq and Iran * Scale = 1:5,500,000 * 4-colour artwork * Features main roads, railways, oil and gas pipelines, plus extra information including national flags, currencies and populations.

☐ ***The Penguin Map of the British Isles*** £2.95

Including the Orkneys, the Shetlands, the Channel Islands and much of Normandy, this excellent map is ideal for planning routes and touring holidays, or as a study aid.

☐ ***The Penguin Dictionary of Quotations*** £3.95

A treasure-trove of over 12,000 new gems and old favourites, from Aesop and Matthew Arnold to Xenophon and Zola.

☐ ***The Penguin Dictionary of Art and Artists*** £3.95

Fifth Edition. 'A vast amount of information intelligently presented, carefully detailed, abreast of current thought and scholarship and easy to read' – *The Times Literary Supplement*

☐ ***The Penguin Pocket Thesaurus*** £2.50

A pocket-sized version of Roget's classic, and an essential companion for all commuters, crossword addicts, students, journalists and the stuck-for-words.

PENGUIN REFERENCE BOOKS